THE REBIRTH OF ANTHROPOLOGICAL THEORY

STANLEY R. BARRETT

The Rebirth of
Anthropological Theory

UNIVERSITY OF TORONTO PRESS
Toronto Buffalo London

© University of Toronto Press 1984
Toronto Buffalo London
Printed in Canada

ISBN 0-8020-5638-5

Canadian Cataloguing in Publication Data

Barrett, Stanley R., 1938–
    The rebirth of anthropological theory

    ISBN 0-8020-5638-5

    1. Ethnology.   I. Title.

GN316.B37 1984   306.01   C83-099139-5

For Kaye, Jason, and Maria

Contents

PREFACE xi

PART 1
THE CURRENT STATE OF ANTHROPOLOGICAL THEORY:
A CRITIQUE

1
Introduction 3

2
An Overview of Theory 8
Theoretical Orientations 9
Clusters of Theoretical Orientations 10
British and American Anthropology 15
Basic Theoretical Orientations 19
Back to the Armchair 50
Conclusion 51

3
Paradigms or Pseudo-paradigms 53
Kuhn's Central Ideas 54
The Two Kuhns 56
Pre-paradigms 57
Pseudo-paradigms 62
Conclusion 69

4
Conceptual Contradictions 73
Ideal and Actual Theory 74
Explaining Theoretical Shifts 76
Some Examples of Conceptual Contradictions 79
Other Conceptual Contradictions 83
Salvage Theory 84
Backward Theory 93
Anthropology and Sociology: An Unrecognized Dialectic 94
Future Orientations 97

5
Theory as Myth 100
What Is Myth? 100
Some Comparisons of Myth and Theory 102
Conclusion 114

6
Structuralism and the Second Burial of Émile Durkheim 115
Durkheim 115
Formal Analysis 121
Promises of Structuralism 122
Problems with Structuralism 125
Structuralism and Positivism 132
Two-Headed Anthropology 135
Structuralism and Marxism 136
Salutary Nature of Field-work 138

PART 2
CONTRADICTION AS THE BASIS OF SOCIAL LIFE: A SOLUTION

7
Contradictions in Everyday Life 145
Contradiction and Conflict: Operational Definitions 146
The Micro Level 150
The Middle Level 158
The Macro Level 169
Conclusion 172

ix Contents

8
Neutralizing Mechanisms 177
Basic Mechanisms 177
Power as the Imposition of Stability 182
Mock Change 189
Conclusion 192

9
The Illusion of Simplicity 195
Defining Complexity 195
The Emerging Synthesis 199
Basic Elements 201
Leach, Murphy, and Bailey 202

10
Reflections on Our Future 211
Rebirth Step 1: Urban-Industrial Society 212
Objections 213
Rebirth Step 2: Social Problems and Inequality 220
Racism and the Failure of Anthropology 222
Objections 228
Ethics and Subversion 234
Rebirth Step 3: The Dialectical Perspective 237

BIBLIOGRAPHY 245
INDEX 263

Preface

My heart lies in field-work, yet here I am writing a book on theory. If blame is to be laid anywhere, I suppose it is on the responsibilities, teaching and otherwise, that prevented me from returning to the field before I had time to reflect on the current state and future prospects of our theory. Just as sociologists take refuge behind methodology in order to avoid dilemmas in their discipline, anthropologists slip off to the field, the enormous challenge of which soon drives away all other problems.

I didn't escape quickly enough, and the deeper I delved into the history of anthropological theory, the more inconsistencies I discovered. Scientific knowledge supposedly is cumulative, yet our theoretical orientations have oscillated between polar positions, advancing, repeating, and retracting, but rarely achieving progress. Our methodology rests on the assumption of an orderly universe; yet social life is essentially contradictory, although disguised by numerous mechanisms. A great deal of anthropological analysis has mistaken these mechanisms for underlying reality, which means that the discipline has itself contributed to a distorted view of behaviour. Since its beginnings, anthropology has expressed a dream, a hope for a universe without hate, rancour, or racism, in which the peoples of the world would live together in harmony. Yet it also has aspired toward science, even at the expense of the dream, and the result has sometimes been a discipline that has lost the capacity for moral judgment.

While my purpose is to provide an innovative analysis of the history of anthropological theory and to point us in a different theoretical direction, I also wish to make a moral statement – to commit the discipline anew and without apology to the betterment of mankind. The basis for doing so is simple: the recognition of the consequences of differential power. Anthropology has almost always focused on the deprived and powerless, usually with the admirable goal of improving their lives, but too often it has lost sight of the larger societal framework in which the deprived are caught. The result, at best, has been a flawed analysis; at worst, an ideological statement passing for theory which blames the powerless for their problems. In this study I shall focus periodically on race and racism, although numerous other examples of man's evil toward man could have been selected. The humanistically inclined scholar may think that I have been too cautious, but I have written with the hard-nosed reader in mind, who will have to grapple with the overwhelming evidence that the attempts of anthropology to explain racism have not only been feeble, but have actually contributed to racism.

Although the ideas for this book took shape in my mind during the last four or five years, they stem from two tensions in my academic background. The first is the tension between my theoretical training and my subsequent extensive field-work on a wealthy theocracy in Nigeria, the vendetta system in Corsica, and white supremacist groups in Canada. Field-work forced me to accommodate the impeccable logic of the deductive model to the actual manner in which research is conducted. The gap between the textbook recipes and the realities of the field is indeed considerable, and anyone who fails to appreciate it is advised to become immersed in research without delay. The second tension is that which exists between the different theoretical orientations to which I was exposed as a student. I was trained in North America and Britain by anthropologists and sociologists who espoused quite incompatible theoretical orientations and images of the discipline. As a result, the 'multiparadigmatic' nature of the discipline was impressed upon me very early, sometimes against my will.

This book also has another, rather peculiar source. I have often been struck by the fact that I seem to know much less about the people and the community in which I have lived and taught for several years than about the Nigerian Utopia in which I first conducted research. Whereas I have been prepared to generalize about virtually all aspects of the Nigerian community, I seem to have nothing important to say about my own. This might confirm the view that the explicit and conscious participant observation that characterizes field-work is immensely more sophisticated than that in which all of us are involved by the mere fact of existing, whether we are anthropologists or carpenters. Yet this study is partly a product of my reflections during the past few years about my own society and my immediate environment, including the setting of the university, the relationships among my colleagues, and their actions in committees, at parties, and with their friends and competitors. Out of this reflection emerged the viewpoint that behaviour is intrinsically contradictory. The lesson I draw is that in order to appreciate the pervasiveness of contradiction one must possess unusually deep insight into the culture at hand. This explains, I think, why comparable understanding is not likely to materialize when conducting field-work in 'other cultures,' especially now that field-work is done for shorter periods, and in turn why anthropologists should do some work in their own societies. Indeed, I would advocate at least two field trips for all anthropologists: one abroad and one at home.

To some extent my intellectual growth has consisted of the bizarre process by which knowledge obtained through formal training in the discipline, culminating with the completion of a PHD dissertation, has gradually been whittled away. It has been a process of slow withdrawal from the ideology of the discipline and from the statements of faith about how one goes about doing anthropology. I know that many academics who experience a similar withdrawal become bitter, lamenting the time and energy they have wasted on inadequate training. I am not one of them. I have been struck by the realization, in regard to both my professional and my personal life, that at one point I have thought x; later, with greater knowledge and experience, y; and, eventually, I have come back again to x. But the new x is not the same as the old x. For example, the argument that we should focus on outstanding social problems or that we cannot ignore the 'soft' side of behaviour (beliefs, norms, emotions, motives) even if it restricts scientific rigour, attains a degree of sophistication that would not have been possible without the exposure to and temporary adoption of contrary ideas. We have here another contradiction: perhaps future anthropologists will be incapable of moving in new and more fruitful directions until they become wedded to the old ones, from which they may not be able to escape. Should this be the case, the outlook for the future is bleak. What it means is that the central ideas in this study are doomed to be discovered, discarded, and rediscovered over and over again. In other words, they will be trapped in the same unproductive rhythm that has characterized the history of theoretical orientations in the discipline. Yet I have written this book with the hope that by recognizing the oscillating character of our theory we can take advantage of it and possibly move beyond it. Those who manage to do so will pay a price: no longer will they have the comfort of belief in a single theoretical approach. Their vision will be greater, including in its sweep the entire range of orientations in the discipline. Such people will be envied, for if my foray into theory has revealed anything, it is that the one-perspective man or woman, the anthropologist incapable of or unwilling to entertain alternative models of mankind, is an intellectual infant.

Several of my colleagues at the University of Guelph gave me the benefit of their critical reactions to an initial draft of the ideas for this study, especially Nora Cebotarev, Ed Hedican, Ken Menzies, Frans Schryer, and Peter Sinclair. At a critical point in the development of my argument, Ken Westhues and Gerry Gold provided me with the confidence that I was on the right track. My students in anthropological theory suffered more or less patiently as I tried my ideas out on them, and their responses forced me to rethink and clarify what I was attempting to achieve. I must also thank Fred Eidlin, who introduced me to several valuable philosophical works, as well as the publisher's anonymous readers whose thoughtful critique contributed substantially to the final product. The constant good humour and tolerance of my wife Kaye and my children Maria and Jason made the time spent writing this book a pleasure, and challenged my argument that family and work must clash. Finally, I acknowledge once again the influence of three of my teachers, F.G. Bailey, P.C. Lloyd, and Peter Carstens, whose standards of scholarship and appreciation of field-work have continued to inspire me. Bailey's work occupies a prominent place in this book, and although my criticisms of parts of it are often severe, it remains an outstanding example of the degree to which successful analysis depends on imaginative flair.

This book has been published with the help of a grant from the Social Science Federation of Canada, using funds provided by the Social Sciences and Humanities Research Council of Canada, and a grant from the Publications Fund of the University of Toronto Press.

PART 1

The Current State of Anthropological Theory: A Critique

1

Introduction

This study focuses on two interrelated themes, with a third one lingering in the background. The first is the non-cumulative nature of anthropological theory. There has been little significant advance in the field since the writings of Marx, Weber, and Durkheim, who laid the basis for a positivistic science of society. This is because positivism was severely restricted from the outset. It was assumed that the social world was highly structured, and that it was amenable to measurement by techniques comparable to those used in the hard sciences. But man is a contradictory, manipulating, choosing creature. The element of consciousness renders behaviour immensely complex, and the social realm is messy if not chaotic. Our techniques have simply not been able to cope with this complexity. Given the limitations of a positivistic science of society, it only required the minds of a few outstanding scholars to establish the theoretical, methodological, and conceptual bases of the discipline. This was the great achievement of Marx, Weber, and Durkheim, complemented by others such as Spencer, Morgan, Tylor, and Boas.

Although there have been numerous theoretical trends in social and cultural anthropology, all of them, with one exception, can be subsumed within the epistemology of positivism. The exception is structuralism, especially as exhibited in the work of Claude Lévi-Strauss. However, structuralism has had its day in the sun. We now must conclude not only that it is essentially a mentalist position, divorced from social organization, but also that some of its basic principles are embedded in the works of the founding fathers. My examination of the history of anthropological theory proceeds in a novel and, I hope, a fruitful manner.

First, the numerous theoretical orientations in social and cultural anthropology are evaluated in terms of Kuhn's work (1970) on paradigms. Although in the other social sciences, notably sociology and political science, numerous attempts have been made to apply Kuhn's framework, virtually nothing has been done in anthropology. My argument will be that the label 'paradigm' must be reversed for disciplines that lend themselves to nomothetic inquiry. Only twice has anthropology come close to attaining this status: first in the social-fact approach of Durkheim, and second in the cultural-materialist approach (in which I include cultural ecology and neo-evolutionism) of Harris, Steward, White, and others. But they fell short of their promises, and the implication is that anthropology is a pre- or non-paradigmatic discipline, and probably will remain so for the forseeable future.

Second, I have worked out a methodology to explain why anthropological theory has been so repetitive and cyclical. As I demonstrate, underlying the various theoretical orientations are a limited number of conceptual contradictions. Each theoretical orientation expresses particular sides of the conceptual contradictions, and new orientations emerge in order to express the other sides. Not only am I able to account for the fact that specific orientations (such as conflict theory) appear, disappear, and reappear, but I am also able to argue that the several theoretical orientations can be run backward. That is, using the same criteria one can measure the degree of theoretical progression from the beginnings of anthropology to the present, or from the present to the past, and the answers are much the same. This is the ultimate proof of the lack of theoretical cumulation in the discipline. In this regard, I have also shown that the history of anthropological theory can be fruitfully analysed in much the same way that Lévi-Strauss analyses myth. Like myth, theories do not become 'better' over time, and are 'good to think' even if they do not explain. I also have a section on salvage theory, which refers to the common practice of tinkering with theoretical orientations that seem to be on the way out in order to keep them alive. We have numerous examples, such as the early Weberian model of development and the attempts to salvage it, which include modernization theory, McClelland's need-to-achieve theory, and the sizable literature on the role of the military in modernization. All of these were attempts to stall the emergence of a Marxian theory of development.

Finally, this scheme of conceptual contradictions not only allows me to explain the rise and fall of the various theoretical orientations in anthropology, but to forecast new ones. For if I am correct, future orientations will consist largely of specific combinations of contradictions that were absent in previous orientations. Obviously, in terms of the sociology of knowledge my position is a radical one, for it downplays (but does not ignore) the links between changes in society and changes in theory. The simple fact is that the numerous, repetitive, and cyclical orientations in the discipline have not closely paralleled social changes. By avoiding this trap, and by refusing to accept the conventional view that our discipline has been cumulative, I am able to make sense of the history of anthropological theory.

The second theme of this study is the contradictory nature of social life. My argument is that social behaviour is both complex and contradictory. Virtually every value, norm, decision, and act has an alternative (or alternatives) that are potentially its negation. Except for the outstanding social problems of an age, such as racism, there is no mechanism, whether theoretical, methodological, moral, or pragmatic, to determine which of the alternative beliefs or actions open to man are intrinsically superior and preferable. Nevertheless, people tend to choose between alternatives in a consistent manner, with the result that behaviour becomes (or at least appears) structured. In other words, the contradictory nature of social life contains within it another contradiction: it is also patterned. I shall offer several reasons for this, one of which is psychological: mankind's felt need for an orderly, controlled, and predictable universe, a need that runs up against another of man's essential features – his striving, achievement-oriented nature, his receptiveness to change. Another reason concerns the consequences of differential power. Power is usually defined as the capacity of one person to force another person to do something, even against his will. It connotes action, change. However, I define power as the imposition of stability. The power élite almost always has a vested interest in stability, and, conversely, the majority of people suffer from it. This partly explains why behaviour, despite its inherent contradictions, exhibits pattern and consistency over time. If it is assumed that differential power in varying degrees is universal, it follows that all social structures perpetuate inequality by the very fact of persisting. From the point of view of most people, social structures are thus repressive institutions. Value systems, as constellations of standards and goals, are indexes of power, and mystifying forces. Normative systems are rationalizations, the purpose of which is to conceal contradiction and maintain inequality. Yet at the same time these social structures, value systems, and normative systems meet man's basic need for order and stability. This is why it is appropriate to describe man as a tragic creature, trapped between irreconcilable forces.

While several mechanisms exist to neutralize the contradictions that permeate the social world, they do not eradicate them. Moreover, such mechanisms render the social realm even more complex, since they disguise its underlying contradictory basis. This partly explains why there has been so little theoretical advance in anthropology: our models have been addressed to a less complex image of the actor. Conversely, the over-simplified model of behaviour that has been necessary for a positivistic approach has helped to conceal the degree of contradiction in the social sphere. In other words, positivism has indirectly provided ideological support for the power élite, which maintains its position partly by camouflaging the degree of contradiction in society. This is another way to arrive at an old lesson: that theory is political, usually in a conservative sense.

The non-cumulative nature of anthropological theory is dealt with in part 1, the contradictory basis of social life in part 2. Present throughout the study is a third theme: the crisis that currently faces anthropology. Self-doubt, introspection, and general anxiety about the future of the discipline have plagued anthropologists for several years. While this has been partly due to the failure of anthropological theory to advance and to its incapacity to cope with a complex and contradictory universe, there has been an additional factor of no small importance: the inability of the discipline to adjust to the social changes that have made a focus on primitive peoples obsolete. There are virtually no primitive societies left, and the Third World countries that have replaced them are modern states, intrinsically related to the international community. Nor can the Third World, primitive or otherwise, still be regarded as the laboratory for Western anthropologists. For several decades Third World specialists have been economists, political scientists, and geographers as well as indigenous anthropologists. Yet the image of our discipline continues to be dominated by a concern with tribes rather than classes, by magic rather than science, and by face-to-face communities rather than bureaucracies. Many anthropologists now select research topics that allow them to work in the most isolated sectors of Third World countries, sometimes under the guise of urgent research. Some have begun to do field-work in urban industrial societies, but usually in a slum or on a street corner, where participant observation is thought to be appropriate. Still others have been attracted to relatively new areas of inquiry such as philosophical anthropology, ethnohistory, structuralism, and the recent brand of French economic anthropology, all of which have sprung up to maintain the discipline's concern with small-scale, rural, non-industrial, pre-state social systems. The price is high. Anthropologists now often focus on a sector of society that is peripheral to mainstream behaviour, or they redefine the discipline as a branch of history and thus relinquish their outstanding methodological device: the participant observation of behaviour as it occurs.

Part of the solution is to swing the bulk of anthropological research to the contemporary world, whether in Nigeria, Afghanistan, or America, and to deal with it in a sophisticated manner. In terms of conceptual territory, the time has come to remove 'simple society' from our vocabulary. That term never was a satisfactory one since it usually referred to only one dimension of pre-industrial societies: the economic realm. Today it is even less appropriate, for virtually all societies in which anthropologists work are complex. In terms of methodology, the reorientation of the discipline will mean using computers, statistics, sampling procedures, and questionnaires. But it will not mean throwing out participant observation, a tool that has always been the strength of the discipline; its use will enrich most studies since almost all behavioural systems have both a formal and an informal dimension. The superficiality of much of quantitative sociology underlines the need for retaining participant observation. In terms of areas of investigation, urban anthropology must flower and expand and a new generation of anthropologists must come to grips with the basic expressions of inequality in the contemporary world. Our failure to focus on major social problems in the past has also contributed to the crisis. For example, it was not anthropology that produced the pioneering critiques of colonialism, although most of us now are prepared to jump on the bandwagon. In this respect, the analysis of élites occupies a special place. The bulk of past anthropological studies has dealt with impoverished peoples, who are often intimidated by researchers. While it is debatable whether such studies have had the unfortunate result of showing governments and their agencies how to control these peoples more efficiently, it is probably true that anthropological studies have done little to improve their lives. The time has arrived, I suggest, to switch our emphasis from the powerless to the élite, from the victims to the victimizers, if only to fill a large void in our knowledge. This does not mean that the discipline's focus should swing entirely to the cultures of advanced industrial societies, and that we should concentrate solely on the power élite. Ultimately our mandate is grander: to embrace both the powerful and the powerless in societies everywhere, rather than to remain tied to an obsolete focus on one part of the world, euphemistically called 'other cultures.' Surely an anthropology of the future that fails to make these adjustments will continue to flounder.

In summary, this study will provide a critical and innovative treatment of anthropological theory, stressing the outstanding accomplishments of the founding fathers, but demonstrating and explaining why our theory has not been cumulative. It will then propose a solution, beginning with the conceptualization of social life as inherently contradictory and ending with a dialectical perspective for anthropology – a perspective that avoids the pitfalls pointed out in part 1 and illuminates the major manifestations of inequality in a post-colonial world.

2

An Overview of Theory

The purpose of this chapter is to outline the major theoretical orientations in the discipline. In doing so, I shall distinguish clearly between British social anthropology and American cultural anthropology, and sketch the central ideas of some of the outstanding figures, such as Radcliffe-Brown, Malinowski, and Boas. Several terms can be used instead of 'theoretical orientation,' such as 'model,' 'school,' 'tradition,' 'conceptual scheme,' 'theoretical system,' or 'paradigm.' I use them interchangeably with 'theoretical orientation' in much the same (loose) way that Kuhn (1970) uses 'paradigm.' Because I shall argue that anthropology is not paradigmatic, I prefer to avoid the term.

Pelto (1970) distinguishes between metatheory (for example, the implicit philosophy of the actor, whether man is a creature of habit or a rational and active agent in the social process), special anthropological theory (such as evolutionism and structural functionalism), and personal theory (the investigator's biases, whether conflict or harmony is emphasized). Theoretical orientation as I use the term is similar to Pelto's special anthropological theory, but the latter is only analytically distinct from metatheory and personal theory; in practice all three are fused. By theoretical orientation I mean (a) the conceptual territory in which the discipline is supposed to operate; (b) the methodology, including research design, criteria of verification, preferred techniques, and assumptions about the balance of 'art' versus 'science'; (c) the implicit philosophy of the actor: whether free or determined, rational or emotional, good or evil; (d) the range of questions considered to be legitimate, such as whether motivation is important or can be ignored, or whether man's genetic make-up is to be entertained; and (e) implicit or explicit assumptions about 'key' factors such as sexual drive, kinship, religion, economics, and social solidarity.

Most field-workers do not consciously choose from among the various theoretical orientations. Instead, they operate implicitly within the intellectual tradition to which they have been exposed. In other words, a theoretical orientation has to be inferred by the analyst; it is a construct made from the existing products of anthropological investigation. I shall begin by listing the various theoretical orientations and then dividing them into several clusters. From each cluster a basic orientation will be selected for detailed examination. In this chapter little attempt is made to be innovative. My purpose is merely to present a baseline from which the subsequent critique of anthropological theory can be developed.

THEORETICAL ORIENTATIONS

A *Deemed of major importance*
1 early evolutionism
2 Marxian conflict
3 Weberian social action
4 Durkheimian social facts
5 historical particularism
6 British structural functionalism
7 culture and personality
8 cultural materialism (cultural ecology + neo-evolutionism)
9 non-Marxian conflict theory (Gluckman, Coser)
10 structuralism
11 formal analysis (the new ethnography)
12 Bailey social action
13 neo-Marxian conflict theory
14 neo-psychological anthropology
15 socio-biology
16 dialectical anthropology

B *Supplementary or minor*
1 Simmelian conflict theory
2 early American conflict (Cooley, Mead)
3 symbolic interactionism
4 symbolic anthropology
5 phenomenological Marxism (Lukacs)
6 scientific Marxism (Althusser)
7 critical theory (Frankfurt school)
8 cybernetics
9 game theory
10 generative models (Barth)
11 ethnomethodology
12 network analysis

13 acculturation
14 material culture
15 socio-linguistics
16 ethology
17 British diffusionism
18 *Kulturkreise* school
19 exchange theory
20 ethnohistory
21 Parsonian voluntarism
22 systems analysis

It is not possible to present the sixteen orientations deemed of major importance in strict chronological order, since some of them (such as Weberian social action and Durkheimian social facts) made their appearances at the same time. Several of the orientations in the second list are placed there not because they are less important than those in the first list, but because they can be subsumed within or are equivalent to one of the approaches in the first list. For example, *Kulturkreise* and the British school of diffusionism can be included under historical particularism. There is an unavoidable degree of arbitrariness about these lists, and some anthropologists would surely insist on placing symbolic anthropology or ethnohistory under the category of major orientations. Others might argue that several orientations in the two lists, especially those normally associated with sociology, do not belong there at all, and would contend that others or at least other labels), do belong there at all, and would contend that others (or at least other labels) do belong, such as configurational theory (Benedict), solidarity theory (Durk-nomics, and stratification. Certainly it would be legitimate to organize a theoretical discussion around these subsystems, but they constitute an order of conceptualization different from the thirty-eight theoretical orientations that have been introduced. Like race relations, they concern substantive issues rather than general theoretical perspectives.

CLUSTERS OF THEORETICAL ORIENTATIONS

1 *Evolutionism*
  – early evolution
  – neo-evolution
  – cultural ecology
  – cultural materialism
  – socio-biology
  – ethology
  – material culture

2 *Conflict*
- Marxian conflict
- neo-Marxian conflict
- Simmelian conflict
- early American conflict
- non-Marxian conflict
3 *Social action*
- Weberian social action
- Bailey social action
- Parsonian voluntarism
- American symbolic interactionism
- generative models (Barth)
- phenomenological Marxism (Lukacs)
- critical theory (Frankfurt school)
- exchange theory
4 *Structural functionalism*
- Durkheimian social facts
- British structural functionalism
- systems theory
- cybernetics
- game theory
- network analysis
5 *Historical particularism-diffusionism*
- Boasian historical particularism
- *Kulturkreise* school
- British diffusionism
- ethnohistory
6 *Psychological anthropology*
- culture and personality
- neo-psychological anthropology
- formal analysis and the new ethnography
- socio-linguistics
- acculturation
- symbolic anthropology
7 *Structuralism*
- Lévi-Straussian
- Althusserian (scientific Marxism)
- ethnomethodology
- dialectical anthropology

Some of the fundamental issues in anthropology are reflected in the labels assigned to these clusters. For example, can man be understood in macro-comparative evolutionary terms (1) or is every culture unique (5)? Do we live mainly in harmony (4) or in conflict (2)? Does man make his own history (3) or is he a cultural dope (4)?[1] Not all the theoretical orientations fall easily within a particular cluster. Gluckman's non-Marxian conflict theory in the second cluster is similar to the equilibrium model usually associated with structural functionalism in the fourth cluster. Marxism itself is represented in the conflict, social-action, and structuralism clusters, and one could make a case for placing it within evolutionism as well. To do so is merely to recognize the wholeness of Marx's vision, which was hostile to conventional disciplinary distinctions. In the next chapter, I shall discuss the work of Ritzer (1975), who considers Marx to be a paradigm-bridger. That is, Marx's vision cuts across and integrates various fundamental conceptions of the discipline, including (according to Ritzer) conflict theory and structural functionalism. However, it is inappropriate to describe a writer as having been a paradigm-bridger before the various paradigms or theoretical orientations actually emerged, reflecting the process of structural differentiation and specialization in the discipline. The fact that Marxism is represented in several clusters might be interpreted as evidence that the distinctions among these clusters lack meaning. In my view, this is wrong, for what it really reflects is the process of differentiation and specialization as it has affected the work of Marx. Regardless of his own synthetic vision, his commentators and disciples have carved up his grand scheme, pressing it into a variety of theoretical traditions. In doing so, several distinct brands of Marxism have been created, rather than one all-embracing scheme.

I have placed material culture under evolutionism, ethnohistory under historical particularism, and symbolic anthropology under psychological anthropology (apologies to Durkheim) simply because they fit even less well elsewhere. Some readers may be unhappy to find neo-evolutionism and cultural ecology lumped together under cultural materialism in the list of major orientations. My argument is that together they represent a distinct and important post-Second World War thrust in American anthropology, one that pushes the discipline's potential nomothetic capacity to the limit. But there are differences among them; I have separated them under the evolutionary cluster and later will discuss them individually.

The combination of cultural materialism, neo-evolutionism, and cultural ecology could have been called the techno-economic perspective since this is its dominant feature. Ethology is concerned with man's biological make-

---

1 'Cultural dope' is a term used by Giddens (1979) to refer to the image of the actor as a robot in the work of the sociologist Talcott Parsons (1951).

up, and thus is linked to socio-biology, which usually is put into an evolutionary scheme. Neo-Marxian conflict in the second cluster is reflected today in dependency theory, French economic anthropology, and, some would argue, in Lévi-Straussian structuralism. Whereas early American sociology was strongly influenced by Simmel's brand of conflict theory, it was not until the 1950s and 1960s that it made an impact on anthropology, notably in Gluckman's work (1963a), which coincided with a renewal of Simmel's influence on sociology, principally as a result of Coser's efforts (1964).

Weber's social-action theory has had a much longer history in sociology than in anthropology, helping to shape Parsons' voluntaristic orientation and more recent writings in symbolic interactionism. Not until Bailey's social-action position became articulated in the late 1960s did anthropology embrace many of the central principles of this orientation, although Barth earlier (1966) had drawn more explicitly from Weber in formulating his generative models, and some threads of Malinowski's work having to do with exchange theory fit into the social-action school. The phenomenological stance adopted by Weber was taken up by Marxists such as Lukacs, stressing the humanist side of Marx, and later elaborated on by what is known as the Frankfurt school of critical theory (see Held 1980 and Jay 1974). Lukacs rejected orthodox Marxism, with its determinist and positivist interpretations of history as consisting of unalterable historical stages fueled by the all-important economic base. Stressing the crucial part played by human subjectivity and class-consciousness, Lukacs was attacked by orthodox Marxists for his Hegelian idealism, or 'Hegelianized brand of Marxism' (Lukacs 1973: xii). In his early work (1971) he also attributed to the proletariat the 'criterion of truth,' arguing that the proletariat was a unique class – one able both to understand and to change society. Under pressure from orthodox communists, Lukacs later recanted, shifting the focus and 'criterion of truth' from the proletariat to the communist party.[2] As we shall see in the next chapter, such fundamental changes in intellectual position are not unusual: subject to comparable pressure, Thomas Kuhn reverted to orthodoxy after challenging the very nature of science.

The school of critical theory, established in 1923 in Frankfurt, centred on the Institute of Social Research. Among the leading figures were Max Horkheimer (philosophy and sociology), Theodor Adorno (philosophy and sociology), Herbert Marcuse (philosophy), Leo Lowenthel (popular culture and

---

2 For a recent statement of phenomenological Marxism which entertains the viewpoints expressed by Lukacs and the critical theorists, see Bologh (1979).

literature), and Freidrich Pollock (economics). Just as the Frankfurt critical school can be traced back to the work of Lukacs, in recent years it has been revived and extended by the work of Habermas (1970).

As a result of the rise of the Nazis, the school moved briefly to Geneva in 1933, and then to Columbia University in 1935. Philosophically and histori- cally oriented, the critical theorists attacked both conventional positivism and orthodox Marxism. Paramount among the interests of the critical theo- rists was praxis, or the relationship between theory and practice. In a world that did not unfold in the manner anticipated by orthodox Marxism, with the proletariat revolution leading to benign socialism (rather than Stalin- ism), what role did theory play in historical development? In part, the answer was that theory – critical theory, at least – could be a revolutionary force contributing to the improvement of society by examining contempo- rary political and social issues, and extending Marxian analysis into previ- ously ignored areas such as mass culture and sexuality. Certainly members of the New Left in the days of the student movement of the 1960s and early 1970s drew intellectual sustenance from the writings of the critical theorists, particularly Marcuse (1964).

Regarding category 4, I see systems theory as tidied-up structural func- tionalism, and cybernetics and game theory as methodological adjustments within the same conceptual territory. Network analysis hardly deserves the label of theory; despite Boissevain's view (1974), it can be tied as easily to structural functionalism as to anything else. Category 5 is self-explanatory. The three orientations listed there share a common and dominant interest in diffusionism, which supposedly disproved evolutionism. In category 6 I link the new ethnography and socio-linguistics to formal analysis dating back to Sapir and Whorf and Boas (but given new impetus in the 1950s with the appearance of componential analysis) and to less sophisticated attempts, especially in Britain, to consider the links between perception, conception, and behaviour. Formal analysis represents a return to mentalism. While writers such as Murphy (1971) and Voget (1975) seem to think that accultu- ration was a distinct and important orientation in American anthropology, in my opinion it was a minor variation within the culture-and-personality school, addressing an issue that has yet to be handled adequately by anthro- pology: culture contact and change.

The orientations placed under the structuralism category require some explanation. Although there are numerous varieties of structuralism, in this study I shall restrict the discussion mainly to the structuralism of Lévi-Strauss, with occasional references to Althusser's blueprint for a scientific Marxism. Ethnomethodology is included here because it is to sociology what structuralism is to anthropology: the only really novel theoretical approach since the turn of the century (see Garfinkel 1967). Dialectical anthropology shares some of the properties of structuralism, especially Lévi-Strauss's variety, but it promises much more. It is a new and exciting orientation, a perspective for the future, best represented to date by Robert Murphy (1971). Dialectical anthropology is a synthesis of phenomenology and positivism, of Marx and Lévi-Strauss, and of others such as Freud and Simmel. Although there are important differences between Murphy's approach and my own, this is the orientation that my position in this study most closely approximates.

BRITISH AND AMERICAN ANTHROPOLOGY

The main difference between British and American anthropology has concerned conceptual territory. Until the last decade or so, the prime impetus behind the works of British social anthropologists was to achieve a narrower and more precise definition of the conceptual territory encompassed by social structure. This was the logical direction of the principles established by Durkheim, and is manifested in the works of Radcliffe-Brown (1964), Nadel (1957), Gluckman (1963b), Firth (1964), and Leach (1961). The idea behind this movement was that only by chiselling out a narrow, precise conceptual territory could theoretical advancement be expected. This movement also was tied to the annoying problem of social change, and led these anthropologists into tortuous attempts to distinguish between analytic and concrete versions of social structure, such as Radcliffe-Brown's discussion of structural form and actual structure in his famous article 'On Social Structure' (1971: chap. 10). In American anthropology, in contrast, social structure has always been considered too narrow a definition of the conceptual territory; another variable has almost always been inserted into the framework, whether it was personality, ecology, biology or techno-economic factors. The assumption in America has often been that the British emphasis on social structure amounted to a one-variable program. That is, social structure was explained in terms of itself; therefore, it was tautological in nature, and did not lend itself to cause-and-effect analysis or nomothetic inquiry.

British Social Anthropology

Social Structure
1 social organization
2 kinship

3 economy

4 belief system

5 political and legal systems

The British focused on social structure, which included the subsystems listed above. There always was a disturbing ambiguity between social structure and social organization, with the illogical implication that they were equivalent. The belief system included more or less explicitly religion, magic, witchcraft, and ritual. Rarely was it conceptualized in terms of ideology in the Marxian sense of reflecting and maintaining the existing relations of production, as was often the case in American anthropology. As we know, social change was underplayed during the era of British structural functionalism, and if considered at all was usually tagged on to the end of a monograph. Of major significance was the assumed dominance of one of the subsystems dealt with by British social anthropologists: the kinship system. The general view was that it permeated all other subsystems, and hence was the key to understanding pre-industrial societies. Later we shall see that the central position occupied by the kinship system in pre-industrial societies has proved a challenge to Marxian approaches to anthropology. Sometimes the effort to present the kinship system as the key to the substructure has distorted the Marxian perspective to the point where it is hardly recognizable.

The restricted conception of the discipline's territory was not very palatable to American anthropologists, and shortly after the First World War one of them, Murdock, delivered a stinging criticism of the British school. The British, he argued, were limited in geographical scope because most of their work took place in British colonial dependencies. They also were limited in their ethnographic scope or their appreciation for general ethnography, which might have been Murdock's way of complaining that American-produced ethnography was receiving insufficient attention. Third, and most crucial, the British were severely limited in the range of cultural phenomena investigated; in Murdock's words (1951: 467), the British concentrated 'exclusively on kinship and subjects directly related thereto' and completely neglected 'such major aspects of culture as technology, folklore, art, child training, and even language.' The British were limited in an additional respect, as Murdock pointed out, one that concerned style of presentation rather than scope and focus of research; moreover, this limitation (if it is one) only emerged after British anthropology had become firmly established as an academic discipline by Malinowski and Radcliffe-Brown. I am referring to the practice of writing monographs around specific subsystems, such as kinship or the economy. For example, whereas Firth (1957) presented a rounded ethnography in We, the Tikopia, Fortes (1945, 1949) took two volumes to present the Tallensi kinship structure, and Evans-Pritchard parcelled his data out parsimoniously, focusing on Nuer political institutions in one monograph (1940), kinship in another (1951), and religion in a third work (1956). Murdock (1951: 466) complains about the 'seeming incompleteness' of the British style, and states that it 'merely reflects an increasing tendency on the part of British social anthropologists to fractionate their descriptions and analyses of social systems.' He was probably correct, but certainly one could not fault a writer like Evans-Pritchard for his overall contribution to ethnography, regardless of how he packaged it for publication. Moreover, the trend away from monographs organized around the several major subsystems and toward those focused on a single subsystem merely took the analytic thrust of social anthropology further in the narrow direction in which it had already been moving: toward an ever-increasing appreciation for the precise properties of social structure.

American Cultural Anthropology
Sometimes it is said that the British are interested in social systems, and the Americans in mankind. The latter suggests a much more inclusive conceptual territory. American general anthropology embraces both socio-cultural and biological systems, and includes physical anthropology, archaeology, linguistics, and cultural anthropology. In his history of anthropology in Britain, Penniman surprisingly argues that the approach there has been similar. Although published originally in 1935, Penniman's study was revised in 1962 and again in 1965, and should reflect the British scene until recent times. In Penniman's view, British anthropology has been as broad as American general anthropology; he regretted the efforts of Radcliffe-Brown to mark off a special domain having to do with social structure. Yet the fact is that cultural anthropology alone, as reflected in the scheme below, has always dealt with a much larger conceptual territory than British social anthropology.

Culture
1 ideology (or culture)
2 social organization (social structure)
3 techno-economic factors (or personality, or ecology, or language, or biology)

Number 2, social organization, is equivalent to the entire territory subsumed within the British conception of social structure. The causal links in American anthropology have either gone from 1 to 3 or from 3 to 1. Social organization has usually been an ill-defined residual category, which is what Murphy (1971) has said about Parsons' social system.

Social structure and social organization overlap and are confused in British anthropology, and the same is true for culture and ideology in American anthropology. At times culture is defined broadly to include ideology along with social organization and techno-economics (or some other factor). When this occurs, ideology usually is treated as the dependent variable, with causal primacy assigned to techno-economics. At other times, culture is defined narrowly to refer to ideology or belief system. When this occurs, culture (or ideology) usually is treated as the independent variable, as an autonomous level of human behaviour, a reality sui generis, much in the same way that Durkheim regarded the collective conscience. This is the manner in which Boas approached culture, emphasizing the fundamental importance of habit and tradition. It also was the approach of his disciples, Kroeber and Benedict. While recognizing the existence of basic culture (that is, social organization), Kroeber, curiously, gave priority to the analysis of secondary culture: value themes and styles. Benedict stressed the consistency of cultural beliefs, opposing what Lowie attributed to Boas as his 'shreds and patches' notion, and treated cultures as irreducible systems, or configurations with their own integrity. The assumption that culture was a reality sui generis was not the sole property of those who conceived of culture in the narrow sense. Leslie White, in his macro-evolutionary studies, also took this position while downplaying personality and biology.

Later I shall use the terms 'reductionism' and 'non-reductionism' to refer to the differences between American and British anthropology. From the British perspective, the American school has been reductionist because it has usually failed to treat the social structure as the key factor or independent variable. It is precisely this narrow view of the discipline's conceptual territory that led Murdock to conclude that the British weren't anthropologists at all (see Murdock 1951 and Firth's reply 1951). As the American anthropologist Fried has argued (1972: 11), any explanation of culture requires some understanding of biological factors. The British have ignored not only biology but culture as well, if Murdock is to be believed. Ironically, Murdock himself has been attacked by his fellow anthropologists (Voget 1975: 796–7; Sahlins 1976: 94–5) for his lack of ritualistic respect for that shibboleth of American anthropology, the concept of culture. In his Huxley Memorial Lecture, Murdock (1971) dismissed culture (and social structure) as a myth, a fabrication: people, not cultures, exist.

If there has been one persistent source of conceptual confusion in the discipline, it has been in the area of culture and social structure (or society). Sometimes it has had its humorous side. Malinowski drove a generation of

British social anthropologists mad by defining the discipline as the study of culture. Parsons traumatized American anthropologists by assigning causal primacy to the social system, with the implication that the British were on the right track. But as Sahlins (1976: 83) has pointed out, culture was cannibalized in Malinowski's scheme, destroyed by a view of man as manipulative and instrumental. As for Parsons' scheme, it is, as Murphy has acutely observed (1971: 56), a cultural approach pure and simple.[3]

BASIC THEORETICAL ORIENTATIONS

From each of the first six theoretical clusters, a specific orientation has been selected for detailed discussion: structural functionalism, conflict theory, social action, historical particularism, culture and personality, and cultural materialism (cultural ecology plus neo-evolutionism). The seventh, structuralism, will be dealt with separately in chapter 6 because it represents a novel approach to anthropological investigations. The six theoretical orientations are presented in an order that reflects differences between British and American anthropology as well as their contemporary significance. The first three orientations are British, the other three American. If we were guided solely by chronology, conflict theory, dating back to Marx, would have to come before structural functionalism, and evolutionism would have to be placed in front of historical particularism. However, I am interested in the position that these perspectives occupy in contemporary debates, especially in the recent versions of Marxism or evolutionism; this explains the order of presentation.

Structural functionalism
Also known simply as functionalism or as the social-structural model, and associated with the equilibrium model, structural functionalism is usually defined in two logical steps. The first is *residual*; social structure is part of what remains after one explains behaviour in terms of human heredity and man's environment. As the outer arrows in the accompanying diagram indicate, heredity and environment encapsulate social structure; in other words, they constitute its general environment.

---

3 Murphy (1971) also argues (correctly, I believe) that the supposed differences between cultural and social anthropology are not meaningful.

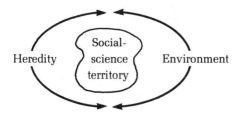

But between heredity and environment we find all the social sciences; thus, to define social structure we have to take the second logical step, which is *analytical*. Social anthropologists working within the structural-functional tradition take a 'slice' out of the social-science territory. This slice constitutes the social structure, shown in the second diagram. Similarly, psychology takes another slice (the personality system), and political science and economics remove still other sections.

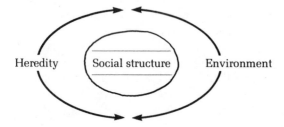

An assumption built into the social-structural model is that in order to expand theory and explanation, there must be a sharp analytic distinction made between anthropology and other disciplines. This orientation is especially hostile to psychological reductionism. Consider, for example, the case of the Igbo (or Biafrans) in Nigeria. Noting the enthusiasm with which these ambitious people adapted to Western values and industrialization, many casual observers argued that they were exceptionally intelligent, an unusually gifted 'race,' far excelling other Nigerian ethnic groups such as the Yoruba and the Hausa. Even trained social scientists sometimes took a similar stance. In *Dreams and Deeds* (1966), for example, LeVine, an anthropologist, measured the need to achieve, a psychological variable which McClelland (1961) contended was directly related to a society's level of economic growth. LeVine found the need to achieve more pronounced among the Igbo than among the Yoruba or Hausa.

From the social-structural perspective, this is a reductionist explanation and hence is illegitimate. Proponents of the non-reductionist model would try to explain the Igbo receptivity to industrialization in terms of properties of the social structure. For example, the Igbo belief system contained significant motivational springs. The Igbo believed in reincarnation. Men who did not achieve greater status, position, and prosperity than their fathers faced a bleak reincarnation: they would be reborn as albinos, as twins, or feet first – all of which were taboo. The Igbo distinguished between *chukwu*, the supreme god, and *chi*, a personal god, an intermediary between an individual and *chukwu*. Everyone had his own *chi*. If one did not prosper, or suffered misfortune, one might blame his *chi*, cast it out, and obtain a new one. Finally, it has been noted that the traditional Igbo status-mobility system was relatively open, with few ascribed positions; emphasis was placed on achieving one's fortune in the economic realm. If this sounds remarkably like American society, we shouldn't be surprised. Most of the work that addressed the issue of Igbo receptivity to change, from LeVine's McClelland-influenced study of achievement motivation to Ottenberg's sound ethnography (1962), was guided by the American-style modernization theory that has now (happily) sunk into oblivion.

Just as psychology takes the social structure as constant and tries to explain behaviour in terms of variation in personality, anthropology takes the personality as constant and tries to explain behaviour in terms of variation in properties of the social structure. Consider Weber's Protestant-ethic thesis, in which it is argued that the degree and nature of work motivation varies with the type of religion. In advancing his argument, Weber entertained the influence of Protestantism (and within it Calvinism, Catholicism, Lutheranism and pietism), Hinduism, and Judaism on orientation toward work. In other words, he was concerned with variations in the properties of the social structure. He was not concerned with variations in the properties of the personality structure, such as whether a person is active or passive or the level of his scores on a scale of need to achieve or affiliate. As Weber found, Protestantism produced a higher degree of work motivation than the other universal religious systems. It should be remarked that the proponents of the social-structural model would not (or should not) argue that motivation is a psychological phenomenon, or that there are psychological as opposed to sociological data. Data are discipline-neutral. They only become 'psychological' or 'sociological' by virtue of the conceptual scheme imposed on them.

The argument, in a nutshell, is that if all social behaviour could be reduced to psychology, there would be no need for the discipline of anthropology; if all psychological phenomena could be reduced to biology, there would be no need for psychology. The proponents of these disciplines contend that behaviour relevant to each of these levels can't entirely be explained at other levels. It should be obvious that reductionism is a highly political term, in the sense that scholars in a specific discipline may be condemned by their colleagues for stepping 'beyond' the discipline's conceptual territory, and also in the sense that it defends the discipline's conceptual territory from practitioners in other disciplines who may claim to speak for it. While by no means an obsolete viewpoint, reductionism has been seriously challenged in recent years by those who contend that existing disciplinary boundaries are outmoded.

Durkheim

The main creator of structural functionalism was Durkheim (1858–1917). Born in the French province of Lorraine, Durkheim was formally trained in philosophy, and in 1887 accepted an appointment in the department of philosophy at the University of Bordeaux. Within a decade he had been appointed to a full professorship in social science, the first position of its kind in France. By then he had published several outstanding works, including The Division of Labour, The Rules of Sociological Method, and Suicide. In 1898 he founded what has been arguably the most famous journal in sociology and anthropology, L'Année Sociologique. Durkheim was directly influenced by others such as Saint-Simon, Comte, Montesquieu, Rousseau, Spencer, and Marx; the influence of the last two was negative, in that Durkheim usually reacted against such things as the individualistic and biological themes in Spencer's organic evolutionism and the materialist basis of Marx's work. The reaction against Marx was certainly more explicit in Weber's work, partly because Durkheim simply legislated problems raised by Marx out of existence, which accounts both for his more (superficially) consistent viewpoint and for his dogmatism.

Durkheim was very much against psychological reductionism, and I suppose every undergraduate student in social anthropology and sociology commits to heart the message that whenever a psychological explanation is given for a social phenomenon, we may be certain it is wrong (see Durkheim 1938: 104). Durkheim argued so strongly against reductionism largely because at the time he was writing it was generally assumed that man was rational and free, in control of his own destiny. Durkheim, on the contrary, thought that to a great extent man's fate was dictated by the social structure: one really had no choice in the language one spoke, or the clothes one wore; to some extent one's choice of spouse and occupation also were dictated. In a work that continues to spark debate in symbolic anthropology (1963), he even contended that the very manner in which we conceptualize is a product of the social structure rather than an intrinsic function of the brain, and is certainly not an individualistic phenomenon. Later we shall see that had Durkheim had the advantage of exposure to modern psychological theory, especially Freudian-influenced work on the unconscious, he might not have taken the position he did.

Durkheim's greatest illustration of the manner in which a person was constrained by the social structure concerned suicide. In his famous book (1951), he showed that every society and every sociologically identifiable group had a specific suicide rate – or a specific tendency toward suicide. The rate was greater for Protestants than for Catholics, for men than for women, for single people than for married people, and for the divorced than for the non-divorced. Durkheim saw the suicide rate as external to the individual, located in society; coercive over the individual's behaviour; and general throughout the sector of the social structure abstracted for analysis, such as divorcées. In other words, it met all the criteria of a social fact as he defined it. However, Durkheim did not argue for complete sociological determinism. He realized that social-structural pressures only accounted for a certain percentage of man's behaviour.[4] He could explain behaviour only to the extent that it varied according to the properties of the social structure; the framework was not deterministic in the sense of being directed to the actions of any particular actor. For example, suicide can never be explained by the social structure alone, but must be complemented by normal and abnormal psychology and biology.

Two features of the social-structural model are highly significant. First, it establishes an explicit conceptual territory for anthropology. Those who learn this orientation have great confidence about the range of questions that can be legitimately raised in the discipline, and the precise limits of explanation. Second, it views the individual as responding in an almost robot-like fashion to the pressures of the social structure. As indicated in the discussion of determinism, this is a distortion of Durkheim's own position. However, he provided room for this distortion partly because of his method of argumentation: stating alternative theoretical viewpoints, proving them wrong, and leaving the reader with the one correct explanation: his own social-structural position. It also must be said that he exaggerated the explanatory range of his model, as Marx did his own, probably because in both cases new ground was being broken. At any rate, there has been a tendency in

---

4 See, for example, his important statement in a footnote in *Suicide* (1951: 325), where he argues that the sociological perspective is not deterministic.

anthropology to explain behaviour solely in terms of properties of the social structure, a tendency that has created the image of the robot, or the over-socialized actor.[5]

This problem relates to an ambiguity that has plagued anthropology from its inception: the relationship between belief and action, between what people say and what they do, between formal and informal codes of behaviour. The ambiguity is at the root of Lévi-Strauss's distinction (1967a: 275) between mechanical and statistical models. In the first, the model and the phenomena are on the same scale; here we are dealing with 'ought' statements, with ideal behaviour, with norms in the sociological sense. If we know one case, we know all of them, for the normative pattern is universal. In contrast, statistical models are based on probability; they are norms in the mathematical sense of averages; the model and the phenomena are not on the same scale. For example, society x may have a preferential matrilateral cross-cousin marital system at the mechanical level; this is the rule that informants will report to the ethnographer. Yet it may well be that less than 10 per cent of marriages actually conform to the rule.[6] Imagine a situation in which nobody in the category of matrilateral cross-cousins is available for marriage. Although Durkheim never wrote on this subject, according to the exaggerated interpretation of his work, one must remain a bachelor or spinster. In reality, one simply marries someone outside the category, either by expanding the category to include others or by ignoring the rule.[7] This problem is also reflected in the distinction between prescriptive and preferential marital partners. Anthropologists have found that marital choice is usually prescriptive at the level of rules, and preferential at the level of behaviour. This distinction is fundamental to the central arguments of this book: the simultaneous existence of a semblance of order at the level of belief, and of flux and contradiction at the level of action.

Radcliffe-Brown

Durkheim's work was incorporated into British anthropology by Radcliffe-Brown (1881–1955), who, until Lévi-Strauss appeared, was usually con-

---

5 In chapter 6 I discuss what I refer to as 'the other Durkheim,' whose concern was with the theory of knowledge and whose approach was almost dialectical.

6 Cross-cousin marriage has been the subject of one of the most important debates in anthropology – that concerning structure and sentiment and alliance and descent. The basis of the debate can be found in two books: Homans and Schneider, *Marriage, Authority, and Final Causes* (1955) and Needham, *Structure and Sentiment* (1962).

7 Of course, this is true for parallel cousin marriage as well, which is a prevalent form in North Africa and the Middle East (see Ayoub 1959, Barth 1954, and Khuri 1970).

sidered to be the greatest theoretician to emerge in the discipline after the groundwork had been laid by Marx, Durkheim, and Weber. Born in England and educated at Cambridge University, where he came under the influence of Rivers, Radcliffe-Brown undertook field-work from 1906 to 1908 in the Andaman Islands, located west of Thailand. However, his flair was for theory; by the First World War he had discovered Durkheim, and set about putting the Frenchman's stamp on British social anthropology. Like Durkheim, Radcliffe-Brown was anti-reductionist, and tried to model the discipline after the hard sciences. Although the positivistic position was certainly not the only one that could have been exploited from Durkheim's writings, it was the one promoted by Radcliffe-Brown. According to Radcliffe-Brown, there are three stages to any scientific investigation:

1 observation (collecting the data)
2 taxonomy (classifying the data)
3 generalization (theoretical excursions)

Durkheim had argued that comparative sociology was not just a branch of sociology, but sociology itself. Radcliffe-Brown reinforced this view by contending that generalization was intrinsically related to comparative analysis. He saw the comparative method as our alternative to the controlled laboratory experiment. One of the ironies in anthropology is that the same man who tried to lay the basis for a positivistic science of society, which necessarily meant comparative (especially cross-cultural) analysis, was also partly responsible for firmly establishing intensive field-work studies within a structural-functional framework, which severely limited comparative work in the discipline. It is often remarked that structural functionalism was anti-historical and conservative, was static rather than dynamic, and helped to prop up colonial rule. While this is certainly true, it must also be realized that, as in the case of comparative work, anthropology failed to be historical and dynamic for an additional reason: the sheer limitations on what one person could do in the field as the ethnographic enterprise thrived. Certainly the virtual absence of systematic comparative work in the era of structural functionalism cannot be explained in the same way that we would account for a similar flaw in Ruth Benedict's writings. Unlike Radcliffe-Brown, Benedict eschewed comparative work on the ground of the assumed uniqueness of each and every culture.

Radcliffe-Brown's writing on the comparative method was addressed to central philosophical, epistemological, and methodological issues in the discipline. For example, can there be an Indian chemistry, a Russian chemistry, and an American chemistry? Or is chemistry the same regardless of national boundaries? Similarly, can there be an Indian anthropology, a Russian anthropology, and an American anthropology? This issue concerns the differences between nomothetic and idiographic approaches to the study of mankind, and has been answered differently since the inception of the discipline. Sapir and Whorf, two American linguists writing in the early part of this century, stressed the links between language, perception, and culture, and Whorf especially came out on the side of the uniqueness of each culture. Benedict followed suit, and others, such as Kroeber, tended to agree. These are American anthropologists, but as we shall see later, the most gifted anthropologist in the era following Radcliffe-Brown and Malinowski – Evans-Pritchard – argued eventually that cultures are not natural systems.[8] Radcliffe-Brown obviously had previously emerged on the other side, arguing for a nomothetic, generalizing, law-like approach to the analysis of social systems. Even those who agreed with him sometimes differed on the preferred range of comparisons. Perhaps the majority of British social anthropologists would have argued that comparisons should be limited to two or three cases involving adjacent tribes. This position was not that different from Boas's, who has been attacked for his anti-scientific and particularly his anti-comparative stance. Often the comparative method was achieved simply by having a number of field-workers address similar issues. This was the case in the famous studies of the village headmen in central Africa (Gluckman et al. 1949), and in important edited works devoted to kinship (Radcliffe-Brown and Forde 1964) and politics (Fortes and Evans-Pritchard 1940).

Comparative analysis presupposed sociological types and classification, but this too was a problem. What were the units of classification? One might select the state, but was it legitimate to compare a state as large as Britain with the Zulu empire? Although there were problems, it made sense to establish sociological types, perhaps arranged according to a scheme such as Steward's (1955) levels of socio-cultural integration, and to restrict the analysis to entities that fell into specific types. But Radcliffe-Brown himself argued that we should also compare *across* types. If a hypothesis held even when the types differed, it was greatly reinforced. For example, if the same

8 As Kuper (1975: 161–2) points out, Evans-Pritchard accepted Radcliffe-Brown's positivistic position until the Second World War, but in his Marrett lecture, delivered in 1950, he issued a declaration of rebellion, stating that anthropology studies moral rather than natural systems and is a kind of historiography. Further evidence of Evans-Pritchard's change in theoretical position is provided by Hatch, who writes (1973: 241) that 'the shift was from a positivistic and functional interpretation of institutions toward an idealistic one.'

rate of divorce accompanied a specific child-rearing practice found in both hunting-and-gathering and industrial societies, we could assign the child-rearing practice considerable causal weight. In similar fashion, Everett Hughes, the noted American sociologist, advocated the comparison of dissimilar roles, such as the psychiatrist and the prostitute: both use the couch, and both must be discreet.

I became aware of another serious problem in the comparative approach in the course of research in Nigeria. On three different field trips (1969–70, 1972, and 1974), I investigated the reasons that led to the remarkable economic success of a Utopia that I call Olowo, founded by Yoruba-speaking fishermen. Located in the depths of the Niger delta along the Atlantic coast, in a region where all houses had to be built on stilts because the land was flooded during the wet season, the Holy Apostles, as Olowo people were known, had constructed several factories and seven fully mechanized sea-going fishing trawlers. The village had been established for religious reasons, primarily to attain immortality (see Barrett 1974 and 1977), and was organized communally. No money was exchanged among members for goods and services, all basic necessities were provided without charge, and profits from the village's industries went to the central treasury. The village was split into male and female sectors, and children were raised by adults other than their parents.

In order to explain Olowo's remarkable success, I undertook a comparative study with a nearby village that had been established at almost the same time. The religious beliefs of the two villages were virtually identical. What was different was the communal system in Olowo, and the private-enterprise system and conventional extended family in the other village. The conclusion I originally drew was that the communal system, since it constituted the basic difference between the two villages, was the key factor in Olowo's economic success. However, further research cast doubt on this explanation, and I began to rethink the comparative framework. A central assumption in comparative analysis is that a constant cannot explain variation. Certainly this is correct; yet an inconstant may be even less important. For example, because religious beliefs in the two villages were virtually the same, they could not account for Olowo's greater economic progress. All that this meant was that religion was not a sufficient cause. It did not specify the degree of influence that religion had, which from a purely logical point of view might have been greater than communalism. As a matter of fact, this was precisely what I concluded after further trips to the field.

Radcliffe-Brown was the high priest of positivistic anthropology in Britain, where he finished his career at Oxford University. He also taught in and left his mark on several other countries, including Australia, South Africa, and the United States. But from today's perspective, his constant harangues for a nomothetic science of society have a hollow ring. Somewhat like Talcott Parsons, he impresses one as a bright graduate student who never grew intellectually after receiving his union card. I think this is partly because he was never really committed to field-work, although compared with Parsons he was an old hand at it. As Davis (1971: 328) had written, 'the "Mediocre" in the social sciences (and probably the natural sciences too) can be defined as those who take the textbook rules of scientific procedures too literally and too exclusively.' To some extent this describes Radcliffe-Brown, but certainly one could not pin the label 'mediocre' on him, because he was engaged in writing the rules themselves.

Radcliffe-Brown was not merely a spokesman for positivism. He began his career under the influence of Rivers and British diffusionism, and only switched to the structural-functional branch of positivism after discovering Durkheim. Despite claims to the contrary by many critics, he was not opposed to evolutionism. Just as Parsons was capable of brilliant work, as reflected in several of his essays (1964) when he put aside his cumbersome logico-deductive scheme, the same was true of Radcliffe-Brown when he went beyond his 'confessions of faith' (Lowie 1937: 222) about a natural science of society; examples are his essays 'The Mother's Brother in South Africa' and 'On Joking Relationships' (1971). Some of these pieces also reflect another theoretical direction that strived to emerge in his work: an incipient structuralist analysis in the Lévi-Straussian vein. Radcliffe-Brown's writings on avoidance and ritual formality, alternative generations (respect and familiarity), and widespread grandparent terminology will become significant later in this book when I try to explain how a semblance of order is achieved in society.

Malinowski

Malinowski (1884–1942) must be dealt with alongside Radcliffe-Brown, not only because together they are considered to be the founders of modern social anthropology, but also because Malinowski was a functionalist. Radcliffe-Brown is thought to be the more gifted theoretician, but far from Malinowski's equal as a field-worker. Most of Malinowski's career was spent at the London School of Economics; in 1938 he left for America on sabbatical and taught at Yale University until his death in 1942. The myth of how

Malinowski became a field-worker is humorously presented by Kuper (1975: 22–3); what is significant is that he put an end, at least for a while, to armchair anthropology or museum moles. It must be remembered, though, that this revolutionary new style in the discipline came about largely through fortuitous circumstances: the effect of the First World War and the co-operation of the Australian government, which allowed Malinowski, a Polish national, to live off and on for four years among the Trobrianders. It must also be remembered that others such as Morgan, Tylor, Bastian, Rivers, and especially Boas had embarked on original field-work even in the previous century.

Although both Malinowski and Radcliffe-Brown were structural functionalists, their theoretical orientations were by no means identical. Malinowski emphasized function, and seemed to lack his counterpart's sensitivity to the potential flaws in the perspective, such as the view that everything has a function. Radcliffe-Brown emphasized structure, or system; at one point he denied that he was a functionalist in the Malinowskian sense, and even that the functional school existed. This was partly because of a terminological quibble: Malinowski defined the discipline as the study of culture, not of social structure. Malinowski also tended to see the universe in a grain of sand, to generalize cross-culturally from a single case, the Trobrianders. But this tendency to view the world as an extension of one's 'tribe,' be it the Trobrianders, the Ashanti, or the Nupe, is a widespread flaw in the discipline. Radcliffe-Brown flatly denied the possibility of generalizing from one society, no matter how familiar the investigator was with it (1964: 38).

There were other differences between the two giants of early social anthropology. Malinowski's theoretical framework (1944), shown in the accompanying diagram, was much broader than Radcliffe-Brown's.

Culture
↑
Social organization
↑
Basic needs (biological and psychological)

Malinowski advocated both biological and psychological reductionism, and assumed that culture and social organization were responses to basic biological and psychological needs; these needs could be met by several different cultural responses, not just by one. In this sense, his orientation was much more similar to American cultural anthropology than was Radcliffe-

Brown's. As indicated earlier, Malinowski also defined the discipline as the study of culture, which again put him on the same wavelength as the North American school.

It is customary to deride Malinowski's contributions to theory. This can be partly explained, one suspects, by virtue of the fact that his work overlaps considerably with the general thrust of the Americans rather than with the direction in which Radcliffe-Brown engineered social anthropology. The seeds of culture and personality were planted in Malinowski's work via his interest in the individual, as well as the seeds of later orientations such as sociobiology. On a purely abstract level, he also anticipated the logic of inquiry in cultural ecology and neo-evolutionism, in positing the different levels of beliefs, social organization, and basic needs. Toward the end of his life, Malinowski was advocating a return to evolutionism. He also was arguing for a reorientation of anthropology toward the study of cultural change, which makes him very much a contemporary figure. With his emphasis on the difference between cultural norms and actual behaviour, on self-interested, manipulating man, he also laid the groundwork for the social-action model that I shall describe later, aspects of which emerged in the work of his student Firth and later in the writings of Leach, Barth, and Bailey. Radcliffe-Brown certainly spoke the language of science, but Malinowski was more flexible; in the end, his contributions to theory may have been greater. Was this because he was also the better field-worker?

No discussion of Malinowski would be complete without referring to the *kula* ring, one of the outstanding ethnographic discoveries in the discipline (Malinowski 1922). The *kula* ring involved the Trobriand Islands, located to the east of New Guinea, and other islands such as Dobu. Necklaces were exchanged clockwise from island group to island group, and armshells were exchanged counter-clockwise. The exchange was ceremonial, for the shells were not intrinsically valuable. However, the result of the exchange was an increased level of social solidarity among otherwise dispersed and potentially hostile island groups. This made possible *gimwali*, which was bartering activity that accompanied the *kula* exchange, involving valuable economic goods such as fish, pottery, and building materials. The rule that *kula* partners could not barter with each other, but could freely do so with the partners of others, ensured that the distinct ceremonial and economic transactions would not be confused. Malinowski's writings played a significant role in the development of an economic theory, such as Polanyi's (1944), that was not restricted to Western market economies. In his own work, Malinowski challenged widely held assumptions in other disciplines, such as the notion of economic man and the Oedipus complex. If he did not succeed in disproving them, his cross-cultural framework at least pointed out the ethnocentrism in existing explanations.

We have seen that Malinowski was much more popular than Radcliffe-Brown among American anthropologists because of his broader conceptual scheme and the central position to which he assigned culture. Malinowski was also more popular among non-anthropologists. This was because he titillated their Victorian imaginations with his writings on the bizarre (at least from a Westerner's perspective), such as the sexual lives of primitives and their views on impregnation by spirits from the sea, funerals, and second burials. But it was the sober Radcliffe-Brown, it must be remembered, who introduced the subject of the exchange of umbilical cords between potential enemies residing in different communities among the Adamandese. These individuals became institutionalized 'best friends' and trading partners, yet were forbidden to ever talk to each other.

The Equilibrium Model

Closely associated with structural functionalism or the social-structural model is the equilibrium model. Structural functionalism rests upon an organic analogy derived from biology, as exemplified in the work of Herbert Spencer (1820–1903), the British sociologist whose evolutionary theory (1876) was made to reinforce individualism and to oppose the state. Structural functionalism sometimes is referred to as the 'big animal' theory of society. Taken literally, the theory is organistic: a society is a real organism, with a heart, lungs, and other vital parts. Taken as an analogy, the theory is organic: societies are *like* animals, and their institutions and functions are comparable to the parts of the body. In the theory's crudest form everything is assumed to have a function, which has prompted criticisms of functional indispensability, functional unity, and functional universality. Merton is usually credited with having cleaned up functionalism, partly by his introduction of terms such as 'latent function' and 'dysfunction.' Actually, Radcliffe-Brown before him had pointed out most of these errors, and it is tempting to agree with Andreski (1972: 56–7), who dismisses Merton's work on functionalism as a proliferation of labels without explanation.

The equilibrium model clarifies essential properties of the structural-functional orientation. Adapted from classical mechanics, it stresses harmony, a tendency toward consensus, a central value system, and change as abnormal and exogenous. It also posits re-equilibrium mechanisms such as Hallowe'en, freshman initiation rites, and youth culture, which let off steam and act as safety valves. Whether referred to as structural functionalism, the social-structural model, or the equilibrium model, it is a conservative perspective tending to provide ideological support for the status quo. It has also been the dominant theoretical orientation in both social anthropology and sociology. Attempts have been made to handle the analysis of change by structural functionalists. The common procedure can be referred to as dual synchronic analysis: one 'freezes' the social structure at a specific time in history, takes an analytic slice, 'freezes' it at a later time, takes another slice, and compares the two to determine the differences. Some writers, such as Parsons, have introduced the term 'dynamic' or 'moving' equilibrium to reflect the fact that while society always is in flux, the change is slow and the overall structural properties of the social system persist. However, Rex contends that dynamic equilibrium is a contradiction in terms: society is either in equilibrium or it is not (1961: 133).

Just as the equilibrium model has been criticized because of its inability to cope with change, it has also been condemned because it downplays conflict; indeed, change and conflict are usually seen as two sides of the same coin. These flaws gave rise to recent trends in conflict theory, but as I shall argue later, even Parsons, the arch-conservative (at least in his academic role), was able to cope with change and conflict as readily as writers such as Coser and Gluckman who introduced a non-Marxian brand of conflict theory. At this juncture it is impossible to avoid one of anthropology's fundamental questions: is society dominated by harmony or conflict? This issue is the basis of the most important replication study in the discipline: Lewis's restudy (1951) of Redfield's Tepoztlan (1930). In a cheeky but penetrating essay, Runciman (1970: 21) has written that there is no evidence that would prove whether society is primarily harmonious or whether it is rent by strain. The history of anthropology is peppered with polarized and seemingly arbitrary arguments. In no small measure this is due to the irresolvable conceptual opposites, such as conflict versus harmony, that pervade the discipline.

Conflict

As it became apparent that structural functionalism was severely flawed, anthropologists began to look around for alternatives, and the one that caught on most quickly was the conflict model. It must be made clear, however, that since the innocent days of assumed harmony and equilibrium models, we have had two very different kinds of conflict models. The first to appear was non-Marxian; it is only in recent years that an explicit Marxist approach has emerged in the discipline.

Type A: Non-Marxian
The conflict model reverses most of the assumptions of the equilibrium model. Conflict is seen as normal and internally generated. It even contributes to the maintenance of the social system. The proponents of the equilibrium model take values as their basic concept. The logical tendency in this model is to employ a single unit of analysis, be it society at the macro level or role at the micro level. Conflict analysts take interests as their basic concept. They regard the social world as dichotomous and rent by opposition rather than united by common values. In other words, they focus logically on at least two units which express different interests. In this model there is a tendency to focus on the individual rather than on the role as the lowest level of abstraction, in so far as conflict theorists are concerned with competing interests rather than with complexes of norms that guide behaviour in particular social roles. Yet both models are systemic in assuming that behaviour is the obverse of random variability.

The conflict model came into vogue primarily as a result of the writings of Gluckman (1963a) and Coser (1964). Their main innovations were to conceptualize conflict as normal and widespread and as positive. Their works were soon to be criticized as disguised equilibrium models, for conflict was seen as functional; it contributed to the maintenance of society. The main flaw in this model was the absence of a dialectic. Without a dialectic, conflict is essentially static, or non-antagonistic. As we shall see later, even in some theoretical orientations that are explicitly Marxian-influenced, such as Harris's cultural materialism, again a dialectic is missing. This is one reason that Harris's cultural materialism has to be dismissed as 'mechanical' materialism – hopelessly insensitive to the strains and dynamism that characterize the institutional framework of society. In many respects a type of conflict theory had been in operation for several years before Gluckman's writings. Quite a remarkable number of anthropologists had had occasion to explain the web of networks that existed by virtue of the fact that the strain expressed in one set of interpersonal relationships was cancelled out in another set, with a resulting overall consistency of the social structure. This explanation can be found in Fortes's writing on the Tallensi, Colson's on the Tonga, and Evans-Pritchard's on the Nuer. It is not accidental that the last two involved feuding societies, for the central tendency in the literature on feuds is the argument that they contribute to the society's equilibrium. Perhaps it is significant that this view of solidarity and equilibrium achieved by cross-cutting loyalties, feuds, and rebellions is expressed by two of the British social anthropologists who remained most faithful to Durkheim and Radcliffe-Brown – Gluckman and Fortes.

The conceptual territory of this model (shown in the diagram) is identical to that of the previous model.

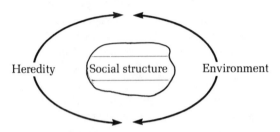

Type B: Marxian

In the Marxian type of conflict model, conflict again is seen as normal and essential; change is normal and internally generated, and the emphasis is on conflicting interest groups rather than a central value system. Unlike the Gluckman type of conflict, Marxian conflict leads to change, even revolutionary change, rather than to the maintenance of the system. This difference is largely due to the central position of contradiction in the Marxian framework. It is contradiction within a system that produces a type of change characterized as dialectical, such as wage-earners versus owners of the means of production in capitalism. Marx's framework is also an evolutionary one, and at the same time shares one aspect of functionalism: change is directional, and the end is a better society; therefore it is 'functional.' This can be called the flaw of optimism in Marxism. As Murphy has said (1971), Weber, a pessimist, was much better at prediction.

This type of conflict theory has rarely been embraced in anthropology; even when it has, the links to Marx often have been denied, obfuscated, or simply unrecognized. As we shall see later, this is the case with Steward's and White's works within the cultural ecology and neo-evolutionary orientations. The Marxian framework also can be found in dependency theory with Frank, as well as in Harris's cultural materialism, and recent French economic anthropology. However, the general trend in recent years has been to pull the teeth out of Marxism, to make it apolitical, stuck to a lifeless class analysis – what I later describe as a castrated Marxism. For example, Harris's cultural materialism does not contain a dialectic, and in French economic anthropology so many institutions apparently can serve as the substructure that Marx's fundamental distinction between base and superstructure has lost its meaning. Althusserian Marxism, as I shall argue, partly amounts to a rediscovery of functionalism. And Lévi-Strauss's structuralism, sometimes described as a Marxian approach, is not only, in the words of the master himself, completely apolitical, but indeed is a mentalist position. The explanation is simple: Marxism is usually ignored by anthropologists, but when it does catch on, steps are immediately taken to turn it into a eunuch.

Social Action

The Durkheim structural-functional approach adapted by Radcliffe-Brown dominated social anthropology for decades – indeed, right up to the 1960s; even today, it would be difficult to say in what way many monographs differ from this early orientation. The approach was modified by the Gluckman–Coser thrust, but not overthrown. This is because their conflict theory turned out to be a disguised equilibrium approach. The first model to which I was introduced as a student was structural functionalism. Suspecting the biases of some of my teachers, I began to read widely in the literature on conflict. Much to my surprise there was little that was new. Conflict there may have been, internal or otherwise, but the overall picture was one of equilibrium and persisting institutions. Perhaps most disappointing of all was the discovery that the model's capacity to cope with change was no greater than that achieved by equilibrium theorists such as Parsons (1951) and Levy (1952). Only later did I appreciate the fundamental differences between non-Marxian and Marxian types of conflict and realize that my reading had been confined basically to the first. This type was closer to Simmel than to Marx, although Gluckman apparently declared that he had never read Simmel's work (see Kuper 1975: 180). This was not true of Coser, who consciously reworked Simmel's propositions, albeit in a particular direction: it now seems clear that he pushed the dialectical parts of Simmel's work far into the background.

Henceforth in this study, when I refer to structural functionalism or to the social-structural or equilibrium model, I intend the terms to include the Coser–Gluckman type of conflict theory. After Gluckman's unsuccessful attempt to replace structural functionalism, some anthropologists took a different tack. They began to argue that the Durkheimian–Radcliffe-Brown approach was too rigid and deterministic. They contended that the individual did more than merely respond to social-structural pressures. They saw the individual as innovative and manipulative, and the social structure as fluid and changing; they stressed that individuals constantly competed for scarce goods to their own advantage and were always confronted with a choice of alternatives. In this model it is not argued that individuals are completely free, but that their behaviour is not simply a reflection of social-structural pressures. Despite the emphasis placed on choice, the model had little in common with Parsons' voluntaristic theory of social action. This is because, as we shall see, the relationship between the normative order and choice is not simple, as in the Parsonian framework. Norms are not conceived of as institutionalized into the social system, and hence explanatory of action; instead, norms are themselves manipulated so as to bring gratification to the actor.

This model can be traced back to both Marx (1818–83) and Weber (1864–1920), the two German-born scholars who created the framework for social anthropology. However, during the long period in which the discipline was dominated by Durkheim and structural functionalism, the works of Marx and Weber were often ignored. Marx had grappled valiantly with the tension between the view that man is free and creative and the view that he is determined by social circumstances. In Marx's work, man is not an automaton but an active participant in making his own history. This tension is certainly intrinsic to Weber's work as well, and if it was never resolved satisfactorily by either of these giants, at least they didn't trivialize the problem by ignoring it as did Durkheim, at least in his positivistic writings. Apart from Marx and Weber, some components of the social-action model were present in a body of writing more accessible to anthropologists – Malinowski's work. He stressed the individual's self-interest, the gap between the rules of the game and how in fact it is played, and the manipulative nature of man. Not until the 1950s did Raymond Firth, one of Malinowski's first students, begin to challenge the Radcliffe-Brown model, although Evans-Pritchard also registered his protest on other grounds, mostly having to do with the role of history and the image of anthropology as a science. Firth (1964) said that an adequate anthropological analysis required two concepts: social structure and social organization. The first was identical to the old Durkheimian conception; the second emphasized choice and innovation. The first concept was analytic; the second was supposedly concrete, in so far as it was tied to empirical behaviour. Actually, Radcliffe-Brown, with his concepts of structural form and actual structure, had earlier flirted with a distinction similar to Firth's. He even separated social structure and social organization, thus anticipating the very concepts later used by Firth.

It was not until the 1960s that some anthropologists discarded the structural-functional orientation entirely. By that time the social-action model was 'in the air,' and could be found in the works of Leach and his student Barth. But it was F.G. Bailey who articulated the new theoretical direction most clearly. Durkheim and Radcliffe-Brown had assumed that the individual's behaviour is constrained by the norms and rules of society. Bailey argues that in real life most of us thread our way between the norms, seeking the most advantageous route. As Bailey himself put it, 'One of the great gaps in anthropology is that we have been too much interested in the "system" and although we know that people live half their lives finding ways to "beat the system" we tend to take serious notice of them only when they are caught out, brought to trial and punished' (1969: 87). It is not that norms and rules don't exist. It is simply that as thinking, feeling, striving creatures, human beings continually manipulate the normative order. In other words, norms are included among the resources available to the actor to be used to further his advantage. An implication is that one cannot explain behaviour simply by erecting a model of the normative order. To do so constitutes a smokescreen; it smooths over the rough edges of everyday behaviour to give it the appearance of order, a theme that will be developed in considerable detail later.

Bailey distinguishes between normative and pragmatic rules, which correspond to norm and act, or ideal and act. These are not isomorphic in Bailey's framework. Instead, they are characterized by an implicit dialectical relationship, approaching the more explicit dialectic in Murphy's work (1971). Bailey (1969: 15) regards the ratio of pragmatic to normative rules as an index of potential social change. When pragmatic rules proliferate, at least two solutions are possible. One is to institute a period of 'cleaning up.' For example, Bailey (1969: 209) refers to accumulated corruption and favouritism in bureaucracies, which are terminated periodically by harsh applications of the rules of impartiality and honesty. Another possible solution is to recognize the inevitability of pragmatic rules and build them into the structure. Rather than having civil servants bend the rules so as to provide places in institutions of higher education for their own children, it might be less messy if places for the children were formally reserved.

A good example of the difference between normative and pragmatic rules, as well as a potential solution, is the issue of adultery in Olowo, the Nigerian Utopia where I conducted field-work. One of the strongest norms in the community was marital fidelity and sexual abstinence for unmarried people. Yet adultery was widespread and punishment severe; those accused of adultery were flogged with small gads (ropes made of twisted fibres), and socially ostracized. However, one could take certain precautions, referred to by some of the Apostles as 'technique,' to reduce the possibility of being punished. For example, a young man would usually not visit a woman alone, but would ask three or four of his mates to accompany him. In this way, he could avoid accusation of any wrongdoing if the woman's husband happened to wander by. Another method was to use a middleman, usually a young boy or girl, who carried messages between the lovers, arranging for times and places to meet. Despite these precautions, most adulterous relationships in Olowo were public knowledge. However, if one made a show of using technique, rather than flaunting one's actions, it was much less probable that anything would be done about it. In other words, technique was a safety-valve that helped to reduce the discrepancy between normative and pragmatic rules of behaviour.

Anthropologists who operate within the social-action model are less hostile to psychological reductionism than the Durkheimians. Their work in effect, if not by intent, often bridges anthropology and psychology. As shown in the accompanying diagram, the social-action territory overlaps all of the social sciences and thus occupies all the residual space between heredity and environment.

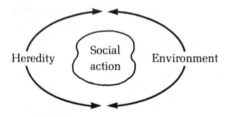

This provides an explanation that is more general and possibly more in tune with empirical reality; but it is also much sloppier than the Durkheimian model – that is, the conceptual territory is not nearly as clear. Because it is assumed in the Bailey model that the individual has an innovative role and exercises choice, it is much more difficult to achieve rigorous scientific analysis. In judging the merits of the Durkheim and Bailey models, one must decide whether it is more fruitful to have an approach that is rigorous but possibly not in tune with empirical reality or one that is more in tune but less rigorous. My own view is that there are benefits to being less rigorous and 'scientific,' but it is difficult to defend this position on rational grounds using conventional criteria to measure scientific progress.

Historical Particularism and Diffusionism
The first several decades of anthropology were dominated by a single theoretical orientation – evolutionism – and indeed it did not begin to crumble until the latter part of the nineteenth century. Part of the challenge came

from Durkheim's structural functionalism, although it did not really penetrate the discipline until the first quarter of the twentieth century. It must also be remembered that strong evolutionary themes remained within the works of Durkheim, Weber, and Marx. Toward the end of the nineteenth century, a challenge came from another direction, and it met the notion of evolution head-on. This was the diffusionist school, or schools, since there really were three distinct branches. The original was the Vienna-based *Kulturkreise* school. As Honigmann (1976: 167) has pointed out, evolutionary theory had taken root less strongly in Germany than elsewhere. The German diffusionists were not satisfied with the assumptions built into evolutionary theory, such as the parallel development of all cultures in the course of passing through identical stages and the arrested development of primitive cultures. Noteworthy was the effort of the diffusionists to examine in detail the prehistory of primitive societies – something that the evolutionists had failed to do. The German diffusionists, such as Schmidt, Graebner, Frobenius, and Ratzel, attempted to explain the growth of cultures through migration and diffusion. An important feature of their framework was the delineation of several distinct cultural areas, the traits of which spread throughout the world and accounted for the current variety of extant cultures. (In this context, it should be noted that *Kulturkreise* literally means 'culture circles.') The noted German traveller and ethnographer, Bastian, had earlier arrived at similar ideas, but had explained the existence of almost identical cultural traits in different parts of the world as a result of the underlying psychic unity of mankind. The diffusionists, on the contrary, thought the cultural traits to be a result of migration and diffusion because they were dispersed geographically.

The second diffusionist school was in Britain; its outstanding proponents were G. Eliott Smith and W.H.R. Rivers. They were less adamant in their condemnation of evolutionism than the members of the *Kulturkreise* school, but nevertheless attempted to account for cultural change in terms of migration and diffusion. Radcliffe-Brown, a student of Rivers, began as a diffusionist, but gave it up for the Durkheimian approach early in his career. Both Seligman and Rivers were psychologically oriented and thoroughly familiar with Freud, and probably influenced Malinowski's views in this respect.

The third diffusionist school – and undoubtedly the most significant of the three in its impact on anthropology – was what became known as historical particularism. This school was established almost single-handedly in America by Boas, who had worked with Bastian in Germany. Boas was strongly opposed to the crude, speculative assumptions of the evolutionists. He also attacked the sloppy use of the comparative method. In Boas's view, in order to comprehend a culture one's study should be limited to a specific area, and the history of the culture reconstructed. He thought that the key process was diffusion. As an element from one culture spread to another culture, it was reshaped in order to fit the new culture. Boas tended to conceive of culture as a patchwork of items diffused from elsewhere and fused loosely together. This view is sometimes referred to as the 'shreds and patches' theory of culture, although the image is traced to Lowie, Boas's student.

Boas (1858–1942) was born and educated in Germany, and taught at Columbia University from 1896 until 1937. He is considered to be the founder of American anthropology, and his importance to the development of the discipline is undeniable, although there are widely diverging views nowadays as to whether he was a healthy or a negative influence. Usually anthropologists trace the advent of modern field-work to Malinowski, but in the 1880s Boas had carried out extensive field-work along the west coast of British Columbia, and before that had been on an expedition to Baffin Island. Boas was also responsible for another of the outstanding ethnographic discoveries of all time – the potlatch among the Kwakiutl, who inhabited Vancouver Island. Beginning with his first visit to the Kwakiutl in 1886, Boas documented (1897) a form of ceremonial destruction and distribution that seemed to revolve around prestige in a manner that defied the image of rational economic man. A person involved in a potlatch might present more blankets or other forms of property to a rival than the latter could return with the expected interest payment. Or a man might organize a ceremonial feast during which he would destroy his own property; his rivals in turn would be required to destroy even more property at a subsequent feast if their prestige was to be recovered. Boas's student, Ruth Benedict, brought the institution of the potlatch to a wider audience in *Patterns of Culture*, and pressed the interpretation of an irrational pursuit of prestige. However, in recent years, beginning with Codere's work (1950) and perhaps represented most forcibly by Harris (1968, 1974), the alternative viewpoint that the potlatch is a rational, explicable response to demographic and ecological factors has emerged. The potlatch served as a focus for debating whether or not anthropology was nomothetic, and Boas himself fluctuated in his opinions. In his early days, he cautioned against loose speculation and sloppy comparison, but he believed that cultural laws could eventually be discovered. As he grew older, he changed his mind and argued that laws were non-existent in the cultural realm. Radcliffe-Brown later would be in perfect agreement: a science of culture was impossible, but a science of social systems, within which culture was a mere aspect, was indeed feasible.

In order to combat the evolutionists, Boas argued for inductive work, and stressed what now is called the emic perspective. He was responsible for the emergence of the view of cultural relativism, again to combat evolutionism. His argument was that the assumption that cultures could be scaled necessarily carried with it the idea of superiority and inferiority. He assumed, on the contrary, that no culture was better or worse than another. Boas stressed the emotional and mental side of man, and especially in his later years was keenly interested in the individual and the way he fit into culture. Boas also stressed the degree to which behaviour can be explained by sheer habit and tradition rather than by utilitarian or rationalistic theories. To a lesser degree, he also entertained the influence of the environment on culture.

Murdock has claimed that Boas was greatly overrated by his students. Murdock's opinion was formed by virtue of the fact that despite Boas's immense production – over 700 articles and numerous books – the Kwakiutl were too inadequately described to be used in the Human Relations Area Files. Perhaps one might wonder today about the publication of gooseberry recipes, but in my opinion Murdock's criticism is ill-founded. The reason that he found Boas lacking was that their interests diverged. Boas was against the nomothetic approach to the study of mankind, and Murdock was in favour of it; hence Murdock asks for a different range of data from those that Boas collected. Ironically, Murdock himself has been strongly criticized by another disciple of nomothetic inquiry – Marvin Harris (1968: 611) – for having stuck too much to Boasian 'soft' principles, stressing the uniqueness and unpredictability of human behaviour, and arriving at correlations rather than cause-and-effect statements.

The diffusionist schools in the United States, England, and Germany provided a healthy challenge to the crude evolutionism that hitherto had ruled supreme. From the roots of Boas's work, contrary directions emerged in anthropology, including the quasi-nomothetic school of cultural ecology, and the opposite trends of culture and personality, configurationism, and integrational studies, as in Benedict's and Kroeber's writings. I agree with critics that the last were theoretical dead-ends; yet the diffusionist period that preceded them played an important part. It brought evolutionism to its knees. If it did not produce a fruitful theoretical direction, it at least got half-way there, with the recognition of the untidiness of behaviour and culture. What was missing was the sense of contradiction and dialectic that is central to the position to be developed in Part 2.

Culture and Personality

Type A: The Old Culture-and-Personality School
Boas had always stressed the emotional over the rational, and as he grew older he became increasingly interested in personality. That interest pro-

duced what became known as the culture-and-personality school. Two of its leading figures were women, Benedict and Mead. Ruth Benedict brought anthropology to a wider audience with *Patterns of Culture*, possibly the most widely read book written by an anthropologist. She also coined the catchy phrase 'culture is personality writ large.'

The early writings in this field stressed a basic personality structure. It was generalizable to all people brought up in a particular culture. Later writings stressed a modal personality, which was the statistically most common personality in a particular culture. The assumption eventually emerged that in a specific culture there might be several modal personality types. While this was a more sophisticated view than the earlier attempt to discover the basic personality structure of each culture, by the 1950s the culture-and-personality school had foundered, with very little of theoretical importance having been achieved. I suppose that it is to be expected, and applauded, that the students of these pioneers have attempted to clarify and extend the works of the masters. Certainly Boas's students, such as Benedict and Kroeber, were not satisfied to leave his untidy conception of culture – the shreds-and-patches image – as it was. Around 1930 Benedict (1932, 1959) introduced what became known as the configurational view, in which the components of culture were interdependent and formed a coherent whole; each culture, like each individual, was thought to have a specific temperament. With this approach, anthropology was reduced to a branch of psychology. Kroeber (1876–1960) took a similar line with his integrational image, and indeed his view of culture has much in common with Durkheim's collective conscience, the most general social fact. But Benedict went a step further. While arguing that each culture constituted a unified pattern, she also insisted that each culture was unique. Here we can see the roots of earlier linguistic work, especially Whorf's, and also Boas's own work; his statements regarding the limits of comparative analysis and his arguments for cultural relativity – in order to reject evolutionary scales – contained the seeds of Benedict's argument. However, it seems that as in the case of other leading figures such as Durkheim, Boas's students and disciples distorted and exaggerated his arguments. A close reading of Boas does not reveal him to be a radical cultural relativist, opposed to any type of comparison and generalization. For example, while *Primitive Art* (Boas 1955) is not a theoretical work in the sense that Durkheim's *Suicide* is, with data filtered through a preconceived system, it nevertheless is based on an exceptionally broad cross-cultural survey. In this remarkable study, theory and data are synthesized and modest generalization attained, albeit in a less formal sense than in Durheim's case. The target of Boas's cautious statements is clear: he merely, and sanely, was against the work of dilettantes in the field.

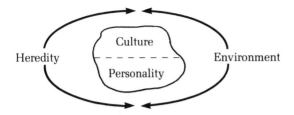

As used by American anthropologists, 'culture' is a highly inclusive term; the culture-and-personality framework occupied, in loose fashion, the entire conceptual territory of the social sciences (as shown in the accompanying diagram) and impinged on heredity and environment when their influences upon personality were entertained.

Type B: Recent Trends in Psychological Anthropology
The early culture-and-personality school was eclipsed by structural functionalism and other emerging orientations, such as cultural ecology and the revived evolutionary framework. However, sporadic attempts were made to resuscitate an interest in the individual and psychology. These attempts were not hindered by the growing realization that Durkheim, the arch-anti-reductionist, actually had erected a framework that was intrinsically psychological in nature. Even Fortes, who remained exceptionally faithful to Durkheim and Radcliffe-Brown, could not avoid psychological assumptions, as Harris has shown (1968: 396). Curiously, Fortes, along with Nadel, was the only prominent social anthropologist at the beginning of the modern era who had been formally trained in psychology, although Malinowski had acquainted himself with the Freudian school. One attempt to revive psychological interests became known as cognitive anthropology, which stressed people's folk cognitive systems or taxonomies. The links between cognition, language, and behaviour as described by Whorf and Sapir were rediscovered, and a new methodology known as componential analysis emerged. Componential analysis first appeared in linguistics; it was a method that supposedly enabled the investigator to differentiate one linguistic form from another. The investigator could identify the criteria used in each language that determined its phonology – criteria such as mode of articulation, place of articulation, and voicing. Each variable has a number of values. Mode of articulation, for example, has the values of 'stopped' and 'nasalized.' Once the limited number of variables has been isolated, the phonemes of a language are readily discerned, since any phoneme is a particular combination of the values of the variables, or phonological components. Componential analysis eventually became associated with the systematic investigation of

semantic domains in general, ranging from kinship terminology (Goode-nough 1956a, Wallace and Atkins 1960) to terms for firewood (Metzger and Williams 1966) and ingredients for making beer (Frake 1964). The advantages, according to writers such as Goodenough, were not limited to rigour and systematic inquiry: componential analysis made possible the discovery of the meaning of terms in the native's sense. A deluge of criticism quickly emerged (see Harris 1968: 568–604). Burling, for example, in a paper entitled 'Cognition and Componential Analysis: God's Truth or Hocus-pocus' (1964), flatly rejected the claim that the method allowed the investigator to penetrate the cognitive processes of peoples.

What was significant about cognitive anthropology was the attempt to handle mentalist problems nomothetically and thus to place the discipline on a scientific footing, which Benedict and others had demolished. This attempt has basically foundered, but in its place has emerged another school simply called psychological anthropology (see Bourguignon 1979). Unlike the early culture-and-personality school, psychological anthropology does not assume that each culture is unique, nor does it decry cross-cultural, nomothetic analysis. Indeed, its aims are exactly the opposite. In many respects, it is difficult to distinguish the new field of psychological anthropology from anthropology in general, or from specializations such as political anthropology. This is because the school appears to cut across almost all anthropological subfields, and usually cannot be distinguished from non-psychological anthropology in terms of its data, except for its more persistent emphasis on problems such as cognition and child-rearing.

Psychological anthropology may be emerging as the focal point in the discipline for the synthesis of all research dealing with the 'soft' side of man: ideology, norms, beliefs, motivation, and socialization. If that is so, there will be a need for another focal point to synthesize the 'hard' side: social structure, social organization, system, institution, and role. The implication is only partly humorous; we may be at the brink of a restatement of the perennial but totally unacceptable distinction between culture and social structure, norm and act, and macro and micro behaviour. Curiously, had Durkheim been born in a later era, when a greater understanding of the unconscious existed and psychological theory rested upon a firmer scientific foundation, he may well have opted for this new version of psychological anthropology rather than for his vague collective conscience and normative social facts. Finally, mention should be made of the degree to which a psychological perspective has been integrated into the recent works of some outstanding anthropologists, such as Murphy and Lévi-Strauss, both of whom are indebted to Freud.

Cultural Materialism

Historical particularism gave rise to an ideographic phase in American anthropology, culminating in the culture-and-personality school. However, the polar-opposite style – a nomothetic approach to the study of mankind – had always threatened to emerge. Indeed, one variety of it grew out of the culture-and-personality school itself: the new psychological anthropology. But the nomothetic style goes back much further to Steward's cultural ecology and White's evolutionism. Cultural ecology can be traced back to Boas, who recognized the broad influence of the environment, even if he did not expand on the notion.

There is a considerable overlap between cultural ecology and what is usually referred to as neo-evolutionism, partly because men like Steward espoused both positions. Steward and White shared several basic assumptions. They both emphasized the etic rather than the emic, thus marking a different perspective from Benedict, Kroeber, and Boas. Both men also pushed the individual and his personality into the background, and assigned causal priority to techno-economic factors, one part of the cultural triad (the other parts were social organization and ideology, and in White's framework sometimes attitudes). Along with Kroeber and Benedict, they also rejected the idea of culture as a fortuitous bundle of disparate traits, a mere mass of shreds and patches. Despite these similarities, there were significant differences in their perspectives. Steward described his approach as 'multi-evolutionism' in order to distinguish it sharply from nineteenth-century uni-evolutionism. Steward's argument was that cultures had evolved along quite different lines, and thus a single, all-encompassing evolutionary scheme was impossible. White denied that his evolutionary approach was any different in principle from Morgan's and Tylor's. For this reason he rejected the term neo-evolutionism. White's approach has been labelled grand theory, Steward's middle-range theory. White was interested in cultural evolution at the macro level, Steward in the evolution of specific cultures. The difference here is methodological, and basically one of taste rather than of right or wrong, although Steward would counter with an argument with which all social scientists must be familiar: before we can have grand theory, the groundwork at a more modest level of analysis must be established. Sahlins (1960) has characterized the difference between White and Steward as that between general evolution and specific evolution. The former refers to the increasing complexity and adaptability of systems, the latter to the process by which new cultural types adapt to their environments.

A final difference between Steward and White, which may be the most significant, concerns Steward's reductionism. In White's view, culture is a reality sui generis, to be explained in terms of the dynamic relationships between its parts, especially the techno-economic realm. To account for the history of mankind, one did not need to step beyond the parameters of culture to consider factors such as human will or desires. Steward, in contrast, was a reductionist. To explain cultural evolution, one had to take into account the environment. We shall see that the links between culture and environment in Steward's work were complex and variable, with the possibility of causal primacy assigned to environment at one stage and to culture at another.

Cultural Ecology
While many of the same writers within the cultural-ecology tradition have also taken an evolutionary line, the combination is not inevitable. On the one hand, Forde (1934) entertained the influence of ecology on social structure, possibly because of his training in geography, without tying it to evolutionary concerns; the same was true for Geertz (1968) in his study of the history of agricultural patterns in Indonesia. On the other hand, none of the nineteenth-century evolutionists dwelt on ecological factors. This does not mean that the ecological focus is brand-new. Montesquieu, for example, tried to explain cultural habits and arrangements in terms of the natural habitat. This kind of environmental determinism has long been discredited, although, curiously, it has been revived in recent times by Boissevain (1974: 74–7), who discusses the influence of climate on social organization and personality, and generalizes that people in warm climates are more gregarious and open than those in cold climates. But Boissevain's perspective can be understood as an attempt to discredit Durkheim at all costs, even if it means adopting an erroneous hypothesis just because Durkheim rejected it.
    Cultural ecology in Steward's hands is considerably more sophisticated. Steward breaks culture down into a core and a periphery. The core includes those sectors of society such as politics and religion that interact directly with the techno-economic base. The periphery is composed of cultural factors resulting from diffusion or simply independent creation that are only fortuitously related to the core. Steward's argument is that environmental factors modify and determine the core, not the periphery. However, this creates an unacceptable gulf between the two. While it is useful to assign greater significance to some social institutions than others, and to argue that they stand closer to the techno-economic base of society, it makes much less sense to argue that part of a society's cultural make-up stands outside the base and core. This is tantamount to stating that society is both systemic and non-systemic simultaneously. Another important concept in Steward's work

is that of levels of socio-cultural integration; examples are Redfield's folk society and the nuclear family. Steward argues that the type of socio-cultural integration in an advanced technological society is qualitatively different from that in hunting-and-gathering society. The concept of levels of socio-cultural integration, however, is most important in the context of methodology, and explains his preference for middle-range theory. Steward's purpose was to erect a taxonomy of socio-cultural types that would allow meaningful comparative work to proceed, in both space and time, cross-culturally and historically. In this sense, his efforts were perfectly consistent with those of most British social anthropologists, at least until Leach's dismissal of classification as butterfly-catching (1961).

Earlier I said that the causal relationship between culture and environment is variable. Usually a distinction is drawn between the natural environment and the affective or man-modified environment. In the latter, no clear distinction can be made between culture and environment; the links, as Sahlins (1968: 367) would say, are reciprocal, or dialectical. Steward suggests that as technology improves, man gains more and more control over his environment, to the point where a calamity such as the demise of Cro-Magnon man, who was too specialized to adapt to environmental transformations, no longer is remotely possible. Culture takes over completely, and cultural ecology as a framework of explanation becomes obsolete. This does not mean that man will be any freer than he is in societies with a low level of technology in which the environment determines culture. As Steward acutely points out, in advanced technological societies, the determinism of the environment may be replaced by the determinism of the culture's superstructure (see Hatch 1973: 120).

The cultural-ecology model (illustrated in the accompanying diagram) occupies a wider conceptual territory than any of the models previously considered:

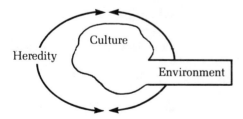

Steward himself has provided an admirable example of the application of the cultural-ecology perspective in his work on the Shoshonean peoples in the western United States (1955: chap. 6). Arid conditions and a simple hunting-and-gathering economy effectively ruled out large concentrations of people, and the elementary family was perforce the basic social unit. A more controversial application concerns primitive warfare, which writers such as Vayda (1961) and Harris (1974) have explained as a mechanism to adjust populations to the carrying weight of the ecological zone.

Earlier I referred to the manner in which adherents of the social-structural model would reject LeVine's psychological explanation of Igbo ambition and receptivity to change. An ecological explanation concerning population density and land productivity may be even more plausible. The Ijebu-Ode people among the Yoruba have often been described using the same adjectives that have been applied to the Igbo. They are said to be exceptionally intelligent and ambitious, well-educated, and prepared to take up jobs wherever they are offered. They also have something else in common with the Igbo. Like most Igbo territory, the Ijebu-Ode is characterized by low land productivity and high population density. In parts of Igbo territory, such as Abakaliki, the land is fertile and the population not dense. Significantly, Abakaliki people are sometimes reputed by other Igbo to be unambitious and possibly less intelligent than Igbo people in general. Some Igbo even deny that Abakaliki people are Igbo. I could go further and indicate the importance of forest density, and even the presence or absence of sand bars on the Atlantic coast of Nigeria, which played a part in determining where Europeans first penetrated the country, but the point surely has been made: any explanation of the so-called Igbo receptivity to industrialization and to the West must take into account ecological factors.

Neo-evolutionism
I use the term 'neo-evolutionism' (with apologies to White) because in my view post-Second World War evolutionism is quite distinct from the nineteenth-century variety. The evolutionism of Morgan, Tylor, and Spencer was characterized by ethnocentrism or Eurocentrism (which meant that evolution had supposedly culminated in the European case and had been retrogressive or arrested in the primitive world); by armchair speculation with little attempt to reconstruct the specific development of a particular culture; by a unilineal scheme of parallel development through a specific order of stages; and by the assumption of inevitable progress. In the nineteenth century, evolutionism was 'in the air,' as academics say, and the

major works in the social sciences, such as Spencer's, preceded rather than followed Darwin's. Indeed, Darwin borrowed the phrase 'survival of the fittest' from Spencer.

Most contemporary writers reject the notion of unilineal development and eschew any idea of progress. Yet this was not true of White. Given his propensity for grand theory, for attempting to understand culture at the most general level, he was less sensitive to the variable ways in which specific cultures evolve. White also accepted the idea that culture is progressive. It is directional, and societal institutions must be understood in utilitarian terms: their purpose is to contribute to the overall efficiency of culture. Although much of White's pronouncements tend to read like a public-relations effort on the merits of science, he did operationalize the definition of cultural evolution in a specific and clear manner. Culture advances according to the increase in the amount of energy per capita per year, or according to the efficiency by which energy is utilized (see Kaplan and Manners 1972: 45). White's famous formula is $E \times T \rightarrow C$; E represents energy, T the efficiency of tools, and C culture. White does depart sharply from the early school of evolutionism with regard to biology. He has been an eloquent spokesman for the contemporary anthropological view that the symbol has replaced the gene in importance as an explanatory tool. In other words, we live in a symbolic universe, guided by culture rather than heredity.

In recent years Marvin Harris has been in the forefront in the attempt to provide a nomothetic footing for anthropology. It is not difficult to understand why he has turned to cultural ecology and neo-evolutionism for support. More than any other American perspective, they represent the major incursions into law-like investigations. Harris rests his cultural materialism on Marx, and supposedly with good reason. Marx too regarded techno-economic factors as primary and the environment as an important condition. His approach also was evolutionary, but was closer to Steward's multi-evolutionism than the unilineal variety, since not all peoples went through the same stages in the same sequence. In addition, Marx embraced the nineteenth-century idea of progress: the final stage, communism, would be a Utopia on earth.

If there is a significant difference between Harris's cultural materialism and neo-evolutionism and cultural ecology, it would seem to revolve around the prominence given to Marx. Most cultural ecologists and neo-evolutionists have ignored Marx, even while rediscovering some of the principal insights. Perhaps the most surprising case of all is White, who toured Russia in 1929. He was thoroughly familiar with Morgan's work, which inspired Marx and Engels, and was acquainted with their writings. Yet the differences between Steward, White, and Harris evaporate because of Harris's peculiar interpretation of Marxism. When Gluckman's brand of conflict theory, or disguised equilibrium model, was discussed, I argued that without a dialectic a conflict model is impossible. Ironically, Harris not only dismisses the dialectical method as hocus-pocus, but also congratulates White for avoiding it. In the end, cultural materialism in Harris's hands amounts to mechanical materialism. The dynamic and variable interaction of the parts of culture are downplayed, and one is left with a neat but monotonous formula in which ideology and social organization are the puppets of technology. Even White, despite a much less self-conscious application of the Marxian framework, allowed for the short-run dominance of aspects of the superstructure.[9] In case these remarks should be construed as a churlish attack on the man who did provide us with the first major textbook (1968) addressed to anthropological theory for contemporary students, let us recognize Harris's genius for tracking down ethnographic examples that so aptly fit his arguments, such as in *Cows, Pigs, Wars and Witches* (1974). Harris is a practitioner, steeped in ethnography (even if it is second-hand), and that distinguishes him from other armchair theorists such as Parsons.

BACK TO THE ARMCHAIR

Since the days of Malinowski and Boas, anthropology has been noted for its emphasis on field-work. Yet with the emergence of neo-evolutionism, anthropologists have retreated again to the library, which makes them similar in style to the early evolutionists. There are several reasons for this retreat. We have masses of good data now; for decades anthropologists have been producing ethnographies, and the argument is that the time has come to put it all together using an evolutionary or cultural-materialist framework. Thanks to Murdock, we also have the Human Relations Area Files and the World Ethnographic Sample; library research, thus, is made all the easier. Then, too, there is hostility in the Third World toward outside scholars; less money is available for research, with the result that distant excursions are less attractive; and primitive societies – the anthropologist's paradise – have virtually disappeared. Note, however, that with the emergence of neo-evolutionism,

9 For a lively reaction to Harris's application of cultural materialism in *Cannibals and Kings* (1978), see Midgley (1980: 31–2).

the dwindling-away of primitive society has not brought an end to a focus on primitives; it merely has put an end to field-work. Whether this is to be applauded is a question to which I shall return frequently in this study.

The neo-evolutionary orientation shown in the accompanying diagram is even broader than cultural ecology.

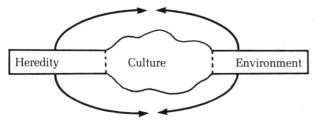

I state this despite the realization that writers such as White stress the autonomy of culture. But the fact is that the neo-evolutionary school, and the related perspective of cultural ecology, are strongly influenced by the framework of general anthropology in America, which incorporates both socio-cultural and biological systems.

CONCLUSION

It is always arbitrary to say exactly when a discipline began. As Murphy has remarked (1971: 6), the social sciences were not invented – they were merely professionalized! If we trace the beginning of social anthropology to Marx, Weber, Durkheim, and Simmel, it can be argued that they anticipated almost every important theoretical issue that subsequent practitioners have dealt with, right up to the present. If we add Morgan, Spencer, and Tylor, and perhaps Fraser and Freud, the same can be said about cultural anthropology. If we are even more generous in defining the time span in which anthropology began, and include Boas, Radcliffe-Brown, and Malinowski, I believe it can be claimed that hardly a single important theoretical issue escaped the attention of the founding fathers. Not even Lévi-Strauss's structuralism, which will be dealt with in chapter 6, is an exception, for many of his ideas come from Durkheim and from others such as Boas and Freud.

One of the significant issues that most of the early giants failed to consider was racism. This may be thought strange in view of the substantial nineteenth-century literature in physical anthropology and biology on race. However, it was during this period that the concept of culture emerged, and with it a reluctance to entertain biological or hereditary factors. Marx had little to say about racism, and when he did deal with the issue, racism was reduced to a class analysis. Tylor's intellectualism carried with it the implication that the primitives were slow-witted. Morgan was devoted to the defence of American Indians, but held blacks in low regard. The one great exception was Boas. It is because he devoted his prodigious powers to combating scientific racism that we are able to maintain that almost all significant theoretical issues were entertained by the founding fathers.[10] As will be shown in chapter 10, in recent years even the mighty Boas has, ironically, been accused of harbouring racist beliefs (see Stocking 1968, Fried 1972, and Willis 1972).

10 The glaring exception is sexism, which may be the only major expression of inequality whose concealing and neutralizing mechanisms are greater than those that obscure racism.

3

Paradigms or Pseudo-paradigms

Although the term 'paradigm' did not originate with *The Structure of Scientific Revolutions* – Merton (1957), for example, had used it in his reworking of functional theory – in Kuhn's hands it achieved a remarkably innovative character. Kuhn was explicitly addressing issues in the hard sciences, notably physics, but scholars in virtually all disciplines, especially sociology and political science, have been captivated by his arguments. Curiously, Kuhn has been virtually ignored by anthropologists. Those who have referred to him, such as Eggan (1968: 120), Hatch (1973: 11), Honigmann (1976: 164), Kuper (1975: 107, 161 and 226), Leaf (1975: 5), McFeat (1979), and Scholte (1966) have made only passing comments. Nowhere does there appear to be an extended discussion of Kuhn's work for the discipline.[1] I reserve the concept of paradigm for disciplines with the potential for nomothetic inquiry. Only twice has anthropology approached this status. On each occasion the anthropologists involved spoke the language of science and claimed to be able to construct law-like statements of regularity, but they failed to produce the goods. This is why I label their work pseudo-paradigmatic. There may be some justification for referring to anthropology as pre-paradigmatic, but for reasons that will be made clear I prefer to describe it as non-paradigmatic.

1 These remarks are addressed specifically to social and cultural anthropology, and do not apply to what has become known as the new archaeology (Binford 1962, 1977, and Renfrew et al. 1982), which Binford and Sabloff (1982) have referred to as a paradigmatic shift. Archaeology provides a fascinating example of the type of paradigmatic battle that has raged in social and cultural anthropology. On the one hand there is the Old World archaeology, positivist-historicist and inductive; on the other, the New World archaeology, theoretically ambitious, deductive, wedded to a systems model. Binford and Sabloff (1982), referring directly to Kuhn, describe these as normative and systems paradigms respectively.

According to Kuhn, contemporary science takes place within the context of a paradigm. A paradigm can be defined in much the same way as I defined theoretical orientation in the previous chapter. Characterized by 'particular coherent traditions of scientific research' (Kuhn 1970: 10), a paradigm includes 'law, theory, application and instrumentation together' (Kuhn 1970: 10), and stands for 'the entire constellation of beliefs, values, techniques, and so on shared by members of a given community' (Kuhn 1970: 175). Commentators on Kuhn's work have defined paradigm as 'the conceptual framework by which the scientist gives initial intelligibility to phenomena' (Westhues 1976: 38) or simply as the 'fundamental image a discipline has of its subject matter' (Friedricks 1970: 55).

Kuhn describes scientific activity that operates within a paradigm as 'normal science,' which does not aim at novelties of fact or theory and, when successful, finds none. Normal science is not innovative. Instead, it is a mopping-up operation; more and more experiments are conducted to subsume more and more data in the form of 'confirmed' hypotheses, within the parameters of the paradigm. In this view, scientists are puzzle-solvers, dealing with problems established by the paradigm. Eventually this kind of activity generates anomalies, which are not merely puzzles, because they can't be explained in terms of the paradigm, and yet won't go away. It is important here to note that it is the very rigour and precision of paradigm-articulated activity that throws anomalies into bold relief. These anomalies lead to a crisis in the discipline, and set the pre-conditions for a revolution. The revolution takes place when a scientist or a group of scientists claim that they can explain the anomalies by a different framework. While cognitive awareness of the anomalies and arguments that an alternative framework has greater explanatory value are important ingredients in the revolution, they are not by themselves sufficient. As Kuhn stresses (1970: 148) there is usually no means by which the new framework can be proved to be superior; instead it is a matter of persuasion and power, as proponents of the new viewpoint try to supplant the existing paradigm.

Usually most scientists are not persuaded; those who continue to espouse the older paradigm simply die off, which allows the new paradigm to emerge victoriously. Kuhn stresses that new paradigms usually are introduced by young people or those new to a discipline, who are less committed to the previous paradigm. He also describes the conversion of scientists to a new paradigm as a gestalt switch, not unlike a religious conversion. The analogy is apt, because in the absence of demonstrated proof, one must accept the new paradigm's promise on faith.

One of the most significant features of Kuhn's thesis is the argument that science is not a cumulative exercise, at least in the conventional sense of that term. Scientific work *within* a paradigm – that is, normal science – is cumulative, since the effect of mopping-up exercises is to subsume more and more facts within the parameters of the paradigm. But the transition from one paradigm to another is not cumulative. Indeed, Kuhn says that successive paradigms often are incommensurate, not simply incompatible. There is no way to compare them to determine which is better. This is because with the new paradigm there are new problems, new criteria of relevance and evidence, new instruments and tools. In a sense, there is a new world, for it is conceived fundamentally differently by virtue of the new paradigm. Although he is ambiguous on this point, Kuhn implies that there is no progress with the change from one paradigm to another. That is, one is no closer to the truth, and indeed, according to Kuhn, we may have to give up the idea that there is any 'truth' to which research is directed. Kuhn readily admits that this is not the picture that dominates the image of science. But he argues that this image is distorted by scientific texts, which almost always portray a discipline as being theoretically cumulative, marked by steady progress.

Kuhn's thesis has been attacked from almost every angle, which is hardly surprising, since it rips away the foundations from several popularly held views of science. The confrontation between Kuhn and Popper has been particularly interesting. Popper conceives of science as a highly rational endeavour, whereas the irrational appears to stand out in Kuhn's work. Even Popper's concessions, such as the argument that scientists proceed by falsification rather than confirmation, are rejected by Kuhn, who contends (1970: 77) that nowhere in the history of science do we find evidence that theories have been dismissed solely because they fail to measure up to the facts of the empirical world. Popper is particularly opposed to the assumptions that there can be little dialogue between proponents of one paradigm and another, and that paradigms cannot even legitimately be compared. This view, which Kuhn describes as the incommensurability of paradigms, is criticized by Popper as 'the myth of the framework.' Popper does not underestimate the degree to which a framework – for example, Marxian or Freudian – can shut off all contradictory interpretations. His argument is that this is inimical to rational and critical discussion, the hallmarks of the scientific enterprise. As Popper (1974: 39) put it, 'our need for theories is immense, and so is the power of theories. Thus it is all the more important to guard against becoming addicted to any particular theory: we must not let ourselves be caught in a mental prison.'

It appears that Kuhn has described scientific activity as it actually takes place, whereas Popper has described it as it ought to operate. Kuhn is, in short, describing a sociological reality, whereas Popper is concerned with the logic of scientific enterprise. Kuhn's 'sociological reality' is characterized by the 'authority' of a paradigm, and by the pressures of the scientific community on its members to conform. Both viewpoints are legitimate. For example, it would be hopeless to try to straighten out the confusing relationship between social anthropology and sociology by examining how particular anthropologists and sociologists have undertaken research, and especially what they have said about one another's disciplines, although notable exceptions (such as Radcliffe-Brown) can be found. Instead, it would be much more fruitful to work out in a logical manner the conceptual territory of each discipline, and forget about the custom and historical accident that have resulted in different preferences for techniques, societal type, and theory. However, an academic discipline is a sociological phenomenon, and is thus to be explained as much by habit, tradition, and historical accident as by logic. It is, in Kuhn's sense, a sociological reality, and in chapter 10 I shall draw upon Kuhn to explain why anthropology will retain its separate identity even if it moves on to the sociologist's turf, urban industrial society.

Kuhn's approach illuminates the scientific enterprise in general. For example, many social scientists, including myself, become disturbed when they learn of research projects that focus on apparently trivial problems involving little imagination and promising little insight. Often I ask my students (usually to their embarrassment) what constitutes a significant research problem. Yet from the viewpoint of normal science, there are no significant problems, only testable ones. Once again, scientists are puzzle-solvers, not innovators. In a sense, from the perspective of normal science, significant problems are the anomalies that constitute the pre-conditions for paradigmatic revolutions, and thus cannot be the focus of normal scientific research. Social scientists who focus on what some of their colleagues dismiss as trivial problems might be said, in the context of normal science, to be operating legitimately. Of course, this interpretation only makes sense if one agrees that paradigmatic status has been achieved in the social sciences, which I do not.

THE TWO KUHNS

Intriguing, unconventional, and revolutionary, the ideas introduced by Kuhn were swept up in a storm of controversy involving scientists and philosophers, and perhaps it is understandable that Kuhn beat a hasty retreat to calmer waters. For retreat he did, to such an extent that a clear distinction must be made between the Kuhn in his 1962 publication and the Kuhn in his

1969 postscript to the new edition (1970) of *The Structure of Scientific Revolutions* and in subsequent articles (see especially Lakatos and Musgrave 1972).

The controversy centred on his definition of paradigm. As Masterson indicated (1972), Kuhn used paradigm in at least twenty-one different senses, which fall into three main groups. First, there are metaphysical paradigms including beliefs, myths, and ways of perceiving the world. A second group is made up of sociological paradigms, which are concrete, universally recognized scientific achievements. The third group, construct or artefact paradigms, is made up of actual products of scientific activity, such as textbooks. Reacting to these criticisms, Kuhn (1970: 175) himself attempted to clarify what he meant by paradigm, focusing on two different definitions. 'On the one hand, it stands for the entire constellation of beliefs, values, techniques, and so on shared by members of a given community. On the other, it denotes one sort of element in that constellation, the concrete puzzle-solutions which, employed as models or examples, can replace explicit rules as a basis for solution of the remaining puzzles of normal science.' The first sense corresponds to what Masterson called metaphysical paradigms, and Kuhn concluded that it was inappropriate. To clear up the matter, he introduced the term 'disciplinary matrix,' which was to replace the term 'paradigm,' especially in its metaphysical sense. Next he focused on 'exemplars.' These are 'the concrete problem-solutions that students encounter from the start of their scientific education, whether in laboratories, on examinations, or at the ends of chapters in science texts' (Kuhn 1970: 187). The exemplar corresponds to Masterson's sociological paradigms. According to Kuhn (1970: 175), it is 'deeper' than the disciplinary matrix, and it is in this sense that paradigm should be employed. By doing away with the larger metaphysical conception, Kuhn removed much of his earlier emphasis on the irrational in science. I cannot comment on the value of this shift to understanding the physical and biological sciences, but many social scientists such as Ritzer (1975: 10) consider it a backward step in explaining their own disciplines.

PRE-PARADIGMS

Inspired by Kuhn's work, a new generation of social scientists (notably excluding anthropologists) rushed in to grapple once again with the scientific status of their disciplines. Predictably, the debate often resolved around semantics, with the illogical assumption that the manner in which a discipline was defined determined its nomothetic capacity. Some sociologists and political scientists interpreted Kuhn's work to mean that their disciplines were pre-paradigmatic, radically different from (and in this sense inferior to) the hard sciences. Others agreed that their disciplines were pre-paradigmatic, but rejoiced in the conclusion, since this supposedly meant that with patience and hard work paradigmatic status would be the inevitable outcome. At least one sociologist (Phillips 1973–4) took the curious position that while his discipline was as paradigmatic as chemistry, it was not scientific. A host of additional interpretations soon emerged in the literature, including Truman's and Almond's contentions (see Bernstein 1979) that political science has occasionally been paradigmatic, Ritzer's (1975) argument that sociology is multiparadigmatic, and Effrat's (1972) conclusion that there have been no paradigms in sociology, at least if the term 'paradigm' is applied rigorously. Effrat does suggest that if it is used loosely, several paradigms – which he equates with theoretical orientations such as structural functionalism – have existed. This is also the manner in which Bottomore (1975) has applied the term to sociology. Yet Ritzer contends that paradigm is much broader than theoretical orientation, and Eckberg and Hill (1979), just to confuse us further, claim that paradigm can only be used in the sense of exemplars, and must be applied to substantive issues within a discipline rather than to an entire discipline. Eckberg and Hill conclude that sociology is not a paradigmatic science since it has few (if any) exemplars, lacks a puzzle-solving tradition, and operates from discipline-wide perspectives.

The widely varying interpretations of Kuhn's work were largely due to ambiguities within it, especially as a result of his change in position in the 1969 postscript to the new edition. For example, in the original 1962 publication he argued that there were no sound, rational reasons for the switch from one paradigm to another; he stressed the politics involved, the irrationality, the almost spiritual conversion. But in the 1969 postscript he recanted. Now paradigmatic shifts took place for 'good' reasons such as accuracy, scope, simplicity, and fruitfulness. As others have pointed out, according to Kuhn's original work these various reasons themselves would be seen as paradigm-influenced. The central thrust of the 1962 publication was to show the differences between sciences and other disciplines. He argued that while the sciences did not possess firmer answers about fundamental methodological and conceptual issues than did the non-sciences, they did possess much more agreement about them. According to Kuhn, this was because only the sciences had paradigms. Yet in his revised position he states that 'a paradigm is what the members of a scientific community share, and, conversely, a scientific community consists of men who share a paradigm' (1970: 16). This is close to being a tautology, and can be interpreted to mean that as long as there is a community of scholars, ipso facto a paradigm exists; but in this sense, all disciplines, from anthropology to art history, are para-digmatic. Kuhn also states that 'in the sciences ... the formation of special-ized journals, the foundation of specialists' societies, and the claim for a special place in the curriculum have usually been associated with a group's first reception of a single paradigm' (1970: 19). Again, by these criteria, anthropology – indeed, all the social sciences – is paradigmatic.

Finally, Kuhn remarks in direct reference to the social sciences that 'maturity' need not be associated with the emergence or acquisition of a paradigm. He goes on to say, 'The members of all scientific communities, including the schools of the "pre-paradigm" period, share the sorts of ele-ments which I have collectively labelled "a paradigm." What changes with the transition to maturity is not the presence of a paradigm but rather its nature. Only after the change is normal puzzle-solving research possible (1970: 179). Yet in his original work, what was peculiar and essential about paradigmatic research was its puzzle-solving character. No wonder myriad interpretations have collected around Kuhn's work. Kuhn himself has readily confessed that his work can mean nearly all things to all people. However, if one restricts the analysis to the original publication, which illuminates the social sciences in a way not done in the postscript, there are four basic criteria that allow us to determine the paradigmatic status of a discipline.

1 *Kuhn states that sciences with paradigms rarely discuss or debate what constitutes legitimate methods, problems, or standards of evaluation.* But in anthropology and sociology we spend a great deal of time doing exactly that. In the hard sciences, far fewer courses are offered to students in theory and methods. Yet social scientists often assume that these courses alone are worth teaching. I used to be amazed that students in the hard sciences knew much less about the properties of science than did anthropology and sociol-ogy students; but the former did not need to be consciously aware of and articulate about them because the rigour of their disciplines made it unnec-essary. These issues were implicit in their paradigms. *Conclusion:* by this criterion anthropology is pre-paradigmatic.

2 *Kuhn states that in sciences with a paradigm, the article is the outlet for creative work, not the monograph, and the textbook is the major pedagogical instrument.* As Kuhn remarks, the hard scientist who writes a monograph usually jeopardizes rather than enhances his reputation. But in anthropology and sociology, the main outlet for creative work is the monograph; the arti-cle is much less important. Whereas the textbook is the main teaching

instrument right up to the PHD level in the hard sciences, it is often said in the social sciences that it is immoral to write one. This is because a textbook is not a creative piece of work, and is meant to be financially rewarding. Edited anthologies often fall into the same category: intellectually suspect, but one means of getting your name known. In anthropology, a textbook may be used at the introductory level, but usually it is supplemented by monographs and articles. As Murphy (1979: v) has recently stated, there even is a movement in the discipline *away* from the use of a textbook. *Conclusion*: again, anthropology is pre-paradigmatic.

3 *Kuhn states that one criterion of whether a discipline has a paradigm is the amount of shared agreement within it.* But as we have seen, both anthropology and sociology embrace several different constellations of beliefs, values and techniques, theoretical orientations, and conceptual schemes, which is the main reason the textbook is inappropriate. Ritzer's argument (1975) that the lack of agreement can be interpreted to mean that sociology is multiparadigmatic is an unacceptable semantic escape route.[2] *Conclusion*: both disciplines are pre-paradigmatic.

4 *Kuhn stresses that anomalies provide the pre-conditions for a paradigmatic shift.* However, the term 'anomaly' is inappropriate to anthropology. The reasons are as follows. According to Kuhn, the normal science activity of puzzle-solving is disturbed when anomalies begin to surface. They create the pre-conditions for a revolutionary shift, which only occurs when a new paradigm, or at least the potential for one, appears on the scene as an alternative. What is significant is Kuhn's remark that it would not be possible to identify anomalies unless a discipline had a paradigm; the very insularity

2 Although Ritzer's work represents the most extensive treatment of paradigms by a sociologist to date, it also is quite wrong and misleading. Unfortunately, I cannot indulge myself in a thorough critique here. Ritzer contends that sociology has had three paradigms: social facts (Durkheim), social definition (Weber), and social behaviourism (Homans). He readily admits that rather than expressing agreement about fundamentals, the proponents of each of these three paradigms continuously try to undermine the other two. In this respect, the discipline would appear to be pre-paradigmatic, but Ritzer prefers to describe it as multiparadigmatic. Kuhn does state that a paradigm can either be discipline-wide or associated with a subcommunity whose focus is on a substantive issue. Yet Ritzer (1975: 18) admits that sociology is a 'science' that has not only failed to achieve paradigm pre-eminence within the field as a whole, but also *within a given area*. Later he states (1975: 131) that the discipline does not even possess any theory. The baffled reader can only wonder how he can call sociology paradigmatic, multiple or otherwise.

and rigour of the paradigm throws anomalies into bold relief. This does not happen in anthropology. We are incessantly plagued with inconsistencies and unsolved problems – I won't call them anomalies. These do not emerge only at the interparadigmatic crisis period and disappear again with 'normal' science. They are always with us. *Conclusion:* by this criterion, anthropology is pre-paradigmatic.

According to these four criteria, it certainly is not legitimate to label anthropology paradigmatic. It may be acceptable to refer to it as pre-paradigmatic. However, I am opposed to this, because one possible but erroneous implication is that eventual paradigmatic status is inevitable, as long as the members of a discipline share a commitment to scientific inquiry. Reacting to the tendency of some social scientists to interpret his thesis as a program for transforming their disciplines into sciences, Kuhn remarks, 'I claim no therapy to assist the transformation of a proto-science to a science, nor do I suppose that anything of the sort is to be had. If ... some social scientists take from me the view that they can improve the status of their field by first legislating agreement on fundamentals and then turning to puzzle-solving, they are badly misconstruing my point' (1972: 245). In my view, anthropology must be considered non-paradigmatic. The reason for this concerns a fundamental distinction between the social and natural realms. This distinction rests upon the notion of order. As Phillips (1973–4) points out, there are three presuppositions in all scientific inquiry: there is order in nature, every event has a cause, and the order and causality can be discovered by man. That, in essence, is the basis of positivism, and diverges drastically from the social world investigated by anthropologists. There may be a semblance of order in the social world, but it is a constantly shifting one. Not only that, our perception and knowledge of the social world itself transform it, because man is a conscious being, capable of symbolic communication, a language-bearer. As it has been said many times, we study not only the social organization of human beings, but also what they think, including what they think of being studied. Dahrendorf (1959: viii) has remarked that a unique human phenomenon is that social structures 'create permanently and systematically some of the determinant forces of their change within themselves.' Van den Berghe (1967: 295) has observed that while tending toward stability, consensus, and equilibrium, societies also generate within themselves the opposite conditions. Friedrichs' dialectical viewpoint (1972a, 1972b) is relevant here. He argues that the social scientist's discovery of order or patterns of behaviour feeds back into the social realm itself, thus altering it. In other words, knowledge of the world modifies the world.

Earlier I referred to Truman and Almond, two former presidents of the American Political Science Association. Truman has argued that from the 1880s until the 1930s, something loosely comparable to a paradigm existed in political science (see Bernstein 1979). Almond, who succeeded Truman as president, contended that a paradigm existed from the turn of the century until the 1950s. This happy state of affairs was terminated by momentous changes in society, such as the Second World War and the breakup of colonialism. These changes ruptured the coherence of political science and put an end, at least temporarily, to paradigmatic activity. Wolin, another political scientist (Bernstein 1979), also stresses that fundamental changes in his discipline have emerged as a result of changes in society. He goes so far as to define political society itself as a paradigm. As political society changes, so does the paradigm. Clearly this is a long way from where Kuhn locates paradigm, and Bernstein (1979: 96) nicely draws this ironic conclusion: by stressing the degree to which paradigms in political science are dependent on changes in society, the authors are admitting that their paradigms are merely ideologies, for paradigms reflect existing, persistent social conditions. For my purposes, the most important implication is that whereas in the hard sciences paradigmatic change comes about as a result of the discovery of anomalies, in the social sciences it is changes in the subject matter that are crucial. Kuhn himself has admitted that he has failed to consider the impact of the social world and its changes on science. This is a serious flaw, yet the fact that he could push his analysis of scientific revolutions as far as he did without considering the social environment merely reaffirms the fundamental difference between the hard sciences and other disciplines. In the next chapter I shall show not only that anomalies fail to account for theoretical shifts in anthropology, but that social changes are inadequate explanations. The peculiar source of theoretical change in the discipline is the presence of several competing and contradictory concepts around which the various theoretical orientations have oscillated.

PSEUDO-PARADIGMS

Only twice in the history of anthropology has the discipline approximated paradigmatic status: once during the period of structural functionalism that dominated social anthropology in the era of Malinowski and Radcliffe-Brown, and once during the period of cultural materialism, within which I subsume cultural ecology and neo-evolutionism. While the two orientations differed radically in many important respects, they shared the view that the social world is orderly, and that they had the tools to discover that order. In other words, both schools assumed that law-like statements of regularity would yield to their investigations, which meant that they proceeded nomo-thetically.

British Structural Functionalism
There are plenty of references to the so-called paradigmatic nature of early social anthropology. For example, Kuper (1975: 9–10) states that it consisted of 'an exceptionally tight-knit professional group, with a revolutionary methodology, shared standards of training and evaluation, and a fairly coherent theoretical framework.' Kuper, a British social anthropologist, adds that an American once referred to social anthropology as 'a mutual admira-tion society of limited intelligence' (1975: 10). But several American anthro-pologists have themselves remarked on the paradigmatic nature of the discipline in Britain. Honigmann (1976: 263), for example, states that British social anthropology in the 1940s and 1950s was characterized by consider-able harmony in thinking and wide agreement on how to proceed in field-work and in the analysis of the data. Redfield (1955–6: 20), referring to the heyday of British structural functionalism, remarked, 'There is no develop-ment in social or cultural anthropology that has comparable precision and coherence.' Although the thrust of Murphy's work is to deny the usually assumed differences between social and cultural anthropology, he does state (1971: 15) that 'the quantity, reliability, and detail of data in any science are a key to its qualitative standards; British anthropology is superb on all these counts. It has carved out a small domain and has excelled in it.' Murdock (1951: 471), with some misgivings, concluded that in British social anthro-pology 'the entire corpus of writings constitutes a perfectly logical, self-con-sistent system which provides answers, or techniques for securing answers, to a number of important scientific questions.' He refers to its highly refined canons of methods and its narrow range of theoretical interests, and states: 'Its voluntarily assumed limitations give British social anthropology the characteristic earmarks of a "school"' (1951: 470). As long as British social anthropologists were prepared to accept his claim that they were mere soci-ologists in disguise, Murdock was quite willing to recognize their achieve-ments.

These comments suggest that social anthropology possessed many of the essential principles and qualities for a nomothetic science of society. It had a 'clean' conceptual territory, which meant that it was easy to distinguish the anthropological domain from other disciplines and to determine which problems could be legitimately handled. It possessed an accepted (if not acceptable) array of research techniques and procedures of verification (loosely related to the quality and length of participant observation, consistency with existing studies, and language competency). Finally, there was a large degree of agreement among British social anthropologists about what constituted the 'core' of the discipline, despite the public bickering of Malinowski and Radcliffe-Brown. Certainly this was the case before Evans-Pritchard lost the faith, and before others, such as Firth and Leach, made the first tentative attacks that later threw the discipline into disarray.

Proponents of the structural-functional model also were not self-conscious about methods, verification procedures, or philosophical implications. Nor was there much emphasis on theory per se, and certainly not on innovative work for its own sake. The British, as Murphy has remarked, were cautious to the point of timidity. Indeed, this school has often been criticized for its crude empiricism, for its paradoxical stance of glorifying field-work while at the same time displaying a singular lack of interest in methodology; the few outstanding replication studies that we have, for example, such as Redfield (1930)–Lewis (1951), Goodenough (1956b)–Fischer (1958) and Bennett's analysis of studies of Pueblo culture (1946), have all been products of American anthropology.

These several features, including an absence of interest in methodological issues, are characteristic of Kuhn's description of disciplines that have attained paradigmatic status. Yet the structural-functional school of social anthropology contained a fundamental flaw. To make this model work, the social world had to be distorted to the point where explanation was futile. Later I shall consider some of these distortions, such as the tendency to exaggerate the degree of simplicity in pre-industrial societies. For present purposes, what is important is that regularities had to be seen at all costs. Conflict, contradiction, and the innovative role of the individual had to be suppressed; where they did appear, as in Malinowski's work, there was an essential logical incompatibility built into the structural-functional framework. Meaning, values, and motivation also had to be reduced to a residual category because of the problems of measuring them and the unmanageable complexity that they imposed on the social realm. This school also placed unrealistic methodological demands upon field-workers. They supposedly were able to disconfirm (if not confirm) hypotheses in a logically impeccable manner; but without the controlled laboratory experiment, and because of the complexity of the phenomena studied, such falsification was simply not possible. The criteria that did exist, such as length of field-work, language competency, and consistency with existing studies, were only remotely related to the disconfirmation process. Indeed, logical criteria for falsification could not even be articulated within the 'paradigm' itself. In other words, the flaw was much more serious than the usual criticisms that falsification criteria or criteria of evidence are paradigm-dependent. It should be added that even the anthropologist's logical alternative to the controlled laboratory experiment – the comparative method – rarely was employed; when it was, it was often for purposes of illustration, not of control. Finally, most social anthropologists during this era did not test hypotheses at all; certainly the practice of going to the field with a hypothesis to test was virtually unheard of. Instead, they were content to gather the data and to carve out a few modest empirical generalizations. I know that this is the preferred model of positivistic science dating back to Comte. The assumption is that the patient gathering of data will lead eventually to a theoretical breakthrough. But as Kuhn has remarked (1970: 16), the history of science shows that this Baconian approach almost never leads to the emergence of a first paradigm in a discipline.

Despite these weaknesses, British social anthropologists acted as if they did proceed nomothetically, and did have the equivalent of a paradigm. How was this possible? It has a great deal to do with the size of the anthropological profession in Britain, and perhaps with the closed, highly stratified nature of British society itself. Whatever the explanation, social anthropology became authoritarian, defensive, narrow, and arbitrary. To maintain the 'paradigm,' the leading figures had to exercise tight control over the anthropological community. As I shall show later, there is much less worship of the elders of the discipline in North America, probably because of the much larger anthropological community; this fact accounts at least in part for the much less unified research interests and theoretical orientations.

It is quite remarkable just how small the British social anthropological community was at the height of structural functionalism. Even in 1939 there were, according to Kuper (1975: 90), only about twenty professional social anthropologists in the entire British Commonwealth. By 1953 there were thirty-eight social anthropologists teaching in British universities, although Firth (1951: 474) indicates that in 1951 there were about fifty members of the Association of Social Anthropologists. In 1968 the ASA, which had been founded in 1946 had 240 members; Kuper (1975: 151) estimates that only about one-third of these were employed in Britain. Even in contemporary times, as Murphy remarks (1971: 20), almost all of the members of the ASA probably know one another personally. Murphy alludes to the obvious social control functions that are possible in such a small, face-to-face community. This seems to be the key to the semblance of paradigmatic inquiry in Britain. As Kuper has stated (1975: 154–5), 'the leading anthropologists had the decisive voice in the appointment of staff and often in the choice of students, particularly graduate students. The professor could effectively withhold or grant promotions, leaves, and other privileges; and his recommendation was crucial in any application for a research grant or for a position elsewhere.' Kuper adds that the leading figures in social anthropology, such as Evans-Pritchard, Firth, Forde, and Fortes, occupied elevated positions in the organizations that gave out funds and prizes, and distributed these to each other.

Murphy stresses the high degree of rigour and criticism that are part of the British style, but points out that these also were means of assuring orthodoxy. He adds that the small size of the British profession also meant that what one said in lectures or in publication became immediately known throughout the anthropological community, which again put a damper on innovation and speculation. Murphy does not deny that the leading figures in British anthropology were excellent scholars, but he contends that they always represented the centre of the discipline's approach, especially those persons selected for professorships.

What is most remarkable, in view of the small size of British social anthropology, is that its accomplishments were so great. How can it be explained that the first students of Malinowski turned out to be men of the intellectual quality of Evans-Pritchard, Firth, and the physical anthropologist Ashley Montagu? Or, for that matter, that almost all the pre-Second World War professional social anthropologists appeared to be so competent – indeed, gifted? I suppose that one could try to explain it in terms of the élitist nature of British education. Perhaps Lévi-Strauss's argument (1974: 408) that only the first stages of any endeavour are truly creative also has some relevance. Certainly, I lean to a similar view regarding Marx, Weber, and Durkheim, who managed to lay the essential framework of social anthropology. Then, too, there is the argument that the times produce the conditions into which genius can step. As Marx said, had he not formulated the basis of dialectical materialism, somebody else would have done so, for the conditions of society created the necessity for such a person. Yet I am not satisfied, for where in anthropology, whose practitioners in the United States alone number over 5,000, can one find today a dozen scholars of the intellectual equivalent of those British anthropologists in the euphoric days of structural functionalism?

Let us come back to the issue of paradigms and control. I have suggested that it was the capacity of the leaders of British anthropology to regulate the profession that explains more than anything else the tightness of that profession, its orthodoxy, and its consistent style. This does not mean that other factors were not involved, such as the capacity of structural functionalism to provide ideological support for colonialism. The last two decades in British anthropology have been racked with strain as its bread-and-butter territory, colonial society, has dwindled away. While there have been some changes in theoretical perspective – perhaps 'fads' is a better word – such as flirtations with Lévi-Straussian structuralism, socio-linguistics, and even Marxian anthropology, there still seems to be a centre, an orthodoxy that has no counterpart in the United States. This explains, perhaps, why many of the most innovative British anthropologists, such as Bailey and Burridge, have moved to other countries, while some of those who have remained, such as Worsley and Mitchell, whose work went against the grain (in terms of Marxism and methodology respectively), have switched to sociology departments. My suggestion is that the job market alone cannot explain this mobility: also relevant is the degree to which scholars have been intellectually stifled. As Murphy (1971) has said, migration to another country has not been as much a brain-drain from Britain as a deportation.

American Cultural Materialism

Compared to British social anthropology, American cultural anthropology is amorphous, or, to use Murphy's adjectives (1971: 35), sloppy, uneven, freewheeling, factually loose, and undisciplined. This condition is mostly due to its much larger membership and to organizational factors. For example, there is nothing in the United States equivalent to the Chair or the Professor, and funds for research are not disbursed by the great figures to younger scholars; instead, one bravely applies for research grants, and prays that the referees share one's theoretical perspective. In contrast to Britain, where every anthropologist probably knows every new PHD personally (Murphy 1971: 20), in the United States a new PHD may not even know all the members of the department from which he graduated. American anthropology is obviously much less controlled than British anthropology; hence its innovative, amorphous character. As Murphy put it (1971: 17), 'The range of interests of American anthropology is so vast that the discipline has almost lost itself. By becoming everything, it threatens to become nothing – this is not a paradox but a true contradiction.'

It is because American anthropology is so diversified that the emergence of a widely held, consistent, and undeniably quasi-nomothetic approach since the Second World War has been so impressive. I am referring to cultural materialism, under which I include cultural ecology and neo-evolutionism. Cultural materialism uses sophisticated research designs and is strong on quantification. An early attempt to place anthropology on a scientific footing was made by Murdock (1949). His efforts in connection with the HRAF are admirable. Yet as Harris (1968) has stated, Murdock produced correlations, not cause-and-effect analyses, and without the latter one has not achieved nomothetic status.

The neo-evolutionary school, as exhibited in White's writings, has been directed mainly toward library studies, with the purpose of historical reconstruction. It is unlikely that such a grand scheme could have any direct effect upon research; the implication is that it must turn anthropology into a brand of history. Steward's middle-range theory would seem to be more promising, at least in its prospects for field-work. However, Steward's own remarks suggest that the cultural-ecology approach may also be doomed to extinction. Recall that he speculated that in advanced industrial societies the superstructure may gain causal primacy over techno-economic and techno-environmental factors, which would mean that the cultural-ecological framework would become obsolete. To the extent that neo-evolutionism and cultural ecology are synonymous with anthropological investigation, the discipline would appear to have little future.

Cultural materialism and structural functionalism differed in many respects. The obvious one was the scope of their conceptual schemes. Another difference was that cultural-materialists stressed the etic viewpoint, and structural-functionalists the emic; the former advocated library studies, the latter field-work; the Americans stressed change, the British stability. Yet both schools made the fundamental positivistic assumptions that the social world was orderly and that they had the tools to reveal the order. Neither school, however, produced any laws, and we are left with the belief that because nomothetic inquiry presupposes an orderly universe, the universe must therefore be orderly.

Earlier I referred to a difference between Kuhn and Popper. Kuhn tended to describe what scientists do, Popper what they ought to do. In many respects there is a similarity between Popper, Radcliffe-Brown, and Harris. The last two can be taken as leading spokesmen for nomothetic anthropology in the two schools on which we focused. Their views constitute little more than 'ought' statements. Friedman (1974), for example, has dismissed Harris's cultural materialism as vulgar or mechanical materialism, lacking any sense of the importance of contradiction, eliminating dialectics, and incapable of producing meaningful analysis.

In summary, both structural functionalism and cultural materialism approached paradigmatic status possessing many of the necessary principles, but they never quite made it. Their leading spokesmen, men such as Radcliffe-Brown and Harris (perhaps more so than others who actually carried out the field-work, such as Steward and Fortes), acted as if a paradigm had been achieved. But this was so much wishful thinking, and led to dogma. For these reasons, both cultural materialism and structural function-alism are best referred to as pseudo-paradigmatic.

CONCLUSION

Sometimes anthropology has been pseudo-paradigmatic, but never has it enjoyed paradigmatic status. On the basis of the arguments I have presented, some readers might want to describe the discipline as pre-paradigmatic, but I prefer non-paradigmatic, in order to stress the fundamental difference between the social and natural realms. Actually, one important index of the non-paradigmatic status of anthropology has always stared us in the face – the degree to which national boundaries have shaped the discipline. Ham-mel (1972) has suggested that there may be national styles of thought, such as the French proclivity for rationalism, universalism, and deduction, the British for social roles and their articulation, and the American for formal-ism and an engineering mentality. Even if this is an exaggeration, it cannot be denied that we do speak of British, French, and American versions of anthropology, possibly a Dutch variety, certainly a German one in earlier times, and signs of the emergence of a Russian one in the future. Sociology appears to be much less influenced by nationalism. American sociology *is* sociology, especially since the European alternative of philosophical sociol-ogy seems to have lost its prominence in recent years, although a variety of it was reborn with the Frankfurt critical school, and Althusser's structuralist Marxism has made its appearance. The American clout may simply be a case of exceptional cultural dominance, reflecting the country's pre-eminent position in the world, rather than evidence of any intrinsic defence in sociol-ogy against the intrusion of national boundaries.

Few criticisms disturb anthropologists more than the claim that their interpretations are culture-bound. The rationale for the overwhelming con-centration of research on other cultures is to overcome ethnocentrism. It is thus understandable why Firth opened his reply to Murdock's harangue against the British school with the argument (or plea) that science is inter-national. However, it appears that anthropology does differ according to national boundaries,and that a more general statement is warranted. The social sciences have basically been a Western phenomenon. Writers such as Jarvie (1975) have said as much, and an important part of Hsu's criticism of racism in the anthropological profession concerns his argument that the dis-cipline has failed dismally to integrate non-Western world views. True, anthropology is the one discipline in the social sciences to concentrate on the non-Western world. But it has done so, according to writers such as Willis (1972), in order to enhance the understanding and welfare of the Western world itself.

The implications of the non-paradigmatic status of anthropology for students and professionals are clear. It explains why so many become confused about the discipline. The problem is not simply that there are numerous competing theoretical orientations; a similar variety of approaches can be found in disciplines such as literary and art criticism and history. The difference is that, unlike these other disciplines, anthropology and sociology are usually introduced to students as sciences. If so, there should be a definite and logically defensible way of doing it. This is why arguments for and against theoretical orientations tend to be vociferous, even vicious. After all, it is not a matter of taste, as in literature; it is science!

Here too it is relevant to refer to the accident of exposure; students tend to accept as 'the paradigm' what they have been taught by instructors who just happened to be employed in their universities at a particular time. The non-paradigmatic nature of the discipline is especially treacherous for graduate students, who often get caught between instructors espousing different 'paradigms.' I suppose that the wise student attaches himself to one school of thought as quickly as possible. This results in a severely limited training, but is the most certain path to graduation. In my view, the serious student must fight against this easy way out. The usual method of doing so is to choose a graduate school noted for a theoretical approach (or approaches) opposed to one's previous training, and to hope for a sympathetic and sophisticated supervisor.

The non-paradigmatic status of the discipline also has important implications for practising anthropologists. One concerns the very choice of a theoretical orientation. As I shall argue in part 2, most people cannot countenance disorder, flux, and contradiction. Anthropologists are little different. As one of my former teachers once remarked, most of us, out of desperation, arbitrarily latch on to systems analysis, networks, action theory, structuralism, or whatever, simply to gain peace of mind. Once this has been done, there is a tendency to exaggerate the rigour and explanatory power of the perspective that has been embraced. The non-paradigmatic status of the discipline also creates many obstacles to publishing. My impression from discussions with biologists and other scientists is that there is not nearly as much divergence of opinion in their disciplines regarding the evaluation of articles, research proposals, and books. This impression is reinforced by a study of Zuckerman and Merton (1971). They found that the rejection rate for articles was much higher in the arts than in the social sciences, and much higher in the social sciences than in the hard sciences.

The analysis of book reviews in anthropological journals is an especially important index of the non-paradigmatic nature of the discipline. The widely diverging standards of evaluation and opinion regarding the merits of any particular book recently prompted Woodbury (1977) to write an editorial on the subject in *American Anthropologist*. It would be rewarding to undertake an extensive analysis of book reviews in anthropology, possibly focusing on works that have won awards or are recognized as major contributions to the discipline. For example, Henderson's *The King in Every Man* (1972) won the Amoury Talbot Award for West Africa, but has been reviewed quite negatively since then. Burridge's *Mambu* (1960) may well be the best work ever done on the cargo cults, but it was dismissed as a so-so study by Keesing (1961). I am not able to do justice here to the subject of book reviews, but in order to stress their importance as indices of the non-paradigmatic nature of the discipline, I shall look more closely at the celebrated case of Silverman's review (1974–5) of three of Bailey's volumes. Silverman reviewed *Stratagems and Spoils*, Bailey's first substantial indication that he had shifted theoretical perspective from his earlier work on India, and *Gifts and Poison* and *Debate and Compromise*, which were edited by Bailey and consist mostly of articles written by his students on their field-work in European communities.

Stratagems and Spoils, according to one reviewer, was a path-breaking study providing anthropology with a new model. In another reviewer's opinion, the book was so good that it rendered Machiavelli's *The Prince* obsolete. Silverman, in contrast, finds little to praise in the three volumes. While she specifically criticizes the articles in the edited volumes, stating that most of them were too low in quality to get accepted in good journals, it is Bailey's approach to politics that she finds wanting. As one evaluates Silverman's critique, it becomes obvious that her interpretation is a result of her different theoretical orientation. Her starting-point is structure, not action. She does not like the image of the innovative actor, the emphasis on values, or the game model. She criticizes Bailey for ignoring what is most important – the structure within which the actors operate. Silverman also subscribes to a conventional and naïve positivistic epistemology: she asks for details on how Bailey's theory of politics can be falsified. Yet as we have seen, the entire issue of falsification is a messy one, and most philosophers of science do not believe falsifying rules can be erected. Popper and Lakatos are exceptions, but Kuhn (1970: 146–7) has undermined their arguments. Not surprisingly, Silverman gives no clues as to how she would falsify a theory. The crux of the issue is reflected in Silverman's remark (1974–5: 114): 'The question of why de Gaulle succeeded becomes "how did he act like a skillful politician?" not "what circumstances made a de Gaulle possible?"' The implication is that Bailey's question is false. What this really shows, however, is that the data have been examined from two different perspectives.

Sankoff (1973: 10), commenting on the widely varying standards and criteria for the evaluation of published works, observes that each school has different criteria of excellence: 'what is taken for granted by one school is perceived as being the question by another. Acceptable proof is another tricky point: demonstration by analysis of a crucial case appears "anecdotal" to those who adhere to a different tradition; what to some is an elegant proof will be criticized by others as "empty formalism".' Sankoff then raises the question whether, within a particular tradition or theoretical orientation, there exist generally accepted standards of excellence, and shows that even there one is in murky waters (although she attempts to clear them up), which brings us back to Bailey's politics. Certainly flaws can be found in Bailey's three volumes, and in some respects he has exposed his flank to attack by reinforcing the positivistic image of verifiable propositions (Bailey 1969: 8, 17). But this is not the point. What is crucial is the degree to which Silverman's criticisms are generated by her different theoretical perspective.

What are the prospects of achieving paradigmatic status in the future, and with it more agreement on fundamentals? It is sometimes said that we have had no geniuses in the discipline since the founding fathers, but that if a genius was to emerge the discipline would no longer stumble along. Sociologists and social anthropologists have a built-in bias against the recognition of genius, a bias that has its roots in Durkheim's anti-reductionism. What is important is not the individual actor, so it goes, but the social-structural conditions that encourage or discourage the emergence of genius. Certainly there is much to be said for this viewpoint, and it may well explain why the current state of anthropology, with thousands of practitioners, is so dull, and why it often fails to attract the brightest students. Whatever the case may be, in sociology there probably has not been a thinker of the intellectual calibre of the founding fathers in recent decades. But in anthropology we have Lévi-Strauss. Certainly he has had a profound effect on the discipline, but as I shall argue in chapter 6, his work on the whole probably adds up to a failure, which means that we are in no better shape than the sociologists. Perhaps the conditions were simply not ripe for the work of a genius. But that is arguable, for the morass of confusion and competing perspectives, the signs of malaise in the discipline, all cry out for solution. Even had Lévi-Strauss succeeded in putting anthropology back on an even keel, his efforts may have been for naught. One of the problems with the geniuses we have had in the social sciences is that they have left us with few methods by which the rest of us can follow them.

4

Conceptual Contradictions

One of Kuhn's most controversial claims was that science has not been cumulative. The conventional image of science as steady theoretical growth has not lacked support in anthropology. Barnes (1966: 159), for example, has stated: 'We have come to realize, perhaps more explicitly than did Durkheim, that one of the distinguishing marks of science is that it is cumulative, and that each generation of investigators incorporates the discoveries of its predecessors into its established corpus of organized understanding.' According to Barnes, this is the main difference between science and the humanities. Sartre and Auden, he remarks, have not superseded Shakespeare and Homer, and in philosophy Aristotle and Plato are never out of print. But the early giants of science such as Euclid and Hippocrates are only of historical interest. Barnes does point out that we do have to return to Durkheim to cope with many current problems. He explains this as a result of Durkheim's lack of clarity, and the still unrealized goal of a positivistic science of society. He does not question the feasibility of the goal itself.

It would not be difficult to spin off a list of prominent names of sociologists who share a similar view of the cumulative nature of their discipline. Coser and Rosenberg (1976: vii), for example, introduce their anthology with the remark that only if sociology can claim that its research results have been cumulative can it develop as a science. A few lines later they say that this happy state of affairs has been attained. Yet a few pages further on (1976: 6) they observe that 'sociology has constantly had to justify its existence. In providing a raison d'être, no one excels the early masters. Only when sight is lost of their reasoning does the field itself become hazy and undefinable.'

How can the inconsistency in their argument be explained? Apparently the cumulative potential has been retarded by the growth of radical empiricism. In other words (1976: ix), 'If such men as Durkheim and Weber still provided us with our best clues, it is because a generation or two of nose counting has supplied us with none that are better.' American sociology has had an engineering rather than a theoretical orientation. As an explanation for theoretical stagnation, this is not very convincing. Quite apart from the fact that the radical-empiricist tradition approximates the essential positivistic style advocated by Bacon, with the assumption that theoretical breakthroughs will emerge from the accumulated masses of data, Coser and Rosenberg conveniently ignore the dominant figure in the American scene at the time of their writing – Talcott Parsons, the incurable theorist.

IDEAL AND ACTUAL THEORY

The distinction between ideal and actual levels of belief and behaviour is intrinsic to the anthropologist's perspective. It also has its counterpart in anthropological theories. The image of anthropological theory as steady cumulation and progress is the ideal pattern; the actual pattern is quite different. The outstanding feature of anthropological theory has been its oscillating, pendulous nature, as it has swung back and forth between contradictory modes of explanation, sometimes reversing itself, sometimes repeating itself. The discipline began with evolutionism and in recent years has returned to it; we had the early conflict theory of Simmel, and its rediscovery in Gluckman and Coser's work; we had a different kind of conflict theory with Marx, and its reappearance in cultural materialism, French economic anthropology, structuralism, and the sociological approach in deviance and criminology known as Marxian ethnography. Weber's social-action framework was eclipsed by structural functionalism and other frameworks stressing the social system, but has been reborn in Bailey's work. The long period of focusing on the individual and the personality gave way to structural functionalism, neo-evolutionism, and cultural ecology, but with the new psychology the individual has made a comeback. With Durkheim, Parsons, and White we had 'cultural dopes,' with Malinowski and Marx an image of the actor as an active, even a manipulating agent, and with Althusser's structuralism a return to the actor as robot. There was the important linguistic work of Sapir, Whorf, and Boas, a long period of relative inactivity, and a rekindling of these interests with the emergence of socio-linguistics and the new ethnography. After years of effort to discredit the biological reductionism of early evolutionism, accompanied by the overwhelming significance attributed to culture, socio-biology appeared on the scene; pioneers such as Tylor and Bastian stressed the underlying similarity of mankind, and after several decades dominated by the view of the immense variation of cultures, accompanied by an unwillingness to reduce one's analysis beyond this level, a similar view of man's universality has emerged in Lévi-Strauss's structuralism. At different periods we have seen a stress on man as a unit in a behavioural system and as a phenomenal creature, as in Weber's work; a view of culture as highly integrated and as a thing of shreds and patches; and, repeatedly, a shifting emphasis on social structure at one period and culture at another; and sometimes the emergence of a framework in which both are downplayed in order to highlight a key factor, be it techno-economics, techno-environment, neurology, sex, biology, or whatever.

Like people in general, anthropologists need a set of ideal beliefs to sustain them; hence the dominant but erroneous view of steady and cumulative theoretical progress. Nevertheless, some support for my description of the actual nature of anthropological theory can be found. Honigmann, for example, has said that rather than being cumulative, the central ideas of anthropology have largely been additive and substitutive. In his words (1976: 8), 'loosely articulated orienting concepts and propositions, even contradictory theories, have accumulated, persisting alongside each other.' Voget (1975: 138) has remarked that anthropology has alternated between a scientific and humanistic orientation, and has characterized the history of the discipline as 'the treadmill of oscillation between extremes of polar theoretical distinctions which have dogged its steps' (1975: 802). Voget is obviously uncomfortable with this description, because he believes anthropology should be cumulative.

In his critical evaluation of socio-biology, Sahlins (1977: 101) has also referred to the pendulous nature of theory. Since the seventeenth century, he argues, we have been caught in a vicious circle, in which alternately the model of capitalist society is applied to the animal kingdom, and the bourgeoisified animal kingdom acts as a model to explain human society. As Sahlins put it (1977: 105), 'We seem unable to escape from the perpetual movement, back and forth between the culturization of nature and the naturalization of culture.' Almost a century earlier, Engels (1940: 18–20) had arrived at an identical conclusion.

In a different work, Sahlins (1976) addresses the distinction between 'the meaningful' and 'practical thought,' or culture and practical reason, which parallels idealism versus materialism, and conventional anthropology versus Marxism. Again he refers to the repetitive, pendulous nature of theory (1976: 55): 'This conflict between practical activity and constraints of the mind inserts itself in an original, founding contradiction, between the poles of which anthropological theory has oscillated since the nineteenth century like a prisoner pacing between the farthest walls of the cell.' The repetitive character of theory is not limited to anthropology. As Mirkovic has stated (1980: 163), in social science in general there is 'a recurring swing from one extreme or opposite pole of orientation to another. It is a sort of pendulum model, or a challenge–response reaction, where one particular conception or paradigm dominates and provokes a reaction of opposite orientation.'

EXPLAINING THEORETICAL SHIFTS

How can the oscillating, repetitive character of anthropological theory be explained? Part of the answer was given in the previous chapter. The non-paradigmatic (or pre-paradigmatic) nature of the discipline allows several competing orientations to exist simultaneously. Under these conditions we would expect theoretical perspectives and methodological innovations to emerge briefly and then disappear, like componential analysis. This stage, at which the social sciences are stuck, is similar to the crisis period in science, in which one is prepared to try anything. While the non-paradigmatic nature of anthropology provides an environment in which a flurry of theories can emerge, it does not explain why the discipline retracts and repeats itself as it does.

A second possible answer concerns the discovery of a superior orientation. Kuhn's arguments make this answer dubious regarding the hard sciences, and it is even less plausible in anthropology. The main reason has already been given: the great deal of repetition in our theories. We keep discovering old truths, and long-abandoned orientations pop up again, often under new labels. By the conventional criteria used to measure theoretical progress – simplicity, elegance, accuracy, scope, and fruitfulness – the discipline appears to have stood still; or, more aptly, to have rocked back and forth without gaining ground. These criteria, in fact, are largely unoperational in anthropology. Kuhn remarks that measurements such as simplicity and neatness or elegance are less effective in the sciences than in mathematics, because of the greater crudeness of paradigms in the sciences. Little wonder, then, that such criteria are not very meaningful in anthropology. For example, how can it be determined whether evolutionism is simpler than structural functionalism, or whether social action is more fruitful than structural functionalism? I personally consider social action to be more accurate in reflecting man's behaviour, but it also is a looser, more ambiguous orientation, and hence possibly less fruitful than structural functionalism. The various American orientations are all superior in their scope to the various British orientations, but they may be less accurate. Even if progress can be demonstrated from one orientation to another in one criterion, such as simplicity, it will probably be contradicted by other criteria, such as scope, fruitfulness, and accuracy. Finally, it must be stressed that each orientation will dictate how one defines and operationalizes these criteria; this suggests that in the last resort it is logically impossible to measure scientific progress, regardless of the discipline, at least by the conventionally accepted criteria.

A third possibility is that shifts in theoretical perspective occur in response to changes in society. This is the conventional explanation in the sociology of knowledge, and there is a great deal to be said for it. 'The principal thesis of the sociology of knowledge,' Mannheim (1949: 2) has written, 'is that there are modes of thought that cannot be adequately understood as long as their social origins are obscured.' Mannheim particularly stressed the link between idea systems and group interests.

Kardiner and Preble (1963: 189) have ventured that 'the history of a field, such as anthropology, is not so much a history of "falsehoods" and "truths," as it is a record of man's attempt to solve the problems that a constantly changing world presents.' Although this view alludes to a social world that is not quite as orderly as the positivists assume, it nevertheless expresses the thesis that theories are transformed in response to changing social conditions. Occasionally a dissenting voice is heard. For example, Honigmann (1976: 248) observed that major events such as the Vietnam war, racial battles, and the proliferation of nuclear weapons failed to alter the discipline significantly. Yet the consistent explanation has been the contrary. McFeat (1979), for example, argues that changing conditions among Canadian native peoples have forced a modification in the models addressed to them. He also stresses the degree to which anthropologists and their jargon have contributed to the changes; indeed, native people have begun to resemble the social organization of the anthropological profession!

Evolutionism is said to have been consistent with the era of European imperialism, with the emphasis placed on expansion, change, the survival of the fittest, and a clear distinction between superior and inferior peoples – all of which were compatible with dog-eat-dog capitalism. While structural functionalism and its anti-historical emphasis was made to measure for colonialism, with the end of the Second World War and the emergence of newly independent nations the conditions were ripe for a new kind of theory, one that emphasized change. What we got was neo-evolutionism, structuralism, and a renewed emphasis on dialectics and Marx. As Mirkovic stresses (1980: 164), that emphasis can be seen as a response to the growing inadequacy of Western positivistic science brought about by a deepening crisis in Western capitalism. Bottomore (1975: 48) claims that positivism itself emerged to serve the ideological needs of technological society.

The thesis that our theories change in response to changes in society is indeed a powerful one. I have no quarrel with it as far as its general influence on the broad theoretical direction of the discipline is concerned, such as an evolutionism to firm up imperialist expansion, and functionalism to take over after the empire had been carved out. However, in chapter 2 I listed thirty-eight theoretical orientations, and in this chapter have described the highly repetitive, oscillating, pendulous nature of the history of anthropological theory. The conventional sociology-of-knowledge approach cannot cope with the degree and character of theoretical changes.

It is possible that the thesis can be salvaged if a modification in the conception of social change is made. Most writers, including so-called radicals who broadcast anthropology's ties to colonialism, accept a straightforward positivistic conception of society as a highly patterned structure of action, slow to change. But there is an alternative conception, a non-positivistic one: the view that society is semi-amorphous, fluid, constantly in flux. If this view of society and social change is accepted, there is less reason to reject the argument that theories are transformed in response to the nature of society. As Giddens (1979: 89) has said, 'The chronic contestation or disputation of concepts and theories in the social sciences is in some part due to the fact that these concepts and theories are caught up in what they are about, namely social life itself.'

This conception of social change approximates more closely the fluctuating, proliferating character of the history of anthropological theory. Yet it remains inadequate, for it does not explain the peculiar character of shifts in theoretical orientation – the fact that new orientations resemble previously discredited ones, and the fact that the discipline swings back and forth between polar-opposite positions such as positivism and phenomenology, each position manifested in a host of theoretical orientations over the past several decades. The social-change argument, whether in the conventional or the revised sense, cannot account for this pattern; to do so, I must turn to the central explanation in this chapter, conceptual contradictions.

The history of the discipline has been characterized by a shifting emphasis on various conflicting concepts and problems. At one point the individual is emphasized, at another point the group, or the micro and the macro. Man is seen first as rational, then as primarily an emotional creature. Emphasis is placed on social organization, with culture viewed as epiphenomenal or unmeasurable; or motivation is paramount, such as in Weber's work, and then considered 'psychological' and beyond the interests of the anthropologist. The discipline deals with the regular, the systemic: it is a science. Then it stresses the particular, the unique, and the complexity of social life. The emphasis is on the observed world, which is then treated as a smokescreen for underlying principles. An effort is made to carve out a narrowly defined conceptual territory, and then the framework is expanded so that social organization and culture become dependent elements of a macro perspective. Change and conflict are stressed, then stability, continuity, and harmony. Man's dreams and values explain first his behaviour, then his orientation to the techno-economic realm. A fuller list of the conceptual contradictions that underlie our theories follows.

SOME EXAMPLES OF CONCEPTUAL CONTRADICTIONS

A *Key Contradictions*
- dynamic   vs static
- conflict   vs harmony
- individual   vs group
- norm   vs act
- qualitative   vs quantitative
- relativism   vs comparison
- reductionist   vs non-reductionist
- emic   vs etic
- value   vs fact

B *Other Contradictions*
- micro   vs macro
- content   vs form
- ideology   vs materialism
- unique   vs regular
- art   vs science
- historical   vs present
- historical   vs analytic
- historical   vs mechanical
- freedom   vs determinism
- emotion   vs rationality
- habit   vs rationality
- habit   vs utility
- process   vs structure
- diachrony   vs synchrony
- applied   vs pure

- unconscious   vs   conscious
- open   vs   closed
- latent   vs   manifest
- unintended   vs   intended
- motive   vs   function
- deep structure vs   surface structure
- specialized   vs   synthesizing
- description   vs   abstraction
- particular   vs   general
- contingent   vs   necessary
- insider   vs   outsider
- complex   vs   simple
- motivation   vs   structure
- culture   vs   society
- continuous   vs   discrete
- literal   vs   figurative
- understanding vs   explanation

Comments

My argument is that all the conceptual contradictions listed above, which have never been resolved, underlie our theoretical perspectives. At different periods some of the contradictions in one column combine to form the basis of a particular theoretical orientation. In time, the suppressed sides of the conceptual contradictions swing to the fore, replacing the previously dominant sides, and in this way a new theoretical orientation is created. The existence of a close logical fit among several of the sides of these contradictions partly explains why similar orientations emerge periodically, albeit often disguised by new terminology. Of course, a fuller explanation would require that other factors be entertained, such as the impact of changes in society on our theories and the underlying conservative drift that seems to pull our theories in a particular direction, I suppose as a means to protect the interests of the powerful.

As in the case of selecting the major theoretical orientations, there is a high degree of arbitrariness in deciding what to include in the list of key conceptual contradictions. If the ones I have chosen do have heuristic value, they should reveal the pattern underlying the changes in theoretical orientations without resorting to the other contradictions. Before applying this scheme, I must point out that several of the contradictions under category B are equivalent to those under category A. For example, dynamic versus static is listed as a key contradiction, and is similar to diachrony versus synchrony, process versus structure, historical versus mechanical, historical versus present, and historical versus analytic. There is on the whole a greater logical fit within the alternatives on the left side and within the alternatives on the right side than between those on the left and the right; in other words, each side to some extent constitutes a logically consistent bundle.

Having introduced the argument that shifts in theoretical orientations can be partly explained in terms of underlying conceptual contradictions, we are confronted with an additional problem: how can they play the role they do? The solution, I believe, has been suggested in an outstanding article by Murray Davis (1971), in which he introduces the terms 'double dialectic' and 'internal dialectic.' After a discipline becomes established, it no longer simply reacts to the empirical base to which it is addressed. It also reacts to its own explanations of the world. Its sensors feed back information without ever having groped beyond the explanatory system itself, and in doing so modify the system. In other words, academic disciplines contain an internal dialectic, or a double dialectic, in the sense of reacting both to the phenomenal world and to theories about it.[1]

A somewhat similar view has been presented by Murphy (1971), who has described Lévi-Strauss's structuralism as a 'frozen dialectic.' It is frozen in so far as it is essentially a mentalist position, divorced from the dynamic interaction with social organization and techno-economic and environmental factors. To the extent that theories change because of internal conceptual contradictions rather than because of changes in society or other causes, they too can be described as a 'frozen dialectic.' Murphy's criticism of Lévi-Strauss, in other words, can be generalized in varying degrees to all the theoretical orientations of anthropology.

A curious implication suggests itself. The constantly changing data base of the social sciences leads some writers to conclude that only under conditions of relatively long-term societal stability is theoretical progress possible, from which a paradigm may emerge. But if I am right about underlying conceptual contradictions and internal dialectics, we should welcome the frequent disruption of our theories that results from changes in society. For when there is long-term stability, there also is time for a significant internal dialectic to develop, so that eventually a theoretical perspective that

---

1 Actually, it may be more appropriate to speak in terms of a *triple* dialectic: that contained within a particular theoretical orientation as the embedded concepts generate their opposites, reflecting the logical sense of contradiction in which A negates itself; that between two or more theoretical orientations; and that between theoretical orientations and the phenomenal world.

APPLICATION OF KEY CONCEPTUAL CONTRADICTIONS TO MAJOR THEORETICAL ORIENTATIONS

Theoretical orientations

Contradictions	1	2	3	4	5	6	7	8	9	10	11	12	13	14	15	16
dynamic	■	■	■		■			■				■	■		■	■
static				■		■	■		■	■	■			■		
conflict	■	■										■	■		■	■
harmony			■	■	■	■	■	■	■	■	■	■		■	■	
individual			■		■			■				■	■	■		
group	■	■	■	■	■	■	■	■	■	■	■	■	■	■		■
norm	■		■	■	■	■	■		■	■	■	■		■		■
act	■	■	■			■		■	?			■	■		■	■
qualitative	■	■	■	■	■	■	■		■	■	■	■	■			■
quantitative								■		■	■			■	■	
relativism					■		■		?							
comparison	■	■	■	■		■		■	■	■	■	■	■	■	■	■
emic			■		■	■	■		■	■	■	■		■		■
etic	■	■	■	■		■			■	?			■		■	■
value	■	■			■		■					■				■
fact			■	■		■		■	■	■	■		■	■	■	
reductionist	■	■			■		■	■		■	■		■	■	■	■
anti-reductionist			■	■		■			■			■				■

KEY

1 early evolutionism
2 Marxian conflict theory
3 Weberian social action
4 Durkheimian social facts
5 historical particularism
6 British structural functionalism
7 culture and personality
8 cultural materialism
9 non-Marxian conflict theory
10 structuralism
11 formal analysis
12 Bailey social action
13 neo-Marxian conflict theory
14 neo-psychological anthropology
15 socio-biology
16 dialectical anthropology

had fed on itself emerges as a kind of monster, inverting the world, seeing it falsely.

As an example of the manner in which the double or internal dialectic operates, consider evolutionary theory. It is probable that early evolutionism did closely reflect social conditions at the time, although a distinction has to be drawn between the evolutionary framework and evolutionary ideology. Obviously, the appropriateness of the evolutionary framework does not vary with specific stages in history; it is either appropriate or inappropriate in general. But in terms of ideology, evolutionism probably was suited to its times. Spencer's survival-of-the-fittest concept and dog-eat-dog capitalism were highly compatible. However, to understand current neo-evolutionary theory we must consider the influence of (a) early evolutionary theory and (b) the reactions against other theoretical orientations that have emerged since then, such as culture-and-personality and structural functionalism. In short, no longer does the discipline relate directly, or even primarily, to the social world; instead there is an internal dialectic generated by the previous theoretical orientations that it created.

Earlier I stated that the key conceptual contradictions, if heuristic, should illuminate the history of anthropological theory. In the accompanying chart, the major theoretical orientations listed in chapter 2 are analysed in terms of the key contradictions.

Assigning the various conceptual alternatives to the theoretical orientations was admittedly a treacherous business. Sometimes it appeared that both sides of a contradiction had been represented in a specific perspective, such as the individual and the group in Weberian social action. The sixteen theoretical orientations are presented chronologically. A brief examination of the chart will reveal that throughout the history of anthropological theory there has been a constant movement back and forth between the opposed conceptual positions. The exceptions are harmony, qualitative analysis, and the comparative framework, which have consistently dominated their opposites.

OTHER CONCEPTUAL CONTRADICTIONS

Before turning to what I call salvage theory, I shall comment briefly on some other conceptual distinctions that seem to be always with us: epistemologies and typologies.

In the first category are a range of concepts that dichotomize science and non-science: naturalism versus phenomenology, positivism versus phenomenology, natural systems versus moral systems, natural science versus formal or mental science, or simply nomothetic versus idiographic inquiry. A more specific set of concepts divides conventional sociological analysis and Marxian analysis; for example, positivism versus Marxism and sociological versus dialectical analysis. Rather than including Marx among sociologists, some writers consider the two approaches to be fundamentally distinct and incompatible. To the extent that positivistic anthropology and sociology emerged in reaction to Marxism, this interpretation carries considerable weight.

Among the main anthropological typologies, the following stand out: mechanical versus organic (Durkheim), gemeinschaft versus gesellschaft (Tonneis), status versus contract (Maine), industrial versus military (Spencer), folk versus urban (Redfield), sacred versus secular (Park), cultures versus civilization (Small), and tradition-oriented ´versus other-oriented (Reisman). To these we might add Parsons' pattern variables and the various terms that identify anthropology's traditional research domain, such as complex versus simple societies, industrial versus pre-industrial societies, or white versus coloured societies.

Again there is ambiguity, for the same concepts have meant different things to different writers. For Evans-Pritchard, the distinction between natural and moral systems corresponded to science versus the humanities. But for Durkheim, the moral and natural systems were epistemologically synonymous. Moral systems were as real as natural systems; social facts were at the same time moral facts. Undoubtedly the discipline has been infused with such epistemological distinctions and typologies. They do not, however, play the same important role in bringing about theoretical shifts as do the more restricted key contradictions. This is because they have hardened into distinct theoretical positions, carrying with them numerous assumptions. The key conceptual contradictions, stripped as they are to the bare essentials, lend themselves to different combinations and thus to the formation of different theoretical orientations.

SALVAGE THEORY

The notion of the internal dialectic composed of underlying conceptual contradictions in combination with the impact of social change constitute powerful analytic tools for explaining the history of anthropological theory. However, there is a type of theorizing not entirely responsive to these tools which makes necessary an additional type of analysis. This concerns the manner in which scholars tinker with discredited theories in order to keep the theories alive. Even if a theoretical approach has been subjected to devastating criticism, there is usually no shortage of devotees who will continue to defend it to the hilt. Often the defence takes the form of modifications of the original orientation. It is in this context that I speak of salvage theory.

Modernization Theory

Modernization theory is one example of salvage theory. The early Weberian-influenced model emphasized the role of the individual entrepreneur, an open class-mobility system, the emergence of a middle class, and democratic political values. Modernization was considered different from economic development, although it usually included the latter. Modernization was a social process. It focused on factors such as secularization, individualism, achievement rather than ascription, a futuristic orientation, and structural differentiation. Although the model also stressed a shift in priority from religious and kinship institutions to the economic institution, it never lost sight of the social aspects of development. In this model, modernization and Westernization were synonymous, as exhibited in Lerner's work (1958) on the Middle East.

A number of critics, most notably Frank (1966), attacked this model, stressing the overwhelming influence of advanced capitalist countries on the underdeveloped world and arguing that underdevelopment itself was 'developed' or 'produced' by world capitalism. Frank emphasized the economic rather than the social aspects of development, and in the process exposed many of the so-called prerequisites of modernization, such as a Protestant ethic, for what they were: Western cultural biases. Not only did Frank argue the greater relevance of Marx than Weber, but he also tied his political values explicitly to his economic analyses. Contrary to popular opinion, political commitment on the part of a Marxist scholar is far from inevitable. Although Frank's critique was exceptionally devastating, it did not immediately bring about a change in development studies. What happened was that a number of new models emerged, many of them before Frank's attack, but inspired by a similar awareness that not all was well with the old modernization model, and determined to protect it. One such response was McClelland's need-to-achieve theory (1961). It attempted to expand the Weberian model by arguing that two critical variables had to be inserted between religious and cultural beliefs and economic growth: child-rearing practices and the psychological level of the need to achieve. By implication Weber was correct, but his theory had to be refined. By de-emphasizing economic factors, stressing certain values such as non-authoritarian child-rearing, and linking the need to achieve primarily to entrepreneurial roles, the theory shared many of the ethnocentric flaws of the Weberian model.

A second response was the emergence of a new modernization model. The individual innovator no longer was the folk-hero of development. Instead, the emphasis was placed on the group or collectivity. There was a shift in priority from the economy to the polity, and with it a stress on a strong centralized authority structure – the state – and political allegiance. A few writers (including myself, although I'm now embarrassed to admit it) even hinted at the emergence of structural de-differentiation (see Nettl and Robertson 1966). A key difference between this model and the old modernization model supposedly was that modernization was intentional. It was directed from the top, rather than emanating from the combined but uncoordinated efforts of millions of splendidly isolated individual entrepreneurs. New nations were in a hurry, and Western scholars, with apparently admirable flexibility, leaned over backward to accept the viewpoint that democracy and individual interests were an unaffordable luxury, especially with pots of gold in the form of international aid waiting to be spent. In the process, they came perilously close to advocating a fascist solution to development.

The third, and last-gasp, effort of liberal–conservative modernization theory was the emergence of the military model of modernization. The military was said to be the most democratic organization in new nations, characterized by a wide social base of recruitment, thus acting as a national melting pot; it was one of the most modern institutions in an underdeveloped society, with many of its personnel technologically trained in developed societies, capable of building roads and schools, reclaiming land, and even running factories. Finally, its defensive role in new nations was supposedly mostly symbolic, and, happily, the autonomy of the civil and military spheres could be dismissed as another example of Western ethnocentrism. In short, the military's potential to act as a vehicle of modernization was apparently enormous. The fact is, of course, that military rule proved to be as susceptible to corruption, bureaucratic ineptness, inefficiency, and the seductive inroads of world capitalism as the civilian regimes had been.

Although the military model took modernization a long way from the Weberian approach, it permitted social scientists to put off their acceptance of a Marxian-influenced dependency model, and to deny priority to economic rather than cultural factors. It is ironic that the dependency model that eventually did emerge, largely as a result of Frank's pioneering work, posed little threat to conventional social science. Whereas for Frank scholarship and politics were entwined, many who followed him, such as Long (1975: 255) eschewed an interest in political action. Some would interpret this to mean that a mature, scientifically respectable Marxism has finally emerged in the discipline. Others might wonder just how extensive conservative forces are in anthropology if they are able to handcuff Marx. 'Mature Marxism,' in fact, may be the most sophisticated example of salvage theory in the context of modernization that we have encountered so far.

It should also be pointed out that the 'new economic order' that has been hailed in recent years in international development and aid agencies was also a clever response to opposition, which met the charge of Western ethnocentrism without really changing anything. At the very time when anthropologists were turning away from culture, stressing the priority of economic factors and international politics and rediscovering that peasants were rational, not tradition-bound, the aid specialists 'discovered' the cultural realm: the problem of development was 'cultural,' related to tradition and beliefs. At a different time in history, I suppose, anthropologists would have been flattered by the prominence given to their bread-and-butter concept.

Conflict theory

A second example of salvage theory was the conflict model that replaced structural functionalism. As in the case of the last varieties of modernization theory, the new conflict theory of Gluckman and Coser looked different; but in fact it was a thinly disguised structural-functional model, which eventually became obvious to most anthropologists. The Gluckman–Coser type of conflict theory was meant to salvage a model that (a) de-emphasized the actor as innovator; (b) stressed system maintenance, harmony, and equilibrium; and (c) prevented the emergence of a Marxian-influenced conflict model in which dialectic, contradiction, and abrupt revolutionary change occupied central positions.

Structuralism

A tension now exists in anthropology between a research emphasis on primitive society, tribal ritual, and kinship, and the recognition that Third World countries have changed so drastically that this emphasis no longer can be defended. Lévi-Strauss's work has riveted the attention of anthropologists to primitive society and to myths, kinship, and the rural setting just when these should be receiving less prominence. Structuralism, then, can be seen as a theoretical adjustment that delays the discipline's adaptation to the contemporary world. In a sense, it is the grandest example of salvage theory, for it justifies the focus on primitive society. Since a detailed critique of

Lévi-Strauss's work will be presented in chapter 6, I shall not elaborate any further at this point. Instead, I shall turn to another brand of structuralism, Althusser's reworking of Marx (1969, 1970).

Born in 1918 in Algeria, and trained as a philosopher at the École Normale Supérieure in Paris, where he has since taught, Althusser's purpose is to erect an epistemological basis for historical materialism, to place it firmly on a scientific footing. This he does by providing a symptomatic reading of Marx – that is, a theoretically informed reading that illuminates a text in a manner not necessarily comprehended even by its author. Althusser stresses that there was an epistemological break in Marx's work from his early anthropological humanism and ideological writings, reflecting the (unfortunate) influence of Hegel and Feuerbach, to his scientific work, in which the actor disappears, the phenomenal world becomes secondary, and the purpose is to elucidate the nature of the hidden structures, much as in the Lévi-Straussian program. Like Lévi-Strauss, Althusser attacks empirical social sciences, with its emphasis on appearances rather than underlying structures. These underlying structures, according to Althusser, are real, and surface phenomena are merely expressions of them. Althusser credits Marx not only with comprehending what is essential rather than appearance, but also with formulating a new problematic: the determination of the elements of the whole by the structure of the whole. The structure as a totality consists of its effects. A social formation consists of several different levels of structures; the three principal structures or 'regional instances' are economic, political, and ideological structures. These structures are relatively autonomous but nevertheless interdependent, and the causal connections among them are complex – Althusser describes them as metonymic, a term used by Lévi-Strauss and by Lacan in relation to his reworking of Freud in a structuralist vein. Althusser means that causality is multidimensional, with each 'regional instance' containing its own contradictions but nevertheless affecting the totality, which in turn affects the parts. In this context, Althusser refers to over-determination, a concept borrowed from Freud, to express the notion that contradictions are never simple but instead are the product of the parts on each other, of the whole, and of the whole on the parts. This emphasizes the epistemological break from the viewpoint of causality as a simple one-to-one relationship between cause and effect.

The critical reaction to Althusser's symptomatic reading of Marx has been aggressive, and perhaps the most interesting line of attack has been the contention that there is nothing really new in Althusserian structuralism, despite its apparent novelty. For example, Giddens (1979: 52) observes that there are many similarities between Althusser's version of Marxism and

Parsons' functionalism. Appelbaum catches the essence of this similarity in his nifty phrase 'born-again functionalism.' He describes (1979: 19) Althusser's structuralism as 'an updated leftwing amalgam of Parsonian systems theory, Durkheimian structural-functionalism, and pluralist political science.' Giddens (1979: 52) points out that just as in the Parsonian scheme people are cultural dopes, in Althusser's they are structural dopes. It is only a short step to Kolakowski's view (1971) that Althusser's framework justifies political repression. It is a form of political ideology, with its emphasis on a 'correct' reading of Marx, that gives a green light to Stalin-like dictatorship. The working class is said to be incapable of articulating the theory, and has to be guided and corrected by a ruling class armed with the 'true' Marxism and with the capacity to nip ideological deviation in the bud. Kolakowski (1971: 127), like Bottomore (1975: 72), dismisses Althusser's work as empty verbosity, in which common-sense trivialities are dressed up in fancy language. Again, the similarities between Althusser and Parsons are apparent.

French Economic Anthropology
While Lévi-Straussian structuralism may constitute the tour de force of salvage theory, and Althusser's Marxism in some respects may amount to a thinly concealed version of functionalism, recent French economic anthropology is a far more subtle example. It embraces Marx wholeheartedly, and at least on the surface would appear to be a radical departure from liberal–conservative development theory. Launched in the 1960s, the new French perspective grew out of the work of anthropologists such as Godelier (1972), Meillassoux (1964), and Terray (1969), who were confronted with the raging debate in economic anthropology between formalists and substantivists. The formalists defined economics as the study of the relationship between ends and scarce means having alternative uses. Emphasis was placed on the individual as a choice-making actor. While monetary profit was usually what was assumed to be maximized, this was not necessarily so, for anything deemed as an end could replace it. The substantivists, led by Polanyi, argued that the formalist position was culture-bound. It was restricted to the market economy of Western society where the economy as an institution and economizing (means–end choice) happened to coincide. The substantivists argued that since economic functions in non-Western societies were embedded in institutions other than the market-place, and since these institutions varied across cultures, a different line of theorizing was demanded. In attempting to construct it, they created another problem: the impression that a different kind of rationality operated in non-market economies (see Prattis 1980).

The French economic anthropologists side-stepped this entire debate by introducing a new problematic. This was the investigation of the mixture of pre-capitalist and capitalist modes of production in new nations. This line of argument was heavily influenced by Althusser rather than by Lévi-Strauss, whom writers such as Meillassoux dismissed as an idealist.

The French economic anthropologists grappled with the problem of how to apply Marx (and especially the distinction between superstructure and infrastructure) to pre-capitalist, kinship-dominated societies. Meillassoux (1964) dismissed kinship as superstructure, as an ideological distortion of the 'real,' economic relations. Others, such as Godelier, did not so glibly ignore the results of half a century of anthropological field-work that had with almost monotonous regularity confirmed the centrality of kinship. Godelier (1970: 355) argued that relationships of kinship function as relationships of production, and that kinship belongs to both the infrastructure and the superstructure. In his words (1970: 356), 'the determining role of the economy will be seen not to contradict the dominant role of kinship but simply to express itself through it.' Some might say that this doesn't tell us anything new; it merely states in other language the old idea that kinship in pre-industrial societies is dominant and multifunctional. Godelier, however, must have thought he was on the right track, because a decade later he was saying much the same thing. The distinction between the superstructure and the infrastructure, he argues (1980), is not that of immaterial and material factors, nor does it concern institutions. Instead it is one of functions. He again suggests that in pre-industrial societies the kinship system functions as both infrastructure and superstructure, or as relations of production. Godelier states (1980: 9) that 'it is only within the nineteenth-century capitalist mode of production that the distinct functions of infrastructure and superstructure existed in the form of distinct organizations. For the first time, the process of production has developed within institutions that are almost entirely separate from the family, from politics and from religion.' One has an overwhelming feeling of having seen all this before. Godelier's partial reduction of Marx to functionalism is not so different from the earlier school that went by this name. Reinterpreted, Godelier has discovered the process of structural and functional differentiation, which has been at the heart of conventional sociological and anthropological theorizing since the days of Durkheim.

One criticism of the two Marxian-influenced approaches – dependency theory and French economic anthropology – is that they can't cope with the macro–micro dilemma, the gap between theory and data. A study is either an elegant but mechanical representation of the model in question, interspersed by inadequate data, or an ethnography that stands uncomfortably next to the theoretical framework, related by a matter of faith. Those who have produced sound ethnography meaningfully guided by one of these orientations are awarded the highest honours. Even those who have not done a very good job are worthy of praise. It is not unusual to hear someone say that so-and-so's work in the general area of political economy may not be very exciting, but at least he or she went out and collected original data. Another criticism is that both orientations have riveted the attention of anthropologists to the rural sector and to a reanalysis of old problems, such as how kinship functions in non-market situations. Godelier (1980) has explicitly stated that he and Meillassoux had embarked upon a program of analysing the accumulated theories and data in anthropology since the beginning of the century. Like Harris, White, and other neo-evolutionists, they threatened to reduce anthropology to a branch of history. Given the kind of book that I have written here, it would be ironic if I did not applaud any attempt to make sense of our theoretical past. I also agree that the problem on which the French anthropologists have focused – how pre-capitalist modes of production are combined with each other and with capitalism – is much more fruitful than the old debate between the substantivists and formalists. However, to restrict anthropology – and it must be remembered that economic anthropology always has contained arguments and assumptions that are potentially applicable to the entire discipline – to the reconstruction of the past, or at least to problems and phenomena in the rural sector, is to smother it. Relying as it does upon the early writings of Marx, which until a few years ago were not accessible, the French school could not have taken shape much earlier than it did; but perhaps it emerged fifty years too late to be really significant.

We now come to the political programs of the French anthropologists. Godelier indicates that one thing that distinguishes him and other economic anthropologists in France from Lévi-Strauss is the wish to translate their scholarly views into political involvement. The amount and variation of Marxism in French intellectual life, compared with that in Britain and America, is remarkable. Meillassoux has been active in Trotskyist circles, Godelier and Althusser in the Communist Party, and Terray and Rey as Maoists (see Godelier 1980: 5). This may mean that the French economic anthropologists have succeeded in combining theory and practice. Yet a Marxian stance seems to be a prerequisite to respectability among French intellectuals – hence Lévi-Strauss's unwarranted claim to be a Marxist – and it is always possible that the apparent militant commitment is window-dressing. Whatever the case in France, in America it is quite different. My impression is that for most Marxist anthropologists there is little connection between one's scholarly pursuits and one's wider activities and interests. In other words, Marxist anthropologists use Marx as a frame of reference, a vocabulary, a conceptual framework and methodology, much as they would the Parsonian or Durkheimian frameworks, while in their non-scholarly life they intrude further into the middle class. This is why we must speak of a castrated Marxism – tame, value-free, divorced from social policy and political action. If castrated Marxism can be absorbed so readily by conventional Western social science, the prospects for any radical body of theory are dismal.

What I have tried to do is to show how apparent changes are often attempts to keep alive a severely flawed body of theory. While the focus of my argument has been on attempts to hold back radical Marxian theoretical excursions, obviously a similar process has occurred with regard to Marxism itself: efforts to defend Marx against any criticisms, especially the criticism that parts of his theory are out of date. The end product is dogmatism. In a curious way, both functionalists and dogmatic Marxists are conservatives, each defending a 'long and proven' theoretical perspective. Nevertheless, the dominant type of salvage theory has been functionalism. More often than not, explicit functional theories have been buttressed, or different theoretical perspectives such as conflict theory or structuralism have been brought into line with functionalism. Friedman (1974: 457), like Sahlins (1976: 87), has described cultural ecology as 'the new functionalism.' He argues that cultural ecology and cultural materialism are rooted in the ideology of functionalism and empiricism that has dominated the American scene. One of the threads that seems to connect the various cases of salvage theory is the persistent attempt to breathe life into the moribund body of colonial anthropology. Any theoretical orientation that contributes to this effort has some of the properties of salvage theory. In this sense, we might include ethnohistory[2] and socio-linguistics, or any new perspective that rivets our attention to old problems.

2 In recent years ethnohistory has been joined by historical anthropology (see McCracken 1982). The former focuses on pre-industrial society, especially in 'other cultures'; the latter focuses on the early industrial periods of Western society. While both represent legitimate lines of inquiry, at the same time they are testaments to the degree to which the discipline's data base has shrunk, and if they gained the centre of the discipline, anthropology as the participant observation of life as it occurs would become obsolete. Moreover, it is one thing to argue that all anthropology should have a historical perspective, and quite another to create special subdivisions such as historical anthropology: the latter may defeat the purpose of the former.

BACKWARD THEORY

I stated earlier that it is very difficult, using the standard criteria, to demonstrate theoretical progress as one orientation replaces another. Even if it can be plausibly demonstrated that progress has taken place in one criterion, such as scope, counter-evidence usually emerges when other criteria are considered, such as simplicity, accuracy, and fruitfulness. As I suggested, one of the problems is that these criteria are variably operationalized in each of the several theoretical orientations. In this section I shall briefly demonstrate that one can just as reasonably measure the discipline's theoretical progress by starting with currently popular orientations and moving backward through time to the earliest orientations. We find the same kinds of evidence when focusing on a single criterion for progress, and the same problems when focusing on several criteria. In other words, whether one starts at the beginning of anthropology and works forward, or at the present and works backward, the results are much the same.

Let us consider scope. Bailey's social action certainly comes out second-best according to this criterion when compared to Marxism or early evolutionism. If the chronological development of the discipline had been from Bailey to Marx, and eventually to Morgan's and Spencer's evolutionism, we could happily conclude that progress had been made. The more confined perspectives such as structural functionalism, culture-and-personality, and historical particularism could then be dismissed as false starts common to all sciences.

What about simplicity? If we again start with Bailey and move on to culture-and-personality studies and finally to Durkheim, we see a steady movement from a model that is complex and indeterminate to one that is simple and specific. Bailey's model, allowing for the influence of the individual as innovator, and stressing a fundamental difference between the rules of the game and how it is actually played, is highly complex. But from Benedict we get culture as a functionally integrated whole, and a neat relationship between culture and personality: culture is personality writ large. Durkheim's framework is even simpler. It has been narrowed down to the properties of the social structure; all else, including motivation, environment, and heredity, has been excluded. Once again, we conclude that the discipline has progressed. But if we had started with Bailey and ended up with Marxism and early evolutionism, as in the first example, we would have arrived at a different conclusion. The Marxian scheme is every bit as sensitive as Bailey's to the tension between the individual and the collectivity. Only by ignoring Marx's insistence that the individual is not a mere puppet but an active agent creating his own history can a less complex, anti-humanistic Marxism be erected. In a similar way, it can be argued that evolutionism, because its scope is so much larger, is even more complex than Bailey's framework. But it could also be argued that it is less complex, for it rests on a simplified view of stages, an a priori argument that primitive societies are simple, and, often, a biological reductionism that glosses over the complexity of cultures and behaviour. Once again, the point is that the criteria to measure scientific progress are ambiguous.

As far as accuracy and precision are concerned, the prospects seem to have improved from the time of Bailey's social action to the earlier period of British structural functionalism and Durkheim's work. One can determine with a considerable degree of confidence precisely the influence of different parts of the social structure on a given phenomenon, such as suicide or divorce. Indeed, statistics comparing countries, religious preferences, and marital status are available. Proponents of the Bailey model can only regard these other perspectives with envy. Finally, we come to the criterion of fruitfulness. While one can take an educated stab at the application of the three other criteria to measure progress, fruitfulness is simply too vague to use at all. Fruitfulness, I gather, refers to the degree to which explanation and insight are enhanced. But how can one explain whether Bailey's social action is more fruitful than neo-evolutionism or cultural ecology? On numerous occasions I have heard British social anthropologists remark that their narrower framework is more fruitful than the more inclusive and eclectic approach of American cultural anthropologists. They 'prove' their point by hauling out assumptions that are intrinsic to their perspective; hence, the argument is circular.

I could go on, but it would be pointless to do so. I have shown that one can begin at the present and move backward to demonstrate theoretical progress in the discipline. It may be argued that my choice of theoretical perspectives and arguments were arbitrary and artificial. I would not disagree. But the same is true for conventional interpretations of theoretical progress. It makes as much (or as little) sense to write the history of anthropological theory backwards as it does to write it forwards. To the extent that the criteria to evaluate progress can be operationalized, an equal amount of proof exists for progress in either direction. To the extent that ambiguity exists, it does so equally for both readings of anthropological theory.

ANTHROPOLOGY AND SOCIOLOGY: AN UNRECOGNIZED DIALECTIC

For present purposes, there are four relevant levels at which a dialectic operates:

1 within particular conceptual contradictions, such as micro and macro, or static and dynamic;

2 between existing theoretical perspectives, such as structural functionalism and conflict theory;

3 between disciplines, especially social anthropology and sociology;

4 (possibly) between social anthropology and cultural anthropology.

The first and second levels are obvious; once one side of a contradiction, such as the micro, has achieved prominence, the other side strives to displace it. At the same time, as soon as a theoretical orientation has been established, its inherent limitations and one-sided biases generate the need for its counterpart. In other words, the transformational method can be used to analyse the rise and fall of theoretical orientations.

The third and fourth levels are not so obvious, and demand elaboration. Writers such as Radcliffe-Brown have argued that social anthropology and sociology occupy the same conceptual territory; it has often been observed that where the one discipline has been strong (such as anthropology in Britain), the other has been weak. This is because the two fields are so similar. The apparent reversal of the relative prominence of these two disciplines in Britain during the last decade or so merely reinforces this viewpoint as well as my argument that anthropology badly needs to be revitalized. In a recent article (1979a), I demonstrated the remarkable similarity of the theoretical trends that have occurred in anthropology and sociology. However, at that time I overlooked an insight that these conclusions suggested: anthropology and sociology may be dialectically related. That is, the discipline of sociology may act as a substitute outlet for theoretical orientations or sides of contradictions that are suppressed in anthropology, and the converse. For example, if an emphasis on the static exists in anthropology, the opposite side of the dynamic may work itself out or be expressed in sociology. Or when structural functionalism rules the day in one discipline, a variant of conflict theory, social action, or evolutionism may do so in the other. A similar dialectical relationship may exist between social and cultural anthropology. If I am right, it is not possible to understand anthropology without taking into account sociology, and vice-versa. It also means that the often-stressed similarity between the two disciplines, as well as the failure of repeated attempts over the years to combine them into a single discipline, will take on new significance; the disciplines are dialectically entwined.

How much of an argument can be mustered to support such a radical viewpoint? Let us begin by recognizing evolutionism and Marxism as common early orientations in both social anthropology and sociology.[3] Sociology then turned to a brand of conflict theory that originated with Simmel, and a phenomenological approach that owed much to Weber. This coincided temporally with the heyday of structural functionalism in social anthropology. In sociology the Simmel- and Weber-influenced approaches gave way to structural functionalism, which was imported into the discipline from anthropology by Parsons (1951, 1964), Merton (1957), Levy (1952), and others. In due time anthropologists gave up structural functionalism, and they adopted in its place first a Simmelian conflict theory in Gluckman's work, and then a variety of Weberian phenomenology in Bailey's writings. By the end of the Second World War, evolutionism had made a comeback in anthropology, thanks to White and Steward. By the time anthropologists were moving in other directions, such as formal analysis and network analysis, the neo-evolutionary framework had caught on in sociology, legitimated by no less a figure than Talcott Parsons (1966). With what was known as the new sociology (see Horowitz 1964), Marx had reappeared, and with him a more receptive environment for the critical theory of the Frankfurt School. But it was not until a decade or so later that similar interests soared in anthropology, as reflected in the ASA monograph edited by Bloch (1975). For years, culture-and-personality dominated the American scene, but it was discarded rather abruptly. Yet there is currently a growing field of social psychology among sociologists (see MacKinnon and Summers 1976) that has some interests in common with the erstwhile anthropological school, although the emphasis is more on quantification, operationism,[4] and a behaviourist twist to exchange theory, such as in the work of Malinowski, Mauss, and Lévi-Strauss. For a short time in the 1960s, game theory (Rapoport 1966; von Neumann and Morgenstein 1947) was a fad in sociology;

---

3 As Murphy stated (1971), it is arbitrary to say when the social sciences emerged, because they were never discovered, merely professionalized. However, there is good reason to trace the advent of contemporary anthropology and sociology to Marx, not least of all because the writings of both Weber and Durkheim were in large part a reaction to Marx. It is in this sense that it is argued that Marxism was a common early orientation in the two disciplines, which draw in varying degrees on Durkheim and Weber. In regard to evolutionism, it was 'in the air' at the time of the formation of professionalized, autonomous social sciences; not surprisingly, it penetrated the theoretical perspective of the times.

4 Operationalism, referred to also as correspondence rules, semantic rules, and rules of interpretation, is a research strategy that interrelates theory, concepts, and data collection. Operationalism means specifying the methods of observation and experimentation by which one's theories and concepts will be related to the empirical world. For an elaborate discussion of the importance of operationalism in anthropology, see Pelto (1970: 47–66).

while it soon dropped out of sight, within a few years it had made a come-back of sorts in anthropology, helping to shape the approaches of Barth and Bailey. Surprising as it may seem, the implication is that social anthropology and sociology are indeed dialectically related. Each discipline can partly be understood as a transformation of the other.

FUTURE ORIENTATIONS

Any attempt to forecast the future orientations of the discipline has to enter-tain the two principal sources of shifts in our orientations: the internal dialectic, in which theories rebound from each other and conceptual contra-dictions clash; and the effects of changes in society, such as a world war or a technological revolution. Solely on the basis of the first source – the concep-tual contradictions – one could predict the emergence of a variant of the Durkheimian model, stressing a narrowly defined conceptual territory and a positivistic (possibly behaviouristic) approach, and viewing the discipline as a science. This orientation, which dominated the discipline through the long period during which structural functionalism ruled supreme, has been sup-pressed for the last couple of decades, and it is doubtful whether it can be kept down much longer. Some readers might think that we already have this approach in socio-biology, Althusserian Marxism, and the behavioural brand of exchange theory. Granted, there are similarities, but there is still room for a positivistic orientation that even more closely resembles the Durkheimian one, especially an orientation that is aggressively anti-reduc-tionist, ambitiously scientific, and implicitly conservative. Such an orienta-tion in the future may favour quantitative over qualitative data, to bring it into line with contemporary research styles, but this will not detract from its similarity to Durkheim's approach; as evidenced by *Suicide*, he was quite in favour of quantitative analysis.

Just as Durkheim's perspective was a conservative reaction to a pre-existing perspective – Marxism – the future orientation that will resemble Durk-heim's will be a conservative reaction to a host of reductionist, anti-positi-vistic, and Marxian-influenced orientations that have emerged since the Second World War. The other principal source of shift in theoretical orienta-tion – the effects of social change – may also be relevant here. The three decades following the Second World War were in many respects radical, reflected in but by no means confined to the student movement of the late 1960s, and amounting to significant realignments in nation-state relation-ships, such as the end of colonial empires. There are many signs that the Western world is now moving in a conservative direction. This will provide further impetus for the emergence of a neo-Durkheimian perspective.

Almost all of the orientations that had emerged by the end of the first quarter of the twentieth century died out, and then reemerged after the Second World War. Included in this category are early and neo-evolutionary theory, Marxian and neo-Marxian conflict theory, Weberian and Bailey social action, and culture-and-personality and neo-psychological theory. One exception was Durkheimian structural functionalism. This orientation did not collapse until well after the Second World War; indeed, the pseudo-conflict approaches of Gluckman and Coser reinforced it. This explains, I suppose, why there has not yet been a neo-Durkheimian perspective, and at the same time alerts us to its potential appearance in the future.

Another exception was historical particularism. To my knowledge there has not been a re-emergence of an orientation decrying cross-cultural analysis, stressing diffusionism and the historical uniqueness of specific cultures and favouring psychological reductionism. My guess is that if such an orientation emerges again, it will be fused to certain features of culture and personality that are incompatible with the neo-psychological perspective: radical cultural relativity and an image of specific cultures as splendidly integrated and self-contained. It is hardly imaginable that such a discredited perspective could regain the centre of the discipline. Nevertheless, on purely logical grounds having to do with the nature of orientations and their underlying conceptual contradictions that have appeared during the past three decades, conditions today are propitious. The determining factor will probably be the social environment. If changes in society occur that foster a climate in which an inward-looking, defensive, self-sufficient and morally relativistic viewpoint can thrive, the prospects for a hybrid of historical particularism and culture-and-personality are enhanced. Should this perspective actually emerge in the future, it probably will be heavily disguised to conceal its connections with the previously discredited schools.

In many respects Lévi-Strauss's structuralism, with its idealist bias, and Harris's dialectical materialism, with its mechanical Marxism, are polar opposites, joined together in the sense that their flaws are exactly the opposite. This creates the possibility of a mediating perspective, one informed by Marxism but not tied solely to a lifeless class analysis or techno-economic priority 'in the last instance.' This perspective will incorporate phenomenological features and may entertain the mind as one of the most important factors that condition culture. This orientation, which I call dialectical anthropology, has been 'in the air' for some time now. Robert Murphy (1971) provided an excellent example of it, and it is essentially the perspective of this book. It represents an attempt to synthesize positivism, Marxism, and structuralism. Where I differ from Murphy is in the significance that I assign to differential power, the role of élites, the range and nature of contradictions (both logical and empirical), and the emphasis on disengaging ourselves from colonial society and engaging in studies of racism and other significant contemporary issues. These remarks suggest a somewhat different line of argument: the possible future substantive, as opposed to theoretical, directions of the discipline. As I argued in the introduction to this book, the world of the primitive is dead, and so too is anthropology if it fails to adjust to the fact. Moreover, what is needed is research on those sectors of society that hitherto have been largely ignored, such as élites, and on those social issues that threaten to strangle mankind in the decades ahead, such as racism, war, and poverty. My guess is that if anthropology does enter the twenty-first century with confidence and capacity, it will be as a result of its success in dealing with these substantive issues. Such an adjustment would of course play back on our body of theory, modifying it and infusing it with renewed sensitivity to power and inequality.

Finally, there is the practice of field-work. As a result of the salutary influence of Malinowski, there was real and significant progress in the field-work endeavour, which lasted for several decades. However, during the last few years the quality of field-work has suffered. The time spent in the field has become shorter, and sound ethnography has been sacrificed in order to make room for the paraphernalia of the contemporary social scientist: the replicable research instrument such as the questionnaire, and the sophisticated analysis of the data, usually with the help of a computer.[5] There has also been a reaction against so-called atheoretical British empiricism, which has encouraged field-workers to delve precipitately into speculative theoretical analysis. My remarks here are more a plea than a forecast, because the forces that have transformed the field-work endeavour are many, powerful, and continuing. Nevertheless, what is needed in the future, if anthropology is to thrive, is a return to the practice of in-depth, long-term, high-quality field-work. No other social science has attained the quality that characterized anthropological research in the past, and none has the capacity to do so at present or in the future. Only anthropology has been able to tell us the meaning of beliefs and practices to the actor himself, and to distinguish between people's own reports about their behaviour and what they actually do. If the quality of field-work suffers even more in the future, anthropology too will have lost its unique capacity.

---

5 I am not against tools such as the questionnaire and the computer; indeed, my view is that the contemporary anthropologist cannot do without them. My argument is simply that the researcher's first priority concerns the quality of the data, not principles of replication or subsequent methods of analysis.

5

Theory as Myth

This chapter focuses on theory as myth, or the myth of theory. Its purpose is to show the remarkable degree to which selected aspects of Lévi-Strauss's method of analysing myths can be applied to anthropological theory. In doing so, it supports the description of anthropology in the previous chapters as a non-cumulative discipline, and anticipates the general critique of structuralism that will be offered in the next chapter.

In the non-technical sense, myth usually means false beliefs; to say something is a myth means that it is wrong or non-existent. As we shall see later, anthropologists, even Lévi-Strauss, sometimes use myth in this pejorative sense. Mythology remains one of the few academic topics that still attract the attention of amateurs, especially as a record and interpretation of historical events and as a theory of origins – of fire, of the family, of a particular people. Myths are the archives of peoples without a written history. Myths often provide an explanation of where a tribe or an ethnic group came from, or where and how life began. (For example, the Yoruba believe that all life started in one of their towns, Ile-Ife.) While anthropologists are less prone than the layman to using myth to refer to false beliefs, they do not dismiss its oral-history function as entirely fanciful; nor do they regard its theories of origins as unrelated to a culture's cosmology and belief system.

The main pre-structuralist theories of myth can be divided into anthropological and psychological ones (see Cohen 1969). For Durkheim, myths symbolized important social values and contributed to the maintenance of social solidarity, much like religion in general. Durkheim also linked myths to the classificatory function, thus anticipating the rudiments of Lévi-Strauss's structuralist interpretation. Malinowski saw myths as legitimating devices (Cohen 1969: 344). Myths were not important for their symbolic value or for their explanation of the world. Instead, they served as a sort of ultimate authority to which one could turn to settle disputes or establish claims of privilege or property in situations of ambiguity. Myths were part of a charter that straightened out the tangles and confusion of behaviour. For Frazer and others of his era, such as Tylor, myths had explanatory value and were to be taken literally, even if the explanation was 'pre-scientific.'

Freud thought myths, like day-dreams, expressed unconscious desires and conflicts. In his explanation of totem and taboo, Freud dealt with basic anthropological issues such as incest, exogamy, and the nature-culture bridge, by which he meant the breakthrough from the horde to the matrilineage. The male child, expelled from the horde by his father, later killed him, thus gaining sexual access to his mother and sisters. Remorse set in and led to the establishment of totems and exogamous groups composed of mothers, sisters, and brothers (see Fox 1968). Both Freud and Jung regarded the unconscious as a reality sui generis, and Jung believed that myths reflected the very nature of the unconscious. Different parts of the unconscious, he theorized, were manifested from race to race or cultural group to cultural group, expressed in the form of myth.

The basic principles of Lévi-Strauss's structuralist approach to myth are introduced in the comparison between myth and theory. Before turning to this, I must say a bit more about psychoanalytic theory, because it is an important source of several varieties of structuralism. Freud has been 'reread' by Lacan to show that he was a structuralist. Lacan (1970) argues that the unconscious can only be approached through the analysis of language, and of course Lévi-Strauss has drawn heavily from linguistics to erect his own framework. He also emphasizes his debt to Freud. There is considerable similarity, as Glucksmann (1974: 53) has pointed out, between Lévi-Strauss's use of 'structure' and Freud's 'unconscious.' Freud also has figured prominently in another brand of structuralism, Althusser's scientific Marxism. Several of the key concepts that Althusser used to reshape Marx were derived from Freud – displacement, condensation, overdetermination, and the notion of a symptomatic reading; the last is comparable to Freud's attempt to decipher what is hidden in a patient's utterances, reflected in puns and slips of the tongue (see Glucksmann 1974: 100). Finally, in his efforts to find meaning in myth, Lévi-Strauss often stretches his explanations to their limits, and throughout this chapter I have endeavoured to remain faithful to the master's example.

SOME COMPARISONS OF MYTH AND THEORY

Myth is the primitive's major intellectual exercise. Lévi-Strauss emphasizes the rational orientation of pre-industrial peoples. Nowhere is this more apparent than in *The Savage Mind* (1966). That study documents 'the science of the concrete' – the remarkable degree of knowledge that people in pre-industrial society have about flora and fauna. At the same time, it is a hymn in praise of the classificatory capacity of mankind. Like modern scientists, primitives demand an orderly universe. Rather than speaking of 'man the tool-maker,' it would be more appropriate to refer to 'man the classifier.'

Unlike Lévy-Bruhl (1966), Lévi-Strauss refuses to accept a distinction between pre-logical and logical thought or between magic as pseudo-science and science proper. Primitive thought is not pre-scientific, not a mere shadow of what is to come. Instead, primitive thought and science are two independent but equally rigorous modes of inquiry (Lévi-Strauss 1967a: 277). Mythical thought and science differ not in the quality of the intellectual process, but in the nature of phenomena to which they are applied (Lévi-Strauss 1966: 13; 1967a: 277). Primitive thought is characterized by its unparalled symbolic thrust, its attention to the concrete, and its interminable classification (Lévi-Strauss 1966: 220). According to Lévi-Strauss (1966: 9), the main purpose of primitive thought is not to solve practical problems, but to satisfy intellectual ones. In his view, mythological thinking reflects a universal need to classify and analyse, to exercise the mind. As he puts it, myths are good to think. The same thing can be said about anthropological theory. Regardless of its explanatory value, it is fun, while ethnography puts most of us to sleep.

Myth can be explained independent of cultural context. If one rule has been generally accepted by anthropologists, it is the rule that a belief or practice must be explained in its cultural context. Yet Lévi-Strauss appears to have rejected this procedure. Burridge (1968: 97) implies that Lévi-Strauss analyses myths 'without reference to the culture which produced them.' Kaplan and Manners (1972: 172) remark that Lévi-Strauss is not very concerned with the social context of myth, and Glucksmann (1974: 78) and Leach (1974: 52) refer to the relative independence and autonomy from the social context that is granted by Lévi-Strauss to myth. Later Leach (1974: 61) refers to Lévi-Strauss's 'astonishing claim' that a myth that defies interpretation in its South American context can be explained when placed alongside myths in North America. It would appear that myth and theory have a lot in common, for in the previous chapter I showed that anthropological theory can be partly explained independent of social setting, as a result of the internal dialectic. In other words, to explain myth we must consider other myths; to explain theory, we must take into account other theories.

It would be unfair to Lévi-Strauss to leave the impression that the social context was absolutely irrelevant to his procedure. He himself has said (1975: 6) that the study of myth apart from ethnography is ineffectual. It is often remarked that a theoretician must know more ethnography than a field-worker. Although this happens rarely, Lévi-Strauss is an exception. While his own field-work may have been a sporadic, brief, hit-and-miss affair, his command of general ethnography is quite remarkable. Lévi-Strauss (1966: 219) has referred to Comte's lack of 'ethnographic sense' which only comes through collecting and handling data. That sense sets Lévi-Strauss apart from theoreticians such as Parsons. Sometimes it is assumed that if one reads too much, one can't be creative. Yet for his path-breaking study, The Elementary Structures of Kinship, Lévi-Strauss said he consulted over 7,000 books and articles! Rarely, however, does he read in order to synthesize and indicate trends in the literature; nor does he worry very much about presenting competing theories in order to balance the picture.

Despite Lévi-Strauss's contention that one can't study myths apart from ethnography, it is not difficult to understand why it is claimed that he ignores the cultural context. He is not reluctant to leap from one section of a continent to another, and indeed across continents, to explain a particular set of myths, even if while doing so he entertains their particular cultural contexts. Moreover, Lévi-Strauss has taken the position that myth constitutes a particular code, a sign system parallel to language, to music, and possibly to art – a sign system that is a reality sui generis, representing the intrinsic operations of the human brain.

Myth is repetitive, giving the same message over and over again, although changing the form, and different versions of myths are always incomplete. Myths can only be explained when an entire set, such as all known versions of the story of the three bears, are put together and their underlying structure decoded. Imagine, for example, stopping your car at the curb during a heavy rainstorm, with the wind gusting around you, and trying to communicate to a friend sitting under his porch that you can't make it to the squash game that evening, but wish to play sometime the following day. You shout different parts of the message over and over again, changing the order, repeating key terms such as 'tomorrow' or 'squash,' with the hope that the general drift of the message will somehow get through. Another example is the kind of dialogue that occurs when one is in a foreign country with only a partial command of the language. Both the foreigner and the native speaker try to communicate by stating their messages in a variety of ways, changing the words, liberally resorting to repetition, and supplementing verbal communication with gesticulation.

Similarly, to understand anthropological theory, it is necessary to consider *all* of the theoretical orientations together. Only then is the underlying pattern of oscillation and repetition revealed, providing a glimpse of the hidden conceptual contradictions.

Myths do not get better (more complete or insightful) with each new version. There are dozens of versions of all the major myths. There is no 'true' version. The earliest version is not the correct one, with all succeeding ones distortions; nor do myths grow so that the latest version is the best one.

Similarly, new theoretical orientations are not necessarily superior to those they have replaced, nor does any particular orientation contain all the answers.

Chronological time is not fundamental to the analysis of myth. Lévi-Strauss distinguishes chronological or historical time from structural or anthropological time. In his poetic comparison of history and anthropology he writes, 'one of them unfurls the range of human societies in time, the other in space' (1966: 256). Structural time is reversible. There is no start or finish, and temporal sequence is not significant. In other words, time is neutral, although closely connected to the notion of structural time are Lévi-Strauss's preferences for synchronic rather than diachronic analysis, and a focus on 'cold' rather than 'hot' thermodynamic societies. Myths are cold. They express reversible time, for they can be run forward or backward and are non-cumulative. Indeed, in the analysis of myth it doesn't matter which version one begins with.

All this is similar to my argument that anthropological theory has not been cumulative. Like myth, it can even be run backward, as I showed in the previous chapter.

Myth, unlike poetry, is eminently translatable (Lévi-Strauss 1967a: 206). Poetry can only be translated at the cost of serious distortion, whereas myth remains meaningful even after the worst translation. The significance of myth is its message, not the style or sequence in which it is told.

If the discipline is considered to be a science, anthropological theory must be similar to myth, not poetry. What is important is its message. One should be able to express that message in axiomatic statements, if not in mathematical equations. Logic rather than literary flair is its basis.

The purpose of myth is to pose and resolve basic contradictions in life. In part 2 I shall show that social life is shot through with contradictions, but for present purposes one or two well-known examples will suffice. Freud pointed out that through the psychological state of ambivalence, love and hate are entwined. He also observed that love is anti-social: to the extent that one person loves another, one turns one's back against society. Incest is a familiar theme in myth; myths express the fundamental contradictions in society that relate to incest. For example, a young man may fully love his mother, but can't copulate with her; put more generally, there may be a desire for natural (blood) sexual relationships, but a necessity for cultural (especially affinal) ones. Myths exhibit such contradictions.

Lévi-Strauss's interpretation of the Oedipus myth (1967a: 209–12) is instructive. How can man's autochthonous (aboriginal) origin be reconciled with the fact that he is the product of a union between man and woman? Is man born from one, or from two? According to Lévi-Strauss, the Oedipus myth exhibits these contradictions, although in disguised form. The incest theme acts as a logical tool to solve the problems: the incest relationship suggests 'sameness,' and the partners are in some sense one; hence man is born from one rather than two.

Another example is Lévi-Strauss's interpretation of the myth of Asdiwal (Lévi-Strauss 1968, Douglas 1968). The Asdiwal myth, set among the Tsimshian Indians of the Pacific coast of Canada, is said to exhibit a contradiction in their society having to do with patrilocal, matrilateral cross-cousin marriage. The myth examines a whole range of alternative marital arrangements and establishes that they are all equally problematic; thus, the Tsimshian might as well stick with what they have. Lévi-Strauss uses the Asdiwal myth to hammer home his argument that one can't reconstruct a people's social organization and belief system from its myths. Referring to Boas (1968: 29), who advocated doing just that, Lévi-Strauss points out that myths can be the exact opposite of real institutions. In the Asdiwal case, the myths speculated on alternative possibilities in marriage and social organization rather than documenting Tsimshian reality.

Similarly, anthropological theory may not reflect the social world; moreover, at the deep structural level it consists of a number of conceptual contradictions. Each theoretical orientation makes a choice among these contradictions, and in doing so supposedly resolves them. As we know, success never is attained; no sooner has an orientation been established than its logical opposite strives to displace it. This does not mean that theory and myth differ in this respect. While myths pose hidden contradictions and mediate between them, they leave them as lethal as before, if the contradictions are real (Lévi-Strauss 1967a: 226).

Myths themselves contain internal contradictions. As Lévi-Strauss states (1975: 332), a mythological system can 'argue with itself and acquire dialectical depth.' It is in this way that innumerable versions of myth are created. In a passage similar to Marx's contention that no stage ever is abandoned until all its productive forces have been exhausted, Lévi-Strauss states that mythological systems usually exhaust all possible ways to code a message – that is, all possible versions of a myth – even if to do so they must resort to inversion (1975: 332). This is similar to my argument that anthropological theory contains an internal dialectic, which at least partly accounts for the different versions of theory that exist. An implication of Lévi-Strauss's views is that a close examination of the underlying conceptual contradictions, which are the elements with which the internal dialectic works, might reveal potential orientations that have not yet been produced. That is what was done in the last pages of the previous chapter.

Myth transvaluates. The normal becomes abnormal, the tame becomes wild, the wild becomes tame. Incest prevails, mothers kill children, jaguars make fire and roast meat. In similar fashion, anthropological theory transvaluates: the social realm is messy, almost chaotic, but our theories are orderly; man is inconsistent, but our theories display the 'hidden' patterns.

At the conscious level, myth is paradoxical, ambiguous. Myths only make sense when they are decoded, revealing the underlying structures. Myths do have the purpose of posing and mediating between unwelcome contradictions, such as being born of one person and yet having two parents (the Oedipus myth, as Lévi-Strauss interprets it), but the message is never apparent.

Similarly, but inversely, anthropological theory is systematic, consistent, and explanatory on the surface; it is when it is decoded that underlying contradictions, ambiguities, and biases are revealed, such as the assumptions that harmony prevails in the world, that change is bad, or that beliefs are merely epiphenomenal to behaviour or to techno-economics.

Myths are anonymous. They come from nowhere (Lévi-Strauss 1975: 18). It might be thought that anthropological theories are exactly the opposite of myths, for the one thing that is certain about them is the identity of their founders. Indeed, we often refer to theories by proper names, such as Marxian or Durkheimian, rather than dialectical materialism or structural functionalism. And yet, with the simple application of a Lévi-Straussian technique, it can be shown that myth and theory in this respect are synonymous. Theory is identical to myth because both are extremes, but in inverse manner; the one dramatically underemphasizes its authorship, the other overemphasizes it to the same degree. It is their opposites that are similar.

Myth is a source of power. Just as native experts in the realms of primitive knowledge such as myth are the brainstormers in their societies, theoreticians in anthropology supposedly are the high priests, the élite. The Marxian notion that knowledge is power, that the ruling ideas are the ideas of the ruling class, is relevant here. Such a view is also consistent with a different theoretical approach to myth, Malinowski's view that myth is used to justify individual interests in situations of ambiguity and conflict.

History is myth is delusion. Lévi-Strauss has often been accused of attacking the discipline of history. He does, it is true, distinguish clearly between structural and historical analysis, which parallel reversible and non-reversible time. Yet in 'History and Anthropology' (1967a: 1–28), *The Savage Mind* (1966: 256), and *The Scope of Anthropology* (1967b: 21), he has referred positively to history, insisting that it complements anthropology, and even arguing that Radcliffe-Brown's mistrust of historical reconstruction may be on the verge of becoming outmoded. But in suggesting that history can be given two readings, one structural and the other chronological, Lévi-Strauss also implies that each nation's history is rewritten from the vantage point of the present, so that past events become compatible with current realities. In this way, the events of the great wars, for example, are rearranged in a perspective favourable to the victor. There is, in other words, no objective history. History is a collective delusion, a myth in the pejorative sense of the term.

In a similar vein, the history of anthropological theory, supposedly characterized by steady, cumulative progress, also has been an exercise in delusion. Relevant here are Kuhn's remarks about the myth-making tendencies of textbooks, which distort the history of a scientific discipline in order to provide a false picture of steady theoretical growth.

Theory is myth is delusion. The previous example indicates that Lévi-Strauss does occasionally use myth in the pejorative sense to suggest false beliefs, rather than in the sophisticated structuralist sense that dominates his work. At this juncture, in view of the periodic focus on racism in this book, it is appropriate to consider another pejorative usage of myth: racial myths. These include the almost benign, such as the belief that certain nationalities or perceived races are well suited for certain occupations – for example, the assumed flair of Italian immigrants to Canada for working with concrete in the construction trade, or the assumed flair of blacks for music or of Jews for business. They also include more vicious myths, such as the assumed intellectual and moral inferiority of non-whites, as well as assumptions that non-whites don't have the same capacity for 'human' feelings, have different and objectionable body odour, and in their sexual drive are more like animals than humans.

More often than not, professional anthropologists attempt to dispel such popular views. The implication is that there is little similarity between anthropological theory and myth in the pejorative sense, at least as it applies to racial myths. However, the situation is not as clear-cut as it might appear. Until the Second World War, physical anthropology, whose major concept was race, probably contributed to racial stereotypes by virtue of its emphasis on what are referred to as phenotypical features as a basis for racial classification: colour of skin, hair type, and other observable physical characteristics. Certainly the body of literature known as 'scientific racism' draws heavily from the work of some professional anthropologists such as Coon (1962). Even concerned, liberal white scholars sometimes reinforce racial myths in the course of their research; for example, one studies a black ghetto, finds the people poor, uneducated, and dirty, and interprets this as proof that black people simply 'are that way.' Finally, as we shall see in chapter 10, the Marxist approach explains racism in class terms: racism mystifies class antagonisms and thus props up capitalism; racism is not a reality in itself. In denying racism as an independent reality, Marxism may have spawned another racial myth – the myth that racism does not really exist. Even in the pejorative sense, myths – in this instance, racial myths – may be similar to theory. Both distort and mystify reality.

The analysis of myth is contained within myth. According to Lévi-Strauss, his work cannot be accused of formalism or idealism because all that he has done has been to discover the nature of myth that is hidden within myth itself (1975: 12).

Similarly, most anthropologists would argue that their theories are short-hand descriptions of, or abstractions from, empirical reality. While both structural theory and conventional anthropological theory consist of relations between elements that are real, the order of reality is not the same. For conventional anthropology, reality is in behaviour and beliefs; it is phenomenal; it lies at the surface. For structuralists, reality lies under the surface; it is not behaviour; instead, it consists of relations between relations, which themselves are abstractions, and which together make up models.

Lévi-Strauss's view that the structuralist interpretation of myth is intrinsic to myth is consistent with his general epistemological approach: the observer's model should correspond to the actor's unconscious (real) model, not to his conscious (rationalizing) model. Another important figure who espoused views contrary to the conventional one, in which a model approximates in logical form to empirical reality, was Leach (1965). In a reversal of Lévi-Strauss, he contended not only that the observer's model corresponded to the actor's conscious model, but also that both models were fictions (not 'reality,' as in Lévi-Strauss's work). With particular reference to the dilemma of analysing dynamic systems, Leach argued that anthropologists, and actors themselves, must act as if there were equilibrium and structure, despite their recognition that society is in constant flux.

Myths don't try to explain natural phenomena, but use natural phenomena to express the logic of mythical thought. Theory is supposed to be quite different from myths, in that it should be a direct outgrowth of (some would say subservient to) the empirical world. At the minimum there should be a relationship between the properties of a theory and those of the concrete realm of behaviour. Yet theory, especially sociological rather than anthropological theory, is often isolated from reality, and enters it only to increase its conceptual range, not to explain a problem on the ground level. My impression is that many sociological graduate programs advance the false notion that research should serve theory and methodology rather than the reverse. My worry is that anthropology is quickly moving in the same direction.

Myths constitute a separate sign system, similar to language, music, and possibly art. It is Lévi-Strauss's argument that myths constitute a sign system parallel but irreducible to language, and approximating the properties of the human brain. In a somewhat similar way, theory is like myth. It constitutes another language, another code, that stands between the mind and the phenomenal world. The trained anthropologist has lost his intellectual innocence. One can never be sure if what one sees actually exists, or if it is seen because one's theory demands that it be seen. Perhaps because I came indirectly to anthropology after studying other disciplines, I became acutely aware of this problem. For two years, before I had ever taken a course in anthropology, I had lived in West Africa, where I taught secondary school in a remote area among the Igbo. Quite apart from the exhilaration of interacting with people in a different culture without having to write it all up for publication and thus reducing human relations to means rather than ends, there was also the thrill of discovery – sacrifice to and nourishment of ancestors during the yam festival, classificatory kinship terminology (the 'father' of one of my best friends, I learned after several months, was not his real father). When I returned to West Africa less than four years later, armed with theoretical and methodological training, I saw things from a radically different perspective. Everything was saturated in theoretical and methodological significance. Like the switch from one paradigm to another, it was a new world that I had entered.

On subsequent field-trips, I have pondered whether the costs of theoretical training are not greater than the benefits. Of course, the obvious retort will be that without such training one simply rediscovers old truths, or gets sidetracked by trivial issues. Besides, it will be said, there is no non-theoretical viewpoint. I agree with all this, but we are still left with the fact that theory distorts. This is a good example of the type of contradiction in behaviour that I shall discuss in chapter 7; like the dilemma over theory and fieldwork, the common property of such contradictions is that they have no solution.

Lévi-Strauss (1975: 12) remarks that his study of myth is itself a myth, another level of code. Sceptics might argue that this is nonsense, for the essential characteristics of Lévi-Strauss's methodology – a combination of dialectical and analytical reasoning – can be found in other writers such as Marx. Lévi-Strauss's defence is that his work on myth is organized in a manner that represents the structure of myth, although the model for The Raw and the Cooked is not myth but music. To the extent that Lévi-Strauss is justified in his view, the same claim can be made for all anthropological theories – not that they all are myths, but instead that they are part of what they investigate: religion, kinship, economics, poverty.

Myths mediate between oppositions. Fundamental to structuralism is the dialectical method, with its binary oppositions and mediators. In the case of myth, unwelcome contradictions are often posed, although in disguise, and mediated by potential resolutions, such as the alternative marital arrangements in the Asdiwal myths.

Similarly, as anthropologists we are caught between the general and the specific, between grand theory and raw data, and we also appear to have the mediator: Merton's middle-range theory, to which most anthropologists subscribe. Andreski (1972: 56–7) claims that Merton has done more harm than Parsons to sociology, and dismisses his functionalism as little more than an elaborate re-labelling program. Middle-range theory itself only makes sense if there is a process by which one gradually but systematically subsumes more and more data under increasingly abstract theorems, with grand theory the eventual logical outcome. Nothing in the history of anthropology suggests that we do operate in this manner: by hit-and-miss attacks, and as a result of the occasional imaginative flair of outstanding thinkers, disparate ideas are synthesized or new ones on a grand scale are created.

If middle-range theory does not effectively bridge the general and the specific, why has it been advocated by so many anthropologists and sociologists? To understand the answer, it must be appreciated that the role of the mediator is a complex one, and comes in different forms. In political anthropology the middleman has the job of communication. In order to keep it, he must make certain that direct communication between two or more groups remains inadequate. In other words, the middleman perpetuates the flaw in the system. A different kind of mediator is found in American mythology: tricksters, such as the coyote and the raven, that play a prominent role in resolving baffling contradictions (see Lévi-Strauss 1967a: 220–1). While middle-range theory may not neatly articulate grand theory and raw data, at the same time it does not seem to sustain the separation. It is not justifiable to describe Merton as a kind of political middleman in the anthropological sense. This leaves us with the mediator in mythology. Andreski's criticisms may have been over-harsh: Merton can proudly take his position alongside the coyote and other noted American tricksters.

Social scientists as bricoleurs. Lévi-Strauss (1966: 17, 21) suggests that mythical thought is an intellectual form of bricolage. The bricoleur, like a tinkerer or handyman, uses whatever materials are available to construct the needed object or piece of machinery; similarly, mythical thought works from a given repertoire of events and restructures them in an almost endless number of combinations in order to express itself. In Lévi-Strauss's words, 'Mythical thought for its part is imprisoned in the events and experiences which it never tires of ordering and re-ordering in its search to find them a meaning' (1966: 22). Similarly restricted, the bricoleur makes do with odds and ends to create what is necessary for the job at hand.

The academic equivalent to bricolage is interdisciplinary studies (and perhaps area studies in an earlier era). The academic involved with such studies can claim no separate body of theory as his own. Instead, he raids disciplines that do possess distinct bodies of theory, taking a hypothesis here, a concept there, and rearranging them according to the problem he is investigating. Bricolage may even be characteristic of anthropological work in general. Runciman (1970: 10, 16) has claimed that anthropology, sociology, and history, unlike psychology, have no theory of their own. They are consumers of theory, not producers of theory.

Theory as magic. Malinowski showed that the Trobrianders turned to magic when contronted with danger or with forces beyond their control, such as when fishing offshore or planting crops. For example, after the crops had been planted, man and wife might engage in coitus interruptus, so that the sperm spilled on the soil would enhance the prospects for a rich harvest. Or a hunter might wait to go hunting until he dreamed his prey had been speared or caught in a trap.

Theory too can be a refuge, although this is true more for sociologists than for anthropologists, who prefer to escape to field-work. Theory can create a sense of pattern and order in the face of actual flux and contradiction. Like the hunter who argues that it is senseless to chase his prey until he has first dreamed that it has been trapped, many social scientists argue that it is futile to conduct research until one's model has been erected. Dream and model are one.

Myth, magic, and totemism explain the world, simplify the world, mediate contradictions, and contribute to the image of a comprehensible, orderly, and controlled universe. Nowhere does the picture of man the classifier show up more clearly than in Lévi-Strauss's interpretation of totemism (1963 and 1966). According to Lévi-Strauss, totemism is an illusion. Properly understood, it is simply a form of classification, and reflects an intellectual impulse and a need for order shared by all of mankind. This does not mean that the world is orderly. It may only mean that we require this image, much as Lévi-Strauss suggests that even if there is no nature-culture gap, we may have a need to conceptualize such a distinction so as to confirm our humanity.

Like myth, magic, and totemism, anthropological theory reflects mankind's effort to impose order, regularity, and control on social life. The implication is that mankind (including anthropologists) cannot endure chaos. That is the meaning of Bailey's (1977) 'basic lie of orderliness' as a necessity for survival.

Most works on theory get around to discussing order at some point, usually in the context of Hobbes. At this juncture I am not interested in the question of how order in society is possible, or how much disorder a viable society can accommodate. Instead I am concerned with the question of why theoreticians are interested in order, and how their views have affected their writings.

What seems clear is that most writers have an intolerance for disorder. 'Freud's ultimate aim,' wrote Hughes (1958: 131), 'was to impose an order on the chaos of reality.' In the words of Kardiner and Preble (1961: 33), 'Herbert Spencer was one of the tidiest men who ever lived. He could not tolerate an inefficient saltcellar any more than he could abide a disorderly universe. His life was obsessed with the need to fit all of nature – the inorganic, the organic, and the 'super-organic' – into a neat, perfectly axiomatized system.' Voget (1975: 79) observes that anthropology's role is tied to the desire among men to discover order in existence: 'Human beings require assurance that life is not pure anarchy and without purpose ...' Voget's remarks can be interpreted to mean not that there is order, but that we have a need for order. A similar view is expressed by Tyler, who states that the anthropologist's task is to find out how people manage to create order out of apparent chaos; he observes that 'we classify because life in a world where nothing was the same would be intolerable' (1969: 6). Murphy (1971: 240) states that 'the individual seeks security and order as a condition of his psychological functioning ...' Referring to Lévi-Strauss's distinction between conscious and unconscious models, Murphy (1971: 110) remarks that the conscious model 'patches up the untidiness of society and produces the appearance of order.' The conscious model may be a deception, but without it life would be intolerable. Once again, we are reminded of Bailey's basic lie of orderliness.

Murphy (1971: 39) captures the essence of the problem: 'Social anthropology is beset by a basic contradiction that perhaps will never be surmounted. This contradiction arises from the fact that, although we search for order, social life is visibly chaotic.' Bailey (1969: xiii), who has admitted to 'a repugnance for disorder' (a repugnance apparently shared by Marx), has described a scholar's life as a contest between his intellect and 'the brute disorderly objective universe of Nature' (1977: 4–5).

Let us return to Lévi-Strauss. 'Since I was a child,' he writes, 'I have been bothered by, let's call it the irrational, and have been trying to find an order behind what is given to us as a disorder' (1978: 11). When he turned to anthropology, he found two realms that were a jumble of confusions and contradictions – marriage rules and myths – and he applied himself to the discovery of order behind the apparent disorder. He goes on to observe that it is 'absolutely impossible to conceive of meaning without order' (1978: 12). This is a seductive insight, even a brilliant one, but it is also wrong. The implication is that there must be order in the universe, because without it there would be no meaning. But Lévi-Strauss has not demonstrated that there is meaning. How then, can one imaginary entity (meaning) be used to demonstrate another (order)? Once again, we are dealing with man's *need* for order, not necessarily with order itself. Lévi-Strauss (1978: 13) claims that such a need for order probably demonstrates that the universe is orderly rather than chaotic, but the logic here appears to be faulty – certainly it is teleologic. Perhaps Henry Miller got to the bottom of the problem. 'The insane have a terrific obsession for logic and order, as have the French' (quoted by Worsley 1968: 141). Are all scholars Frenchmen at heart?

CONCLUSION

The overwhelming concern of anthropologists with order has special significance for this study. As Davis (1971: 314) has remarked, the thrust of a young, growing discipline is to show that what seems to be disorganized or unstructured is actually organized and structured; the thrust of older, stagnating disciplines is to show that what appears to be organized is really disorganized. Most anthropologists still are involved with the attempt to discover pattern in a disorderly world. Perhaps a stage has been reached where the opposite kind of analysis is required. Those who successfully tackle it may be able to sever the existing links between theory and myth. Drawing from the linguist's vocabulary of phonemes, morphemes, and sememes, Lévi-Strauss coined the term 'mythemes,' and Foucault has given us the term 'epistemes.' With all the advantages of a special vocabulary in mind, I now introduce a new term for anthropology in general: theoremes. Theoremes are gross constituent units, constructed from the repertoire of conceptual contradictions, which by substitution, combination, inversion, and transformation have permeated the entire range of anthropological theory. Henceforth, no attempt to make sense of the history of anthropological theory can hope to succeed without taking into account its theoremes.

6

Structuralism and the Second Burial of Émile Durkheim

Structuralism is the only novel theoretical orientation in anthropology to have emerged since the turn of the century. With its distinctive episte-mology, it promised to cope with many of the difficulties inherent in a positivistic science of society. In the previous chapter I drew heavily on Lévi-Strauss's structuralist approach in order to analyse anthropological theory, and may have given the false impression that structuralism is our salvation. Despite its novelty and early promise, it is not the New Jerusalem, although many of its proponents do approach it theologically. The very strength of structuralism – its capacity to explain other anthropological the-ories – is also its weakness. Structuralist analysis works best with mentalist data, within which are included our various theories. Theories are not sim-ply the imaginative playthings of scholars. They are articulated with the phenomenal world, but they do not necessarily reflect it. As particular kinds of ideologies they invert and distort it, and as a result of their internal dialec-tic, in which theories rebound from other theories, they become increasingly artificial. Structuralism is merely an advanced case of this general anthropo-logical malaise.

DURKHEIM

Although this chapter focuses on Lévi-Strauss and structuralism, Durk-heim's name is included in the title for two reasons: first, to emphasize the degree to which Lévi-Strauss draws from the work of his countryman; second, to stress that structuralism is not entirely new. It represents the other Durkheim, the one concerned with the theory of knowledge and belief systems, rather than the positivist that most sociologists know.

Lévi-Strauss turned to anthropology almost by accident, after studying law and philosophy. He had initially rejected Durkheim's positivism, and the first anthropologists to have a real influence on him were Americans: Lowie, Boas, and Kroeber. But Lévi-Strauss turned increasingly to Durkheim. In Tristes Tropiques (1974: 59) he stated that he probably had become more faithful than anyone else to the Durkheimian tradition. He dedicated Structural Anthropology to Durkheim. In The Scope of Anthropology he remarked that Durkheim represents the essence of French social anthropology (1974: 8), and he referred repeatedly to Durkheim in his general review of French sociology (1945). His commentators also connect him directly to Durkheim. Goddard (1975: 111) states that Durkheimian sociology was the main precursor of structural anthropology. Clarke (1978) argues that the impetus behind Lévi-Strauss's structuralism was the adaptation of Durkheimian sociology to the new individualism that sprang up in France after the First World War, which is another way of saying that structuralism is a kind of salvage theory.

It is in Primitive Classification (1963) and The Elementary Forms of the Religious Life (1968) that Durkheim's 'hidden dialectic,' as Murphy (1971: 163) puts it, is found most readily. Durkheim and Mauss contend that classification is a product of social life. Because men were organized, they were able to organize things. Durkheim and Mauss denied that classification was in any way an a priori condition to social existence. It was not an inherent capacity of the mind. In his introduction to Primitive Classification, Needham reveals the obvious weaknesses of this theory, especially the fact that Durkheim and Mauss allow for the a priori existence of several principles of classification, such as space and time. It will be apparent that Lévi-Strauss's view, which insists that classification is a function of the intrinsic operations of the mind, especially binary ones, is directly opposed to Durkheim's. Nevertheless, Durkheim's focus on classification provided a platform from which Lévi-Strauss could advance to his own ideas.

One can find numerous specific comments in Durkheim's work that are directly related to Lévi-Strauss's structuralism. For example, Durkheim alludes to the importance of contradiction in mythology (1968: 12), and comes close to dialectical analysis in his statement that 'when a classification is reduced to two classes, these are almost necessarily conceived as antithesis' (1968: 13). Then, too, he distinguished between many oppositions such as the sacred and profane and the individual and the group, at least in his less positivistic writings, and focused on topics such as totemism that have been of central interest to Lévi-Strauss.[1]

---

1 It is, of course, all too easy to read into passages such as these meanings and directions not intended by the author, which is partly why various attempts to reread the early

Durkheim and Lévi-Strauss both advocated totality or wholeness, emphasized binary oppositions and synchrony, and downplayed conflict. However, where Durkheim highlighted emotions and sentiments, Lévi-Strauss stressed logic and rationality. Durkheim saw totemism as the precursor of science, while in Lévi-Strauss's view they were equal but distinct, two parallel modes of investigation. Durkheim regarded man's mythical thinking as faulty thinking; Lévi-Strauss saw it as rigorous logic. For Durkheim, knowledge and classification were epiphenomenal to social structure. For Lévi-Strauss, they were a product of the inherent operations of the mind. Durkheim was anti-reductionist; Lévi-Strauss openly advocated neurological reductionism. For well over half a century Durkheim tortured anthropologists and sociologists with an enigmatic half-truth: the external, coercive, collective conscience. Lévi-Strauss pulled it down from the clouds and placed it firmly in the unconscious, an entity about which Durkheim was ignorant.

It is important to stress the degree to which Lévi-Strauss goes back to Durkheim, for Durkheim is not always included in the list of founders of structuralism. De George and De George (1972: vii), for example, say the founders were Marx, Freud, and de Saussure. According to Lévi-Strauss (1974), Marxism, psychoanalysis, and geology are his three mistresses. Yet as Clarke has remarked (1978: 425), there is little evidence that Lévi-Strauss ever studied Marx seriously. While the influence of Freud is reflected in Lévi-Strauss's focus on the unconscious and in his deterministic orientation, it is not nearly so clear as in Althusser's brand of structuralism, in which several key concepts have been lifted directly from Freud. Lévi-Strauss (1975: 11) is even happy to accept the criticism that his concept of the categorizing unconscious is more Kantian than Freudian. In contrast, Lévi-Strauss's reliance on Durkheim and his disciples has been considerable. From Mauss he developed his ideas of exchange and reciprocity, from Hertz the notion of binary oppositions, and from van Gennep the concept of the symbolic function of rituals.

Durkheim was first buried intellectually when social anthropologists rejected his brand of structural functionalism for a more voluntaristic model of action, such as Bailey's. He was not buried with the appearance of Gluckman–Coser conflict theory, which modified but did not transform the

masters, whether Freud or Marx, in terms of a contemporary theoretical orientation such as structuralism should not be accepted uncritically. As far as Durkheim is concerned, all I wish to show is that some of his interests were compatible with some of those that eventually emerged with structuralism. The data are merely suggestive; they do not prove anything.

Durkheimian framework. In recent years Durkheim has been revived with the ascendency of Lévi-Strauss. But because of the crippling problems in structuralism, which leans so heavily upon Durkheim, it is now time for his second burial. Unlike the second burials described in the anthropological literature, this one is not intended to be a laudatory ritual aimed at intensifying the solidarity of the social unit from which the deceased departed (in this case Durkheim's intellectual heirs). It is intended to mark his final passage from the intellectual centre of the discipline, which belongs more legitimately to Marx and Weber, who together set the discipline on the most direct route to scholarly progress.

There is a tendency among scientific disciplines, as Kuhn has observed, to revise the theoretical positions of earlier scientists so that they fit into the current paradigm. This may explain the recent attempt to prove that most of the early giants in the social sciences were structuralists in disguise. Certainly if it is acceptable to describe Marx and Freud as structuralists, then Durkheim too must be included in that category. As in the case of positivism, there are several varieties of contemporary structuralism, although these have not crystallized to the same degree into distinct schools; we usually refer to them by proper names, chiefly Lévi-Strauss (anthropology), Althusser (Marxian sociology), Chomsky (linguistics), Barthes (literary criticism), Lacan (psychoanalysis), and Foucault (philosophy). By no means is there agreement among these men. The Lévi-Straussians and the Althusserians are at each other's throats. Piaget has rejected Lévi-Strauss's synchronic focus, and Chomsky has declared that Lévi-Strauss has not made legitimate use of linguistics. Lévi-Strauss has denied any similarity between his work and Foucault's, and Foucault has refused to call himself a structuralist at all; Piaget (1970: 132) suggests that Foucault's 'epistemes,' the archaeology of thought of each era, are actually similar to Kuhn's paradigms. Just as Marx denied being a Marxist, Lévi-Strauss has declared that he is not a structuralist (see de Gramont 1970: 9), at least as the term usually is understood, and Althusser doesn't readily accept being included within the structuralist fold (Giddens 1979: 159).

The infighting among structuralists is partly due to the lack of a clear definition of the approach. As Lane (1970: 11) has observed, no one who calls himself a structuralist has ever clearly set out the fundamentals of the approach. With specific reference to myths, Cohen (1969: 345) has complained that Lévi-Strauss has never fully stated his theory. Many famed anthropologists, including Leach, Maybury-Lewis, and Burridge, have bravely confessed that they can't always understand what Lévi-Strauss is trying to say. Such ambiguity is not peculiar to structuralism. As Clammer observes (1975: 219), Dupré and Rey, two French economic anthropologists, nowhere explain what they mean by 'mode of production.' It is doubtful that such a remarkable lack of clarity exists in other branches of knowledge, notably the hard sciences and philosophy. Yet Kuhn implies that his central concept – the paradigm – can't even be defined, which draws applause from others, such as Phillips (1973–4: 15).

In Lévi-Strauss's view, structuralism is not a theory but a method, which is how it is defined by others such as Lane (1970: 13), Nutini (1970: 72), Piaget (1970: 136) and Ehrmann (1970: ix). Yet Leach (1973: 37) declares that it is neither a method nor a theory, but simply 'a way of looking at things.' Leach probably does not mean to be derogatory, but others do. Runciman (1970: 46) reduces structuralism to the conventional notions of interconnection of parts and form apart from content, and evokes Kroeber's whimsical comment that the term 'structure' adds nothing to our analysis 'except to provoke a degree of pleasant puzzlement.' Lévi-Strauss especially would take exception to Runciman's remarks on form apart from content, for he claims that structuralism collapses this distinction (Caws 1970: 203). There is no separate content apart from form (Kaplan and Manners 1972: 176). Form and content convert into each other, and must be analysed by the same method (Glucksmann 1974: 59). Form is the property, or content, of the real (Clarke 1978: 407). The issue at stake here is a structure apart from or beneath the observable empirical world, which is as 'real' as concrete behaviour. It is this level of reality that interests them. For example, structuralists are not so much concerned with the pattern on a sweater as with the knitting rules that produced the pattern: knit one, purl two, and so on. Thus, when Lévi-Strauss claims to have broken down the distinction between form and content, it is not empirical content to which he refers, but a content lying at a different order of reality: the underlying structures.

This leads us directly to the priority that Lévi-Strauss gives to the unconscious over the conscious, which parallels his distinction between deep structure and surface structure. Home-made models (the actor's models) cannot be ignored, because they are part of reality and at times are insightful. Yet an analysis restricted to the surface structure or concrete behaviour and the actor's beliefs is exposed to two major flaws. First, at this level the facts are almost limitless and chaotic. Second, rationalization is a characteristic of conscious behaviour and beliefs. People's explanations of their beliefs and behaviour mask what they really believe and do. This is why Lévi-Strauss would be opposed to the sociological approach of tapping people's reports of their behaviour with a questionnaire. In his view, attitudes and emotions are consequences, not causes; they mystify rather than explain (see Lévi-Strauss 1963: 71).

In order to avoid getting bogged down in the data, Lévi-Strauss turns to the unconscious; here we see the influence of Freud and, especially, of linguistics. Linguists found that people were capable of speaking a language correctly without any understanding of the rules. They concluded that these rules must exist at an unconscious level. For example, consider two lists of fish: trout, cod, herring; suckers and sharks. Notice that the plural form of the fish in the first list is the same as the singular, but in the second list 's' is added. The reason? We eat the fish in the first list, but not those in the second. The point is that in our language we have unconsciously made this distinction in order to separate edible from non-edible fish.

Lévi-Strauss (1966: 204–7) ingeniously shows comparable distinctions in the names given to birds, dogs, and cows. We give birds human names, such as Jennie Wren or Robin Redbreast; dogs have names that are almost but not quite human – Bowser, Shep, Pal; cows have names that describe their coat or character – Rusty, Red, or Douce. Why these differences? Bird society is like human society, but is apart from it; birds form an independent society. Names stand for a whole species, not for an individual bird. Dogs are human subjects, part of human society. Cattle are also part of human society, but are objects rather than subjects. The different systems of names are unconscious distinctions. Lévi-Strauss is receptive to the suggestion that the codes will vary with the cultural context. He remarks that among African pastoralists such as the Nuer, cattle will be treated the way Westerners treat dogs.

Structuralism is not only a method, according to Lévi-Strauss, but one that cuts across all disciplines rather than being restricted to anthropology, and one that has been with us for a long time. What he means is that the idea of structure is intrinsic to the scientific enterprise. Lévi-Strauss has no doubt that anthropology at least the structuralist tradition, is a science. It is his view that the human mind is like a computer, structured in terms of binary oppositions (up–down, left–right). All social organization and culture are conditioned by the nature of the mind. All mankind is rational, in the sense that behaviour and beliefs are imprisoned within the confines of the mind's operations. By a series of transformations and inversions the fundamental binary operations of the brain are reproduced in social organization and culture. Separate domains – from kinship systems to architecture, music, eating and drinking customs, and myth – are logical transformations of one another whose underlying patterns supposedly can be decoded by following the structuralist procedure. Lévi-Strauss has claimed that the human sciences can become as rigorous as the natural and physical sciences. One has only to map the circuits of the brain to bring this about.

FORMAL ANALYSIS

Referred to variously as the new ethnography, cognitive anthropology, ethno-semantics, socio-linguistics, ethnoscience, or componential analysis, formal analysis has much in common with structuralism. Indeed, several writers such as Kaplan and Manners (1972: chapt. 4), Kuper (1975: 222-3), Scheffler (1970: 66-7), and Harris (1968: 493 and 598-9) examine both together. The successors to Boas had to choose between two different directions, both of which were implanted in Boas's work: the humanistic versus the scientific, the idiographic versus the nomothetic, the emic versus the etic. Boas was not anti-scientific. His training in the hard sciences, if anything, imposed on him the burden of exact methods, and made him sceptical of sloppy comparison. Although he was aware of the impact of the environment on culture, he was concerned with habit, emotion, and the individual. Out of these ideas two orientations emerged. One was the culture-and-personality school, which exploited the 'soft' side of the Boasian tradition. The other was the cultural-ecology school, which developed the 'hard' side. Kroeber, one of Boas's illustrious students, represented the soft side (but not the culture-and-personality school) in his emphasis on value culture. Ironically, his own student, Steward, represented the hard side.

The significance of formal analysis, or the new ethnography, is its demonstration that the 'soft' side of Boas could itself be made 'hard.' Drawing on advances in linguistics, and using computer hardware and the formal approaches of cybernetics and systems analysis, the new ethnography purported to be capable of producing a scientific analysis of meaning. It defined anthropology as the study of man's mental makeup, which presumably explained his beliefs and actions. Concerned with cultural maps, cultural categories, and with the quasi-mathematical analysis of narrow domains such as kinship terminology, the new ethnographers claimed to be able to get inside the heads of informants, and, like Lévi-Strauss, to determine the logical properties of the human mind. As Tyler states (1969: 14), 'Cognitive anthropology is based on the assumption that its data are mental phenomena which can be analyzed by formal methods similar to those of mathematics and logic.'

Kuper (1975: 223) has observed that not one prominent British social anthropologist was converted to the American school of formal analysis, although watered-down versions using some of its concepts (such as cognitive map) did appear, as in Bailey's work (1966). The reason, suggests Kuper, concerns the pseudo-scientific pretensions of the new ethnography. In contrast, Lévi-Strauss's impact reverberated throughout British social anthropology. This was partly because of the man's genius and partly because of the grand design of his work, much of which related directly to existing research interests, such as Lienhardt's and Evans-Pritchard's in systems of thought and Turner's in ritual and symbolism (see Kuper 1975: 224–5).

PROMISES OF STRUCTURALISM

1 Structuralism made general questions about mankind popular again, as reflected in Lévi-Strauss's concern with the nature–culture bridge. Social anthropology in particular had become very narrow, dominated by ethnographical detail and a focus on kinship, which almost passed for social organization in general. Lévi-Strauss's structuralism lent new scope and significance not only to topics that had dropped into the background, such as totemism, but also to kinship studies themselves. In The Elementary Structures of Kinship (1969) Lévi-Strauss raises the question of how man leapt from a state of nature to culture. Old explanations such as man's opposable thumb, language, and writing were inadequate. Lévi-Strauss focused on the incest taboo, which he thinks is universal (although others such as Leach disagree). Lévi-Strauss argues that if man and woman did not marry out, it would be impossible for society to exist, for it would be broken down into opposed biologically based units. The incest taboo results in exchange and reciprocity, the creation of affines, and social solidarity. It is the instrument that transports man from nature to culture.

In Lévi-Strauss's early work the distinction between nature and culture was ontological. In later years it became methodological or conceptual. As Lévi-Strauss put it, there may be no distinction at all between nature and culture, but man may have felt a need to invent such a distinction (see Glucksmann 1974: 69). This explains, he argues, why cooking food, while not necessary for man's survival, is nevertheless universal. It conveniently marks man off from other animals.

2 Structuralism revived the cross-cultural method, and did so in a novel manner. Most British social anthropology after the First World War was comparative only by virtue of being non-Western. Lévi-Strauss, expressing more the style of Frazer than Malinowski, undertook macro-comparative investigations. Unlike Radcliffe-Brown, Lévi-Strauss did not see compari-

son as an alternative to the controlled laboratory experiment; nor was comparison done for purposes of illustration. Instead, the comparative units were non-empirical structures, linked by virtue of the process of transformation and inversion.

3 By stressing the underlying similarity of all cultures, structuralism corrected what appears to have been an exaggerated picture of the range of cultural variation in the discipline. Because so much weight has been given to the importance of new ethnographic discoveries, there has been a tendency among field-workers to emphasize how their 'people' are different from others rather than similar.

4 The view that mankind is similar under the surface has been encouraged by another promising principle, neurological reductionism. The idea of the psychic unity of mankind is not new; it can be found in the works of Bastian, Muller, Tylor, and Frazer. But it achieved greater sophistication in Lévi-Strauss's hands. He argued for the explicit recognition in our analysis of 'the uninvited guest': the human mind. The contention is that social organization and culture, regardless of the setting, are limited and shaped by the fundamental operations of the mind, which Lévi-Strauss has attempted to identify. He is concerned with man's inherent structuring capacity – with how man thinks, not what he thinks.

As both Jarvie (1975: 256–7) and Hammel (1972: 4) have pointed out, a basic problem in anthropology is how to reconcile man's apparent diversity and his underlying unity. While Jarvie appears to have little admiration for Lévi-Strauss's structuralism, and Hammel has stretched parts of it to argue that myths do become more nearly perfect over time, it does offer a solution to the problem. Cultural diversity is real, but so is the underlying sameness of culture. Surface-level diversity, or cross-cultural institutional variation, is merely the expression of transformations and distortions of the mechanisms of the mind.

5 Emerging from this neurological base is a fifth structuralist principle, the reduced-model concept. Again, the argument is that under the surface all cultures are the same, largely because man's mental operations are universally identical. From this starting-point, it is only a short step to the idea that there are models of socio-cultural organization models reduced to their simplest and yet universal forms. The outstanding example is primitive society, which is said to be less complex than modern society, and yet contains all the essentials of the latter. The reduced-model concept reaffirmed the valid-

ity of anthropology's ties to non-Western, pre-industrial society at the very time that they were being questioned.

6 Structuralism held great attraction because it recognized the basic weakness of a positivistic science of society, and indeed was an attempt to erect a new epistemological basis for the discipline that would be less affected by the variation and flux of observable behaviour. Structuralists accepted the highly complex and semi-chaotic empirical world, but directed their investi- ~ gations toward the underlying structures, where relations are logical rather than causal.

This is reflected in Lévi-Strauss's conception of social relations and social structure. Over the years anthropologists such as Nadel, Radcliffe-Brown, and Firth tried to clarify the term 'social structure,' particularly to make it serve as both an analytic tool and a descriptive statement of concrete behaviour. They could only do so by introducing two terms, such as structural form and actual structure, or social structure and social organization. Lévi-Strauss redefined the field in order to avoid becoming distracted by the data. For Lévi-Strauss, the term 'social relations' does not refer to concrete behaviour, as in Radcliffe-Brown's work. Social relations are abstractions, equivalent to phonemes in linguistics or perhaps the diacritical features, such as voiced or unvoiced and nasal or non-nasal, that lie behind phonemes. Social structure is also quite different from the conventional usage. Most earlier social scientists, such as Radcliffe-Brown and Parsons, consistently conceived of social structure as the sum total of social relations. Even those who argue, like Durkheim, that the total is greater than the sum of its parts assume that the form of social structure approximates to that of the empirical world. Lévi-Strauss, in contrast, treats social structure as an abstraction that lies below social relations, which are themselves abstractions. Social structure concerns models in which relations between social relations are manipulated by transformation and inversion in order to reveal their underlying messages. Social structure in this sense is 'real,' but it is an order of reality apart from the empirical realm.

7 In an age of apparent scientific and technological progress, structuralism transported anthropology into the modern world by establishing the basis for scientific inquiry. Earlier I remarked that Lévi-Strauss believes that he has found the key to open the doors to a scientific anthropology that will be just as rigorous as the hard sciences. This rigour is not reflected simply in the epistemological and methodological bases of structuralism, but also in its techniques. For example, Lévi-Strauss describes the method of plotting myths on large boards, achieving a three-dimensional picture, and ultimately of coping with the material by using a computer.

8 In the previous chapter, evidence was presented to underline the scholar's incessant search for order, the attempt to find relationships in apparent chaos. Lévi-Strauss has not only discovered pattern and order in marriage rules, but has done so where little had been previously detected: in mythology. Certainly the functionalist explanations of Malinowski and Durkheim are crude and superficial in comparison with the logical properties attributed to myth by Lévi-Strauss. As he has concluded, if there is order in myth there is order everywhere.

9 Neo-evolutionism and cultural ecology can both be regarded as library orientations rather than guides to field-work. Structuralism's value, as Glucksmann remarks (1974: xii), may also be partly related to its capacity to serve as a post-fieldwork model. Lévi-Strauss is basically an armchair anthropologist. Since we are indeed running short of primitive societies, and since the new masters of Third World countries often won't let outsiders in to conduct research, surely we should welcome any means that would sustain the discipline. What bothers me is that this bankrupt viewpoint is probably fairly widespread among anthropologists.

PROBLEMS WITH STRUCTURALISM

Structuralism, despite its promise, presents more problems than solutions. Most of what is worthwhile in structuralism, except its application to myth (and to kinship, which Lévi-Strauss abandoned), existed in the writings of Marx, Weber, Durkheim, and their principal disciples. Some of its features, such as the revival of the comparative method, were shared by other approaches, such as neo-evolutionism. The main value of structuralism may ultimately be the rediscovery of old concepts such as contradictions and binary oppositions, and its success in finally making dialectics legitimate in mainstream anthropology. Had Gluckman and Coser built these concepts into their conflict models, those models would not have been so easily demolished.

1 One problem with structuralism is that it appears to lead to a mentalist position, and possibly is applicable nowhere else. The fact that some of its principles, especially those related to myth, could be used to illuminate the nature of anthropological theory merely confirms this criticism. Some anthropologists may be satisfied to reduce anthropology to a branch of hermeneutics, or to the theory of signs, as Lévi-Strauss has advocated, but surely the majority would find it stifling and futile to do so.

2 Rules for transformational analysis are vague. This does not mean that Lévi-Strauss has neglected to spell them out. He explains the operations as follows (1963: 16):

1 define the phenomenon under study as a relation between two or more terms, real or supposed;
2 construct a table of possible permutations between these terms;
3 take this table as the general object of analysis which, at this level only, can yield necessary connections, the empirical phenomenon considered at the beginning being only one possible combination among others, the complete system of which must be reconstructed beforehand.

Despite this apparently explicit program, we are still left in the dark, and even Piaget's explanation (1970) of how to carry out a transformational analysis doesn't throw much more light on the problem. The structuralist method can be compared to that by which the sex of new-born chickens is identified. There is, I believe, a Japanese method of sexing chickens which when mastered allows one to proceed at a tremendous rate, yet the method can't really be explained or codified. One simply learns by doing it. Similarly, structural analysis, and in particular the transformational method, can't be taught as straightfowardly as one teaches a student how to do a genealogy. Instead, neophytes simply plunge ahead blindly, trying to force a structural interpretation on the data, and suddenly they are on to the trick.

3 Contradiction is used sloppily, often to connote opposition, conflict, inconsistency, or even ambiguity. Moreover, one is never certain whether the contradiction consists of a logical relationship or is embedded in behaviour. The uncertainty is largely due to the confusion between form and content discussed earlier. Lévi-Strauss candidly admits that many of his central concepts, such as inversion, equivalence, homology, and isomorphism, are used very loosely (1975: 31), and welcomes future efforts to refine them. Actually, I am sympathetic to Lévi-Strauss on this point, and later will argue that there is good reason to broaden the meaning of contradiction beyond the logical sense in which the term is usually used.

4 The emphasis on the mind is merely another example of a single-factor theory. The history of anthropology reveals that the search for a key cause, whether the innovative actor, social facts, the sexual animal, or techno-economics, has been irresistible. But this oversimplifies social life. We need a model that is capable of ranging from the macro to the micro, one that can

embrace structure and event together and cope with the etic and the emic and naturalistic and phenomenological properties, one that stresses multi-directionality and feedback and has a tolerance for a zone of unknown or uncontrolled variables and a lack of closure. That is asking a lot. Perhaps Marx came closest to attaining it – not the 'real' Marx of Althusser's imagination, but the real Marx who grappled with both man as determined and man as free and creative. The fact that Weber too struggled with the same dilemma explains why he deserves to stand beside Marx as a creative giant.

5 To argue that the empirical world is extremely complex does not necessarily mean that it is defined as amorphous, uncharacterized by cause and effect, and irrelevant for analysis in so far as it is said to express only superficial and fortuitous relationships – the anthropological equivalent to the linguist's dictum that at the vocabulary level there are no necessary relationships. My critique of anthropology has been that we have made very little progress since the turn of the century. I have not argued that we know nothing. To the contrary, the insight and sophistication of Marx and Weber, and to a lesser extent of Durkheim, were nothing short of remarkable. As Kuhn (1970: 163) has pointed out, to argue that philosophy has not progressed is to contend not that Aristotelianism has failed to progress, but simply that there still are Aristotelians. Similarly, what progress we have enjoyed has taken place within the frameworks established by the early masters such as Marx, Weber, Durkheim, Morgan, and Boas.

6 This is the obvious point to reflect on Lévi-Strauss's effort to put anthropology on a scientific footing. Several writers have questioned the validity of structuralism if it is not open to empirical disconfirmation (see Burridge 1968: 114, and Maybury-Lewis 1970: 161). After all, if time is reversible, there can be no cause-and-effect analysis, and by what criteria does one evaluate the transformations that structuralists supposedly demonstrate? This criticism holds despite Mepham's (1973) argument that a different methodology must be used in the human sciences compared to the physical sciences, and that criteria of verification or disconfirmation are vague even in positivism, indeed even in the hard sciences. There is a world of difference between a situation in which verification is difficult and one in which it is logically ruled out. Despite all the hardware and appearance of rigour, one has the feeling that the numerous insights that Lévi-Strauss has produced – and they are many, especially regarding myth – have been due primarily to his imagination and genius and only secondarily to his methodology. Some intimation of this viewpoint comes from Lévi-Strauss him-

self. Early in *The Raw and the Cooked* (1975: 30) he advises us that we shouldn't take his logico-mathematical symbols too seriously, for they are used unrigorously, and only superficially resemble the equations and formulae of mathematicians.

The scientific status of structuralism can be attacked from another angle. In one of his early and classic essays, 'Social Structure,' Lévi-Strauss (1967a: 281) referred to a fundamental dilemma. Should one study many cases superficially, or a small number of cases thoroughly? Here he allows himself to be guided by Durkheim (1968: 415) who stated, 'when a law has been proven by one well-made experiment, this proof is valid universally.' This is exactly Lévi-Strauss's procedure in his early work on kinship (1969: xxv–xxvi) and his later work on myth (1970: 1). Many contemporary anthropologists would place this procedure in the same category as Durkheim's claim that whenever it can be shown that two phenomena vary with each other, a sociological law has been demonstrated: both belong to the kindergarten stage of sociological investigation; mature science requires that we explain what has caused the correlation.

As Scholte (1970: 115) has said, the implication of Lévi-Strauss's position is that the counting of cases is unimportant; what is important is the underlying concrete universals that justify 'the one well-done experiment.' Leach, in his customary cheeky manner, has been even more blunt. Lévi-Strauss, Leach (1974: 110) contends, is inclined to argue that if there are any ethnographic facts consistent with his theory, that is enough to prove him right. While I am not enthusiastic about the idea of underlying universals, I am sympathetic to Lévi-Strauss's procedure of selecting a few cases for thorough analysis; the realities of research often drive us to this second-best procedure. It does, however, play havoc with Lévi-Strauss's attempt to set anthropology on a scientific course. At the same time it confirms my own view that we remain in the shadow of science, trying to locate it, but never quite seeing the real thing. The irony is that if the philosophers of science are right, perhaps there is no real thing; or, like the perfect portrait-sitters in Henry James's short story, the real thing when it is located is a curiosity, one that stifles imagination and creativity.

7 In its emphasis on deep structure per se, structuralism is no different from previous theoretical orientations in anthropology; as Marx stated, if outward appearances corresponded to inward essences, all science would be superfluous. Structuralism does differ sharply in its neurological reductionist stance and in its refusal to search for cause–effect relationships (or even correlations) at the level of surface or empirical phenomena. Yet the empha-

sis on the mind is either heuristic or not; it is not a demonstrated truth. Lévi-Strauss can only work at the level of supposition, inference, and metaphor; he does not have access to the mind itself. The denial of cause and effect at the empirical level, moreover, amounts to throwing the baby out with the bath-water. To stress that we are baffled by the complexity of social behaviour does not define that behaviour as totally random.

8 Todorov (1973) has pointed out that essays devoted to the subject of structuralism, to the definition of the approach, exist in much greater quantity than those that actually perform a structuralist analysis. The problem is that the merits and flaws of the orientation are debated around quasiphilosophical issues, and not around the products of investigations informed by structuralism. This type of theoretical work, in which an orientation rises and declines around philosophical and logical issues without having been adequately employed in actual research, is not restricted to structuralism, but perhaps is characteristic of a larger proportion of the writings associated with it than with other theoretical orientations. In my view this kind of work does not constitute legitimate theorizing. Another type of illegitimate theoretical work is widespread in the social sciences. It revolves around what can be labelled as 'false starts.' What passes for theoretical work is the article or book that shows why particular hypotheses or sets of assumptions in the literature are wrong. One example is the attack on the analytic distinction between racism and prejudice, which suggests that the former is a structural and the latter a personality phenomenon. The writers (see White and Frideres 1977) who argue that this distinction, which is an example of the macro–micro dilemma, is not useful may well be justified. Yet, as the case of most attacks directed against 'false starts,' at the end we are back to first base as far as explanation is concerned.

9 Another danger of structuralism is that it has trivialized the anthropologist's task by restricting the focus to problems that do not intersect with the human predicament, or at least by restricting the analysis of them. For example, structuralism throws little light on racism or colonialism, and while it deals with entities as significant as life and death, the analysis is abstracted out of the arena in which we live and die, catapulted into the clouds of logic.

10 A related problem is Lévi-Strauss's statement that the purpose of anthropology is to dissolve, not constitute, man (1966: 247). If he means simply that anthropology is the study of decaying societies (hence his suggestion that it

be renamed entropology), one might be sympathetic. He apparently means that man the actor, the living and breathing phenomenal creature, must be excised from the anthropological endeavour. This line of reasoning can be traced directly back to the neurological position. One expects to find anti-humane elements in positivistic, etic approaches in the social sciences such as socio-biology, mainstream structural functionalism, and evolutionism. What is curious is its appearance in so many avowedly non-positivistic schools, ranging from Lévi-Straussian and Althusserian structuralism to Parsonian voluntarism with its over-socialized conception of the actor. The problem is the old one: how to conduct systematic inquiry without assassinating the living actor?

11 My final criticisms concern Lévi-Strauss's idea that primitive societies (and children) represent a reduced model of mankind (see Leach 1974: 18). Such an image is extremely attractive, for it suggests a short cut for dealing with the baffling complexities of cultural forms around the world. It also is a fallacy, and a particularly dangerous one for anthropologists. As I shall argue in chapter 9, anthropologists have been all too disposed to viewing pre-industrial societies as simple. The notion of the reduced model may be interpreted as support for this position, although to do so is to distort what Lévi-Strauss had in mind, at least in regard to belief systems. He refers to the 'relative simplicity' of small societies (1967b: 25), but he does so in the context of social organization. Rather than sharing the fallacy that primitive society in general, including its belief system, was simple, he laments the consequences of this error for the discipline: the absence of adequate data on primitive thought (1966: 40). A consistent theme throughout his vast writings has been the incessant documentation of the complexity of primitive belief systems. How, then, are his reduced models flawed?

Let us deal with children first. Lévi-Strauss suggests (1969: 94) that 'infantile thought represents a sort of common denominator for all thoughts and all cultures.' In each new-born child can be found the entire range of possible human mental structures. The thoughts of children are undifferentiated, polymorphic. The opposite is true for the thoughts of adults. As one mental mechanism is selected, the range of remaining choices is restricted, because there is a logical fit between different combinations of mechanisms. Socialization is a process of increased restriction, as each culture draws out specific mental mechanisms from the infant's generalized capacity. This explains not only cultural variation, but also why there appears to be more similarity among children than among adults from various cultures. Children's thought, because it has not yet been selected and restricted in accordance with the cultural idiom, approximates more closely the unconscious, the hidden properties of the mind.

Children from various cultures may not have more in common than adults, but they may have less that is different. In other words, everything that children have in common adults have in common as well, but adults possess additional factors reflecting advanced socialization which distinguish adults of one culture from those of others. This interpretation turns Lévi-Strauss upside-down. Rather than viewing the child as the fulcrum of all possible mental operations and the adult as a specialized choice from these, it portrays the socialization process as one of enrichment rather than restriction. My argument is a logical one, but it is no less speculative than that of Lévi-Strauss.

If children are more similar cross-culturally than adults, it does make sense to regard them as a possible source of the fundamental properties of mankind. Yet my own field-work experience makes me wary of this argument. The Yoruba, Igbo, Corsican, and Canadian children among whom I have lived do not seem to be much more similar culturally to one another than do the adults of the four cultures. This is not surprising, since the socialization process in each culture begins at birth, and to some extent culture intrudes even while the child is still in the womb, such as a particular culture's definition of when life begins, or the effect of culture-specific narcotics. Piaget and others have plausibly identified the performance of certain functions at certain ages. Yet as far as I am aware, there has been no satisfactory answer as to when the child's polymorphic mind gives way to the restricted adult's mind. Piaget (1951: 197–8) has suggested that the effect of the child's thought process lasts longer on the individual in primitive society than in modern society. As Lévi-Strauss himself states, this argument is merely a variation on the outmoded theme of pre-logical and logical thought.

Even if Lévi-Strauss is correct in attributing to children the whole range of possible mental operations and social arrangements so that less stands in the researcher's way between the child's thought and the unconscious, it would mean little to anthropology. A research focus on the attitudes of children in order to lay bare the unconscious would simply be beyond the technical capacity of the vast majority of anthropologists.

The legitimacy of treating primitive society as a reduced model also is questionable. Lévi-Strauss seduces one into accepting his entire framework on the strength of the attraction of part of it. He stresses the complexity of primitive thought and refuses to regard modern society as superior. So far so good. But if we accept this part of his argument, we must also go along with the preference for synchrony over diachrony, the view that primitive societies are timeless (coinciding with a central tenet of structuralism), and that there are fewer conscious models overlaying and obfuscating the unconscious in the primitive world than there are in complex societies. It is this last factor that supposedly provides the anthropologist with a justification for focusing on primitive society. With fewer conscious models to worry about, the investigator can more easily probe the underlying mechanisms shared by all mankind. At the level of the unconscious, both industrial and pre-industrial societies are complex, but they also are identical. If one can decode the latter, one has decoded the former.

The concepts of conscious and unconscious models, however, are problematic. The conscious model that the anthropologist discovers in the depths of the Niger delta is merely his initial attempt to make sense of a society. In the course of field-work, this kind of model is erected and discarded over and over again. Indeed, what one reads in a monograph is merely the latest – not necessarily the real – version. What passes for the conscious model of the actor is merely the first tentative stab at generalization by the anthropologist. The argument that pre-industrial societies are less characterized by conscious models also is suspect. Ward (1965: 124) showed that in China every person carries several conscious models in his mind. She remarks (1965: 136) that Lévi-Strauss's substitution of conscious model for the more conventional terms of ideal pattern or norm is misleading, since it suggests that people in a society – whether industrial or primitive – possess a single uniform version of their own social system.

Finally, Lévi-Strauss may be correct in his assertion that mythical thinking is as complex and rigorous as modern science. Yet this does not mean that primitive thought approximates more closely the hidden operations of the human brain. There is even some reason to question whether Lévi-Strauss really believes that primitive thought and modern scientific thought are distinct but equal systems of analysis. His reference (1966: 16) to a 'prior' rather than a 'primitive' form of science may be a euphemism, a slippery way around the terms 'pre-logical' and 'logical' mentality. If Lévi-Strauss's assumption of reduced models could be defended, anthropologists would be delighted, because it would make our job a lot easier. Examined under the cold light of logic, however, the blemishes in the assumption stand out.

STRUCTURALISM AND POSITIVISM

The accompanying diagram reflects the different procedural approaches of structuralism and positivism.

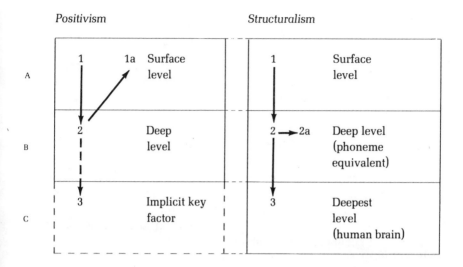

In the positivistic approach one starts off by collecting empirical data, and then goes 'below the data' in order to search for explanation and pattern; this search consists of conceiving of relationships between variables which are formally stated in terms of hypotheses. Finally, one returns to the surface level for empirical confirmation. The obvious criticism that these remarks only hold for the inductive approach is incorrect. It is impossible to proceed deductively without *any* exposure to the empirical world; one's hypotheses must have rebounded from data, no matter how loose and distant the link. Structuralists also perform steps 1 and 2, but rather than returning to the surface level, they move in either of two directions (both of which are often confused and confusing): one is horizontal, permitting manipulation of models. Models are decoded systems or 'languages' contained in domains ranging from kinship terminology to mythology, and consist of relations between variables, which are abstractions rather than perceived empirical reality. The other direction is vertical, permitting assumptions to be made about inherent mental operations. Note, however, that in positivism there is often an implicit c level. Many theoretical orientations contain a 'key' factor that impinges on the analysis, such as techno-economics, sex, or social solidarity. That key factor is usually smuggled into the analysis under the guise of stereotypes such as economic man, psychological man, or the harmonious universe.

Can structuralism and positivism be synthesized? This same question has been repeatedly raised with regard to the equilibrium and conflict models, and usually the answer has been negative, except when the pseudo-conflict of Coser and Gluckman is entertained. A similar fate would appear to attend any effort to combine structuralism and positivism, at least if their respective epistemological claims are taken seriously. In chapter 3 I argued that anthropology is non-paradigmatic. However, if I was pressed to identify potential paradigms in the discipline, I would suggest the following: positivism, Marxism, and structuralism (and possibly phenomenology). These are on a conceptual plane much higher than equilibrium and conflict models, or social action and evolutionism. Some writers would pose positivism and Marxism as two distinct approaches to sociological investigation prior to the emergence of structuralism. After its emergence, those who follow Althusser would subsume Marxism within structuralism, again leaving two paradigms, positivism and structuralism. My own inclination is to place Marxism within positivism, with positivism and structuralism constituting two fundamentally distinct approaches – paradigms, if you will.

If positivism and structuralism did in fact constitute paradigms in Kuhn's sense, then it would be impossible to reconcile them, for by definition paradigms are not just different conceptual entities – they are incommensurate. Quite apart from the fact that it is probably more appropriate to regard positivism as an epistemological and conceptual approach independent of any particular theoretical perspective, neither positivism nor structuralism meets the requirement of paradigmatic science that I set out at the beginning of chapter 3: the capacity for nomothetic inquiry. In addition, despite the apparently irreducible differences between positivism and structuralism, the work of Robert Murphy suggests that a loose dialectic and an appreciation for contradiction, hidden structures, and the influence of the human mind on culture and behaviour can be brought together with a positivist's respect for the phenomenal world. The obvious criticism of such an approach is that the structuralism is no longer recognizable, and the positivism has relinquished all its rigour.

The potential synthesis of positivism and structuralism is confronted by a disturbing feature to which reference has already been made: structuralism may ultimately be restricted to belief system and positivism to behaviour. If this is the case, the emergence of structuralism has widened the unfortunate conceptual division between culture and social organization. Yet as Murphy strongly argues, both mind and act are necessary dialectical components in an analysis. Giddens (1979: 60) points out that structuralism and functionalism share some general characteristics, partly because of Durkheim's influence over each of them. Freud and Marx demonstrated that the dialectic and structural need not be divorced from behaviour. In his diatribe against Sartre

(1966: 245–69), Lévi-Strauss admits to combining analytical and dialectical reasoning, and argues that Sartre also does so. More important, in his early work on kinship and on the myths of Asdiwal, Lévi-Strauss showed how to integrate the principles of an empirical science and structuralism. Contrary to what many critics have argued, Lévi-Strauss has never been opposed to observation. What he has advocated is a clear distinction between observation and experimentation (see Lévi-Strauss 1967: 272 and Glucksmann 1974: 37). Observation is the first stage of investigation. The next stage is experimentation, which means manipulating models that consist of relations between social relations, the latter being themselves abstractions from the surface level of observable social action. Empirically oriented anthropologists such as Radcliffe-Brown ignore or fail to recognize the distinction between these two stages of investigation. This explains, so Nutini (1970: 85) argues, why Radcliffe-Brown confused models of social structure with the raw data of surface-level behaviour itself.

TWO-HEADED ANTHROPOLOGY

Earlier I referred to the two Durkheims. It is now popular to speak about the two Radcliffe-Browns, the positivist and the virtual dialectician of joking relations and totemism, and the two Marxs, the early humanist and the later systems theorist (or structuralist, if Althusser's viewpoint is accepted). I also pointed out that there have been two Kuhns – the early radical philosopher of science and the rather tame one of later years.

One could argue that almost every major figure in social anthropology has presented at least two different programs. We have Evans-Pritchard's early focus on natural systems and his later focus on moral systems.[2] We have Leach the functionalist and, sometimes, Leach the structuralist; Bailey's early systems position and his eventual Goffman-like symbolic-interactionist approach; Parsons the structural-functionalist and Parsons the social-action theorist, plus Parsons the eventual evolutionist! Certainly we have had Weber's institutional framework alongside his action program; with no

2 That Evans-Pritchard clearly sided with Radcliffe-Brown's natural science of society approach before the Second World War is reflected in his statement (1937: 73) that social anthropology deals with 'functional interdependencies,' which sets it apart from art, history, and other humanistic studies. It was only a few years later, in his Marett lecture of 1950, that he reversed his position. In his review of British social anthropology, Kuper (1975: 162) refers to the article published by Evans-Pritchard in 1937, as well as to the Marett lecture, and concludes that 'clearly there has been a complete reversal.'

greater effort than required for Marx, a structuralist position could be read into his writings. For example, the impact of Calvinism on the development of capitalism was unintended; it was the result of the underlying structural and value congruence of the religious and economic realms. The process of rationalization, so important for Weber, can be viewed as a series of transformations from one domain or level to another, including bureaucracy, music, mathematics, and religious and economic institutions.

Verstehen, often criticized because of its subjective character and lack of rigour – despite Weber's argument that one strives for averages of projective empathy, not simply data based on a single projective case – can also be given a structuralist twist. Like myth or music, it constitutes a separate language, and in even more obvious ways it provides the investigator with an opening into the human mind, which is the goal of structuralist anthropology. A similar argument can be made for ideal types. Unlike models, they are never demonstrated to be valid or invalid, either directly by their fit with the empirical world, or indirectly by extrapolating and testing hypotheses. Ideal types are useful or not useful, rather than right or wrong in a cause-and-effect sense. They are composed of one-sided accentuations of salient but fortuitously related characteristics, to be found in reality only by accident. In some senses, they resemble the underlying structures in the works of Lévi-Strauss and Althusser. The point of all this is not to claim that Weber was a structuralist. I merely wish to suggest that there is as much reason for calling him one as there is in the cases of Marx, Freud, and Durkheim. Marx and Freud probably were reread as structuralists because of their stature in the development of Western thought. Durkheim rather than Weber was reread as a structuralist partly because anthropologists have tended to ignore Weber.

STRUCTURALISM AND MARXISM

Is Lévi-Strauss a Marxist, and is Marxism a form of structuralism? Since Lévi-Strauss has said he is not a structuralist, and since Marx denied being a Marxist, we are obviously working on shifting sand. Lévi-Strauss claims to be a Marxist, and defends himself against assertions to the contrary (1967a: 333). He describes Marxism as one of his three mistresses, and says (1974: 57) he rarely begins a piéce of work without first seeking inspiration from *The 18th Brumaire of Louis Bonaparte* or *The Critique of Political Economy*. He claims that he only wishes to do for the superstructure what Marx did for the infrastructure (1966: 130). He even purports to give priority to social transformations over ideological ones, and confesses that his theory of superstructures is merely 'the shadows on the wall of the Cave' (1966: 117).

Certainly numerous commentators have gone along with Lévi-Strauss's claim that structuralism and Marxism are shared, complementary programs. Friedman (1974), for example, suggests that while Lévi-Strauss's structuralism is not quite Marxist, it can be readily converted to that framework. Godelier is even more positive. He points out that Lévi-Strauss and Marx share the view that the structures of scientific interest are hidden below the surface, not to be confused with observable social relationships (1970). Marx's analysis of surplus value serves as an example of his structuralist approach. Both the owner of capital and the worker are under the impression that wages pay for all the work that is done. But the secret of capitalism is the surplus value consisting of unpaid labour that is siphoned off by the capitalist. The appearance and the reality are at odds. This leads Godelier (1970: 343) to conclude that Marx was 'a forerunner of the modern structuralist movement.'

Despite Lévi-Strauss's claim to be a Marxist, as well as the support he receives from others, the arguments to the contrary carry more force. Lévi-Strauss himself has said that structuralism is apolitical; many commentators, including Leach (1974) and Harris (1968), have disputed Lévi-Strauss's claim to be a Marxist. As Zimmerman (1970: 233) puts it, Lévi-Strauss's work is as conservative as historical Catholicism. Marxists such as Sartre have seen in structuralism an attempt by liberal scholars to put off the acceptance of a Marxian analysis of society. Some, such as Burridge (1968), have argued that Lévi-Strauss has confounded Hegel's contradictions and contraries, and used them in a very non-Marxian manner. Goddard (1975: 105) claims that structural reason is fundamentally opposed to dialectical reason, and therefore Marxism and structuralism can never be synthesized. This certainly must come as a surprise to Lévi-Strauss, who all along has assumed that he has used the dialectical method. Goddard (1975: 121) is prepared to admit that he does indeed employ it, but in a way that falls far short of the Marxist usage, for it is merely a formal procedure, limited to the analysis of binary discriminations. Even Godelier, in a later paper (1980: 11), shifts his position and rejects Lévi-Strauss's claim to be a Marxist. As Godelier says, Lévi-Strauss's statement that priority belongs to infrastructures has no effect on his work; in addition, he ignores completely the concept of relations of production. Goddard (1975: 105) classifies structuralism as an equilibrium theory, one that ignores history and produces synchronic analyses of a presumably static universe. How this view could possibly be compatible with Marx's emphasis on historical change would seem to be baffling, but not apparently to Althusser.

Lévi-Strauss's brand of structuralism may have little in common with Marxism, but surely this can't be said about Althusser's structuralism, which is synonymous with his reading of Marx. Yet there is much shared ground in the works of Lévi-Strauss and Althusser. Both purport to be scientific. Although Althusser regards science as a progression of ruptures with previous knowledge, each successive advancement comprehends all previous ones (Applebaum 1979: 22); in this sense he appears to accept the obsolete view of science as cumulative. Both brands of structuralism are anti-humanistic and ahistorical, and stress synchrony and structural transformation rather than cause and effect. Like Lévi-Strauss's structuralism, Althusser's is also a form of conservative ideology. In chapter 4, I referred to several critics who had pointed out the parallels between Althusser's structuralism and the older mainstream functionalism. This may seem surprising, since Althusser, unlike Lévi-Strauss, apparently wishes his brand of Marxism to fuse with his political views and activity. Yet as Glucksmann (1974: xii) has remarked, Althusser's later work is characterized by 'a theoreticism, intellectual elitism and virtual contempt for political practice.' The conclusion seems to be inevitable: Lévi-Strauss is not a Marxist, and Marx was not a structuralist, at least not as defined by Lévi-Strauss or Althusser.

SALUTARY NATURE OF FIELD-WORK

A fitting end to this chapter is a brief discussion of my attempt to employ the structuralist framework in a study of Corsican society, particularly the vendetta. During the Genoese occupation of Corsica (1562–1729), the vendetta at its peak claimed nearly 1,000 lives annually (Carrington 1971: 283) in a population of 110,000 to 120,000. In the nineteenth century, it still accounted for 161 deaths in a single year. In 1823 the chances of being murdered in Corsica were thirty-six times greater than in continental France. There were about the same number of crimes against property during this period in Corsica and on the mainland, but crimes against persons were fourteen times greater in Corsica. As Blanqui (1841: 11) put it, in Corsica one kills more than one steals. While the dishonouring of women was a major cause of vendettas, they could be set off by seemingly trivial reasons, such as insulting a neighbour's dog or merely looking at a person in a peculiar way.

In recent years the vendetta, which meant murder and counter-murder between two extended families (including affines) over several generations, has diminished greatly, but interpersonal relationships in Corsica remain exceptionally intense. Many men continue to arm themselves with pistols and knives. I knew one elderly man who slept with a loaded pistol under his pillow. Another carried explosives in his jacket pocket. A young man, who had returned to the island after living several years on the French mainland, sometimes wore a knife strapped to his leg for protection. Corsicans today still are hypersensitive to supposed wrongs and insults. For example, one day in 1977 a quarrel developed in a village over the rights to a parking place. Later that evening one of the disputants entered a bar and shot the other dead.

Another notable feature of Corsican society is the relative absence of laughter and casual horseplay. As Corsicans have explained to me, one must always be on guard against an affront to one's honour. Joking is dangerous, because it can easily be construed as an insult. Sometimes the Corsican character is said to exhibit the Napoleonic complex. Not only have Corsicans been prone to violence, but they also have a strong sense of their own identity and superiority, an arrogance that leads them to look down on others such as Italians, whom they call 'macaronis.' Certainly they are not subservient or obsequious to tourists or other outsiders.

This image of Corsican society took shape in my mind during a brief field-trip in 1977. It just happened that around the same period I had saturated myself in the literature on structuralism; in attempting to formulate a research hypothesis out of the Corsican pilot study, I turned to structuralism. Robert Murphy (1971: 238), drawing from Lévi-Strauss, had suggested that attention be paid to situations in which order breaks down. Under such conditions, one has an ideal laboratory for the study of rules. In other words, such situations constitute another kind of reduced model of mankind. With Corsica's widespread strain in mind, and guided by Murphy's remarks, I posed the following research problem: did Corsica represent a cultural extreme, or did it exemplify underlying basic cultural mechanisms shared by all peoples? I opted for the latter alternative. The widespread and persistent conflict over the centuries suggested a case in which the edges of the culture had been eaten away, exposing the inner core. In other words, it gave a glimpse of the mental infrastructures, unconscious models, or basic cultural mechanisms to which structuralists allude.

Support for the structuralist interpretation appeared to be abundant. Basic social relationships fell neatly into a framework of binary oppositions: men against women, husband against wife, brother against brother. On the public stage, Corsica is a male-dominated society. A man often openly adores his mother, providing her with a place of honour in his home after her husband dies, while treating his wife with unconcealed disdain. Even the climate and the geography of the island are dualistic. Transhumant shepherds winter on the warm coast, then move with their flocks to the mountain plateaus in the summer. There are the impenetrable mountains of the west coast and the flat plains of the east coast; the more rugged and inhospitable the terrain, the more frequently vendettas appear to have occurred. Most villages were split into two feuding sections, usually a higher and lower one geographically, since settlements had been located on the sides of mountains for defence purposes.

Of even greater significance was the strong possibility that the vendetta in particular and Corsica's widespread strain in general could be explained in terms of a key principle in structuralism: the solidarity function of exchange and reciprocity produced by marital exogamy. Corsica has the highest rate of endogamous marriage in France (Pomponi 1976: 341). Although considered incestuous by the Catholic Church, first- or second-cousin marriage was preferred, especially among the Corsican notables or nobility (Lafaye 1972: 40; Pomponi 1976: 343). Wherever the vendetta occurred most frequently, so apparently did marriage between cousins. Marital endogamy, especially patrilateral parallel cousin marriage, is a feature of Mediterranean societies, and there is a considerable literature dealing with its effect on feuding (for example, Ayoub 1959, Barth 1954, Khuri 1970). Forced marriages between members of feuding families was formerly one of the major means of establishing peace in Corsica. Black-Michaud (1975: 92) states that forced marriages were also used as a peace mechanism throughout the Mediterranean and the Middle East. This was a clear recognition that marital endogamy was closely connected to the vendetta problem.

The structuralist framework appeared to fit the Corsican case usually well, especially from my vantage point in a Canadian library. It was only after I returned to Corsica for more intensive research that it became clear that the question I had asked – whether Corsica represented a cultural extreme or underlying basic cultural mechanisms – was the wrong one. This question was only tangentially related to the vendetta as a phenomenon; moreover, it deflected my attention from the more penetrating questions and more plausible (albeit prosaic) explanations. What one really wants to know is the following: what is the nature of the vendetta system, and why does it emerge in some societies and not in others? Certainly marital endogamy, a significant factor for structuralism, was related to the vendetta; but it was only one of several variables that together explained why people so readily killed each other off. As I learned, the rate of vendetta deaths varied within Corsica as a result of regional differences in the degree of marital endogamy, the degree of commerce, the degree of feudal persistence, the degree of colonial contact, and even the level of land productivity. In addition, the vendetta emerged under specific historical conditions at a particular time in Corsican society: prior to the formation of the nation-state and technological society, as serfdom gave way to peasantry. Much more significant than any of the principles of structuralism are Corsica's colonial past, the clash between pastoralists and the agriculturalists who attempted to close off the communal pastures, class and status differences within Corsican society during the slow transformation from feudalism to capitalism, and the relationship of the vendetta to other types of blood vengeance, such as the feud.[3]

As I remarked earlier, theory is fun, and reading the works of Lévi-Strauss certainly can be stimulating. But a theory appears attractive on paper as long as the only measuring rod is logical elegance; it may not look so good when it is brought face-to-face with data. Had I not tried to apply the structuralist procedure in the course of intensive research, I would probably now have a much higher regard for it. The lesson is clear: field-work is fundamental to the anthropological endeavour.

3 For a discussion of the distinction between feud and vendetta, see Black-Michaud (1975) and Peters (1967).

PART 2

Contradiction as the Basis of Social Life: A Solution

7

Contradictions in Everyday Life

Part 1 of this book focused on various theoretical orientations, showed that change from one orientation to another could be explained partly in terms of underlying conceptual contradictions, and argued that the discipline has not been theoretically cumulative. Part 2 will focus on behaviour and beliefs, and will point us in the direction of a theoretical solution to the problems dealt with in part 1. The basis of that solution is to recognize, accept, and employ the contradictory nature both of our conceptual schemes and of our behaviour. We must come to grips with the fact that our theoretical orientations are riddled with conceptual contradictions, and must build this feature into our theories rather than suppress it. If we do so, our theories will begin to approximate in form the content of behaviour in a way that hitherto has escaped our grasp; this is because behaviour itself is permeated with contradiction. Bailey's message, like Malinowski's, is that people spend as much or more time breaking, bending, and twisting norms as being guided by them. Thus, the simple Durkheimian notion of the collective conscience and social facts, impinging on and coercing behaviour, is inadequate. Bailey's work is aimed in the right direction, but does not go nearly far enough. I shall argue that contradiction is a central characteristic of our behaviour. That is not the image of society that most people perceive. Numerous mechanisms exist to conceal the contradictory basis of social life, as we shall see in the next chapter. Anthropologists too have been blind to the degree to which contradiction exists, which is why they have suffered from an illusion of simplicity, a theme that will be developed in chapter 9. This image of social life is exceptionally complex, and in order to cope with it our theory must be equal to the task. In my view, the most promising candidate for the job is the dialectical perspective. The chapters that follow clear the stage for this perspective, which in the final chapter is marched out to make the concluding statement of the study.

CONTRADICTION AND CONFLICT: OPERATIONAL DEFINITIONS

Before attempting to demonstrate the contradictory basis of social life, we must be clear about our terminology. Multiple and often conflicting definitions of key concepts in the social sciences are the rule rather than the exception; this is no less true of contradiction, a term which has made somewhat of a comeback in recent years. Is contradiction solely a tool of logic, or is it rooted in behaviour? If the latter, is it ontological or confined to class society? These questions lead us directly to the contrasting viewpoints of Hegel and Marx. Hegel conceived of contradiction as both a characteristic of logic and inherent in thought and language, which subsumed behaviour. For Hegel, the logical and the real were not distinct. Marx, with Feuerbach's help, turned Hegel upside-down, restricting contradiction to a structural principle of class society. In doing so, he not only denied contradiction ontological status, but also rejected the Hegelian correspondence between a contrary and a contradiction, or between a semantic contradiction (a statement about behaviour) and a social or objective contradiction (behaviour itself).

Much of the current debate revolves around these issues. Friedman (1974), following Godelier, distinguished between intrasystemic and intersystemic contradictions, and argued that Hegelian contradictions, which always are produced within a unity, can't cope with the latter type. In a manner reminiscent of Parsons, Friedman then proceeded to define intersystemic contradictions in terms of the limits of functional compatibility. Piaget (1970: 126), with Althusser as his guide, observed that Hegel's dialectic was reducible to the identity of contraries, while Marx's was characterized by over-determination. What this means, at least to Althusser, is that Hegel's contradictions are simple: at a given moment all thought and history are compressed into a single contradiction. In contrast, Marx's contradictions reverberate back on each other, producing further contradictions, primary ones and secondary ones dynamically interacting, leading to the possibility of revolution. Burridge (1968: 99) suggests that part of the confusion of Lévi-Strauss's work is a result of his tendency to mix contraries and contradictions while emphasizing the former.

Many writers have tried to clarify what Marx meant by contradiction and to restrict its usage accordingly. In my view, however, there is no a priori reason why we should remain faithful to Marx, and throughout this book I have used 'contradiction' in an unapologetically wide and loose sense. I have found contradictions in our conceptual schemes, and will shortly locate them at all levels of behaviour. At times these contradictions have resembled their logical usage, in which A negates itself, and at other times they have consisted of oppositions that do not necessarily negate each other.

I do suggest that an analytical distinction be made between contradiction and conflict. I restrict the former to a single unit, whether an individual actor, an institution, or an entire social formation. Conflict is reserved for interaction. This can be between two or more actors, two or more institutions, or two or more social formations. Thus, an individual who finds himself torn between turning the other cheek and revenge is in a contradictory state. But an individual who attacks another person, verbally or physically, because of an insult or some other reason, is in a state of conflict with that other person. Similarly, the goals of research versus teaching may be contradictory within the university setting, but they are not in conflict if the unit of analysis is the institution of the university. Rationality in the university setting, however, may well conflict with faith in the religious setting; 'conflict' is the applicable term because two institutional spheres are involved. Finally, the production of the bourgeoisie was a contradiction built into feudalism, not a conflict, because a single unit, or social formation, was involved; or the production of the proletariat was a contradiction built into capitalism. But the proletariat and bourgeoisie are in a relationship of conflict to the extent that they, and not the social formation, are our units of analysis.

The point is that contradiction is always used when a single overarching unit is in mind. In other words, A contradicts itself; it does not conflict with itself; every unit or system is its own contradiction (or contains the seeds of its own destruction). Except at the micro level, as explained below, every contradiction can be transformed into a conflict, and vice-versa, depending on the investigator's point of reference. It is thus extremely important to be clear about the level of generalization of one's analysis, and to be explicit when changing from one level to another.

While contradiction occurs at the micro, middle, and macro levels, it is less apparent at the latter two becaue (a) choice no longer is an existential problem for the individual; (b) moral communities have sprung up around particular sides of contradictions at the middle and macro levels; and (c) these moral communities are in conflict with each other. In other words, it is at the middle and the macro levels that the individual is cloaked in normative attire, and structured into and out of certain kinds of behaviour by virtue of the properties of the institutional sphere; it is at those levels (not the micro) that the 'self' is provided with consistent meaning and identity. Little wonder, then, that people are prepared to destroy the world for reasons varying from religious belief to political affiliation.

Contradiction and Conflict

1 *Micro level*

2 *Middle level*

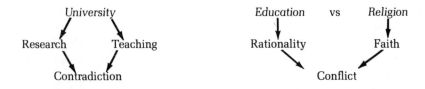

3 *Macro level*

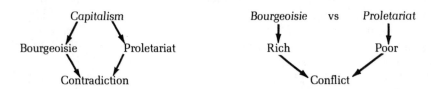

The preceding diagrams show that contradiction can exist at all three levels, and that each contradiction can be transformed into a conflict. At the macro and middle levels, all behaviour can potentially exhibit the properties of both contradiction and conflict. This is also true of the micro level when ego and alter are involved, but not when the unit of analysis is the single individual. In that case conflict is impossible, because it requires a minimum of two units.

My argument, reflected in the diagram below, is that while contradiction is found at all levels of behaviour, it is more apparent at the level of the individual actor, where the mechanisms that conceal contradiction are less effective. Certainly, there is no such thing as 'free' choice, which might result in random behaviour; but at that level, the mutually supporting actions characteristic of a dyad or collectivity, which restrict the range of possible choices, are relatively absent. Indeed, the greater the size of the social unit, the less choice is exercised. This is because one side of the contradiction(s) will already have been elevated into an inviolable moral principle, which will serve to define a moral community. The same will have happened to the other side of the contradiction(s). The groups of communities will stand in a relationship of mutual hostility, or conflict. In this context we can understand why Bailey (1977) uses the term 'myth' to describe the goals of specific groups in the university setting; those goals are myths because they are imbued with the sacred and because they conceal contradiction, which in turn releases the brake on action.

Transition from Contradiction to Conflict

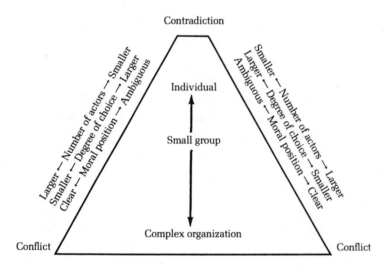

A somewhat similar but certainly not identical distinction between conflict and contradiction has been made by Giddens (1979). Starting with Godelier's distinction between intrasystemic and intersystemic conflict (involving, for example, capital versus wage labour and private appropriation versus socialized production respectively), Giddens restricts conflict to the first and contradiction to the second. Unlike Marx, he argues that contradiction is ontologically embedded in the relation of men to nature, and not confined to a particular era in history, that of class-based society.

Several years earlier, Bailey (1960) also separated conflict and contradiction in order to make sense of the complexities of village life in India. When speaking of a single structure, he used the term 'conflict'; when dealing with two or more structures, such as ritual behaviour and political behaviour, he used 'contradiction' (1960: 8). This usage might appear to be the exact opposite of my own, in which contradiction is restricted to a situation involving a single unit and conflict employed in connection with two or more units. Yet a close reading of Bailey suggests that our approaches are similar. He states that two or more structures, such as ritual and political behaviour, operate within a single social field. In other words, the overall unit, a requisite for contradiction in my terms, is envisaged in Bailey's framework. In the end, however, the analytical distinction I have drawn between contradiction and conflict is heuristic or not. There is nothing about behaviour itself that favours the one term in some situations over the other. All that is important is that the distinction between two types of strain be made – that within a single field of social action, and that between two or more fields. Readers so inclined could define these terms in exactly the opposite way without causing them to lose explanatory capacity, as long as the terms are used consistently.

In order to document systematically the degree of contradiction in social life, a distinction will be made between the micro, middle, and macro levels. In quite different ways, Marx and Lévi-Strauss wrote brilliantly about contradictions and oppositions at the most general level of behaviour and beliefs. This explains why my emphasis will be on the individual actor, dyadic relations, and middle-range institutions. Nevertheless, a brief overview of Marx's dialectical approach will be presented, because without it the picture that I wish to draw of a contradictory world would be incomplete. That picture will not resemble the neat and tidy systems of oppositions characteristic of Lévi-Straussian structuralism. Instead, the emphasis will be on a world of 'cluttered contradictions,' themselves at times messy, lopsided, loosely integrated, ambiguously located, and devoid of ultimate rational design. If this view makes the philosophical hair of French rationalism stand on end and drives the logician zany, the only solace to be offered is that it moves us closer to the actual character of social life itself.

THE MICRO LEVEL

My main purpose is to show that virtually every value, norm, act, and decision has one or more plausible alternatives that contradict it. All social action involves choice between alternatives. But I wish to make an even stronger claim: not only is contradiction ubiquitous at the micro level of behaviour, but in addition in almost all cases there is no mechanism – theoretical, methodological, moral, or pragmatic – to justify the choice between alternatives.

I hasten to qualify this claim because I do believe that there are some exceptions, such as racism. I am not a radical cultural or moral relativist. I am prepared to take a moral stand on those issues such as racism that appear to be unambiguously right or wrong. It is true that what is unambiguous to one person may not be so to another, and that an anthropologist writing about racism a few decades ago might well have adopted a different position from mine. My views obviously reflect my times, and it may be thought that this is about the best that can be done. Yet there is one guiding principle that allows us to sort out the issues: power. I am prepared to argue that differential power always contains the capacity for immorality. Racism is merely one (albeit major) aspect of differential power. The same argument can be made if racism is replaced by other issues, such as colonialism, sexism, poverty, slavery, or child abuse. It follows that those centres of suffering humanity whose condition appears to be blatantly generated by differential power should be, if not the foci of the discipline, at least the subjects of serious research. An anthropology that decides otherwise has surely broken its early promise.

Among the following examples of contradictions at the micro level, three classes are identified: rules, roles, and attributes. Rules, in turn, are separated into three types: logical contradictions, in which A and B are mutually exclusive, or in which A negates itself; contradictions that are in opposition but not logically exclusive; and normative versus pragmatic rules. It is tempting to add another category consisting of rationalizations for behaviour and beliefs, but that category fits better with the mechanisms to conceal contradiction that are dealt with in the next chapter.

Rules
Logical Contradictions

– the grasshopper	vs	the ant
– gather ye rosebuds while ye may	vs	prepare for old age
– people are unpredictable	vs	man is a creature of habit
– wisdom comes with age	vs	old people have closed minds
– be secure	vs	take chances
– live life to the full	vs	stress kills
– the greater the contribution, the greater the reward	vs	share and share alike
– think before you act	vs	be spontaneous and free

– exercise to keep fit	vs	act your age
– be faithful to spouse	vs	enjoy 'natural' desires
– strive for the top	vs	the contented man is the happy man
– labour is fulfilling	vs	labour is alienating
– freedom of speech	vs	laws against libel and slander
– accumulate material possessions	vs	don't tie yourself down
– don't be aggressive	vs	stand up for your rights
– be tolerant of 'different' people	vs	stick to your own kind
– respect authority	vs	don't be browbeaten by bureaucrats
– a man's home is his castle	vs	to be settled is to vegetate
– be open-minded	vs	be decisive, have strong opinions and the guts to take a stand
– consider the facts	vs	the heart knows better than the mind
– be one of the gang	vs	go your own way, be independent and self-sufficient
– no man is an island	vs	he who stands alone stands the tallest
– old people should not be ignored	vs	give the young a chance
– in vino veritas	vs	it's only the booze talking
– actions speak louder than words	vs	it's the thought that counts
– do not kill	vs	the just war

Oppositions

– children are fulfilling	vs	children get in the way of one's career
– be devoted to your work	vs	don't sacrifice your family; get your priorities straight
– children need love and self-expression	vs	children need discipline
– television is educational for children	vs	television is detrimental to a child's socialization
– travel is educational	vs	the family needs stability
– blood is thicker than water	vs	sibling rivalry
– welfare is humane	vs	welfare is degrading
– village life is friendly	vs	village life is suffocating
– city life is enriching	vs	city life is alienating
– the hunter's love of nature	vs	the thrill of the kill
– don't be proud or boastful	vs	confidence is half the battle

Normative versus Pragmatic Rules

– be your brother's keeper	vs	look out for number one
– turn the other cheek	vs	an eye for an eye

– be honest	vs	everybody fiddles the system a bit
– the world is in your grasp	vs	know your place and limitations
– clothes don't make the man	vs	appearance is half the battle
– work as hard as you can	vs	don't be a ratebuster
– whatever you do, do well	vs	don't be sucked in by the system
– play the game fairly	vs	nice guys finish last
– live a good life	vs	it's a dog-eat-dog world
– the Lord will provide	vs	God helps them who help themselves
– stick up for your principles	vs	better red than dead
– be poor but happy	vs	happiness is wealth and power

Discussion

How much support for this argument can be found in the literature? Festinger (1957: 1) refers to people who think blacks are the equal of whites, but wouldn't want to live in the same neighbourhood with them. Others agree that children should be heard not seen, but are proud when their own children's antics draw the attention of guests. These are the kinds of inconsistent values and opinions that concern me. As Festinger writes (1957: 5), 'the existence of dissonance is undoubtedly an everyday condition. Very few things are all black or all white; very few situations are clear-cut enough so that opinions or behaviours are not to some extent a mixture of contradictions.'

Bailey (1977: 198) remarks that people who interact frequently will likely be divided by irreconcilable contradictory beliefs. He asks (1977: 41), 'How do we set up trade-off statements for different kinds of values? Given that people have conflicting demands on their allegiances and their resources, what circumstances make them decide in favour of one rather than another claim? How much credit are you willing to lose with your family and neighbours in order to make a big name? How far will you risk alienating all the old people in the interests of modernity?' Part of Bailey's response (1977: 41) is that such questions concerning basic values 'allow no single *reasoned* answer (emphasis in original). This conclusion reinforces my argument that we generally lack criteria by which to make choices. Later I shall deal critically with the other part of Bailey's answer, his argument that compromise rules the day.

Lynd is best known for his contention that sociological research and knowledge should be socially useful. But he also made an elegant statement about the contradictory nature of social life (1964: 60–2). Some of his examples in relation to the United States:

Democracy, as discovered and perfected by the American people, is the ultimate form of living together. All men are created free and equal, and the United States has made this fact a living reality.

But: You would never get anywhere, of course, if you constantly left things to popular vote. No business could be run that way, and of course no businessman would tolerate it.

Everyone should try to be successful.

But: The kind of person you are is more important than how successful you are.

Religion and 'the finer things of life' are our ultimate values, and the things all of us are really working for.

But: A man owes it to himself and to his family to make as much money as he can.

Life would not be tolerable if we did not believe in progress and know that things are getting better. We should, therefore, welcome new things.

But: The old, tried fundamentals are best; and it is a mistake for busybodies to try to change things too fast or to upset the fundamentals.

Hard work and thrift are signs of character and the way to get ahead.

But: No shrewd person tries to get ahead nowadays by just working hard, and nobody gets rich nowadays by pinching nickels. It is important to know the right people. If you want to make money, you have to look and act like money. Anyway, you only live once.

Honesty is the best policy.

But: Business is business, and a businessman would be a fool if he didn't cover his hand.

Patriotism and public service are fine things.

But: Of course, a man has to look out for himself.

The American judicial system ensures justice to every man, rich or poor.

But: A man is a fool not to hire the best lawyers he can afford.

Poverty is deplorable and should be abolished.

But: There never has been enough to go around,

Most of these examples, which amount to less than half of those in Lynd's text, fall into my category of normative versus pragmatic rules, although Lynd also deals with rationalizations, such as the last example quoted. As he (1964: 105) observes, from the individual's perspective u.s. culture is complex, contradictory, and insecure.

Further support for these views will be given later in the chapter, but now I turn from rules to roles.

Roles

husband	vs	father
husband	vs	son
wife	vs	mother
wife	vs	daughter
scholar	vs	citizen

Discussion

The first thing to note is that we are dealing with contradictions in the various roles played by a single actor. For example, a man who is a husband is also a son, and probably will be a father. While these roles overlap, they certainly are not isomorphic, and are at times contradictory. A grown man may well continue to enjoy the company of his father, and may choose to spend his annual vacation with him on a fishing expedition. But if he does so repeatedly, his wife and children are going to be not a little miffed. Or, a man may spend all his spare time taking his children to sports events or the movies, and simply be too pooped out to wine and dine his wife. Again, somebody is going to be unhappy. Similar contradictions are built into a woman's role.

A sociologist studying labour unrest in bureaucratic creations such as the Canadian postal service might well conclude that its cause is perfectly rational: it represents a neo-Luddite movement, a last defence against the onslaught of machinery. But this same sociologist, in the role of citizen, might nevertheless be disgusted at the slow and undependable postal service, especially if an application for a research grant doesn't arrive on time, or if galleys for an article are held up. Several other contradictory roles are played by the scholar; they will be discussed when I focus on the university per se.

I have not here dealt with contradictions between roles occupied by different actors, such as husband versus wife, because these are examples of conflict. As I pointed out earlier, contradiction is restricted to a single unit, such as an actor or an institution, while conflict involves two or more units, such as man and wife or universities and the church. Obviously, at the micro level the line between contradiction and conflict is not a sharp one. For example, Merton and Barber (1976) focus on contradiction and ambivalence built into a single role, such as that of the medical practitioner, who is supposed to show concern for the patient, but also must keep his distance. But to make sense of the physician's role, one also has to take into account the roles and demands of his patients. The attitude of a patient who is prone to anxiety will fluctuate, ranging from exaggerated esteem and respect for the physician to outright distrust and hostility. Such fluctuation impinges upon the physician's role, causing him to alternate between impersonal detachment and compassionate concern.

In many respects, Merton and Barber's analysis constitutes an admirable example of the degree to which contradictions, or norms and counter-norms, are built into social roles. However, even in this non-functionalist perspective their analysis is flawed by a reactionary, conservative bias. In effect, what they have done is to offer an apology for professionals such as medical practitioners, who are often targets of hostility from the general population. This is not to deny the kinds of ambivalence built into the roles of the 'sensitive' professionals (1976: 552) that Merton and Barber describe. But the fact is that they virtually ignore the sheer power of professionals and class factors, including the barriers that keep others from entering the ranks of the profession. Merton and Barber state, 'Unlike the bitter relatives of the deceased, physicians will maintain that "the operation was a success but the patient died" just as they will maintain (among themselves) that "the operation was botched but the patient survived"' (1976: 560). They fail to see in this a major source of the anger toward professionals, because, professionals themselves, they grossly underestimate the capacity of non-professionals to see through the façade. An important implication of their analysis is that the mere focus on contradiction does not tie one to a radical position. Some anthropologists will be relieved to learn this.

Before leaving Merton and Barber, it should be pointed out that they describe the contradictory demands of a particular role in terms similar to my characterization of theoretical orientation. Not all norms can be expressed simultaneously. Influenced by the fluctuating effect of other roles, such as the patient's, the norms in the physician's role will oscillate between the poles 'of detachment and compassion, of discipline and permissiveness, of personal and impersonal treatment' (1976: 545). Similarly, Lynd (1964: 59) observed, regarding the contradictions that I quoted, that at one moment one side of the contradiction may hold the floor, and a moment later the other side. It seems, then, that not only our theories are pendulum-like; our beliefs and behaviour are also.

Attributes
- beautiful   vs   intelligent
- big   vs   fair
- might   vs   right
- rich   vs   ethical
- fat   vs   sad
- thin   vs   contented
- black   vs   professional
- white   vs   poor

Discussion
The attributes listed above are logical contradictions inasmuch as each attribute in the opposed pairs is the obverse of the other. But they are of a special nature: they represent stereotypes, simplifications, and distortions of reality. For example, popular belief often has it that one can't be both beautiful and intelligent – the 'dumb-blonde' syndrome. Similarly, big people have an unfair advantage, which is almost the same as saying might is right. According to my faded introductory-psychology notes, the managers and leaders of industry do tend to be oversized. Yet the number of variables that determine who gets to the top are many. The most obvious are race, class, and sex, but there are others. Some people are super-aggressive *because* they are small. One doesn't have to go back in history to Napoleon to prove the point. Virtually every athletic team of any note has at least one obvious candidate. Ordinal position of birth also seems related to one's motivation, although the number of exceptions to the theory seems to be sizeable. The class variable is especially intriguing. Young people from wealthy families obviously have a head start. But the business barracuda, and the university's too, is likely to be the young man or woman from the slums. Representatives of the middle class often don't know which way to go – to chase the buck or buck the system; hence their proneness to alienation and rebellion (albeit short-lived). This reinforces the notion that we have a tendency to think in terms of binary oppositions, to push toward polar extremes.

Shakespeare immortalized the stereotypes of the merry fat man and the agitated skinny one with the creation of Falstaff and Cassius. They are probably untrue, and quite possibly just the opposite. We come now to the contradiction of the black professional. How does a white person treat such a curiosity? Black people are supposed to be poor; they are slaves, or field-hands, or migrant labourers, or factory workers. When one comes across a black physician, which of his (or her) statuses domniates, race or profession? Hughes (1976) refers to this dilemma, as does Lenski (1954), and states that race is a 'master status-determining trait.' Lenski develops the argument further by suggesting that individuals subject to a high degree of status discrepancy are especially prone to social change and liberal politics. Like Merton and Barber, Hughes falls into a conservative bias. His essay begins with an affirmation of the unusual openness and fluidity of the status-mobility system in America. The reader is prepared for the argument that the dilemmas and contradictions of status are due to the dynamic social system. Yet the remainder of the article documents the rigidity of the system, the degree to which it is dominated by ascription rather than achievement. He pays attention especially to ascription because of racism (a term he avoids). For example, he says (1976: 289) that despite the high degree of mobility in America, it 'remains a white, Anglo-Saxon, male, Protestant culture in many respects.' Most patients, as he explains, would accept or prefer 'a white, male, Protestant physician of old American stock and of a family of at least moderate social standing' (1976: 286). Hughes's analysis of status contradictions is reasonable. One wonders why he referred to the old myth of the open, achieved society at all, for it only obstructs his argument. Perhaps this is an example of the pitfalls of doing research in one's own culture, or maybe it merely reflects the ideology, in the guise of theory, of his time.

The final mutually conflicting attributes, white versus poor, are included in order to reinforce what was said earlier: the oppositions in this list constitute stereotypes. From the perspective of most black people, the idea that white people can be poor may be a source of bitter mirth. But the facts are contrary to the stereotype. Stereotypes are of a special nature. They are not only contradictions but also distortions. That makes them doubly complex, and possibly explains why they are so difficult to uproot and destroy.

THE MIDDLE LEVEL

Three cases will be dealt with: universities, the black movement, and the West African Utopia that I call Olowo. I begin with the university, that citadel of rationality, for if it can be shown to contain widespread contradiction, so probably can most other institutions.

Universities
1 Knowledge as inherently revolutionary in the Weberian sense vs knowledge as adult socialization in the Durkheimian sense, and thus inherently conservative;

2 knowledge as enlightenment, humanistic vs knowledge as power in the Marxian sense;

3 education as an end in itself vs education as a means to higher income and status;

4 mass education vs élite education;

5 education as a source of liberation vs education as a source of alienation;

6 the capacity to understand the world vs the capacity to engage in the world;

7 the university as the source of new ideas vs the university's emphasis on tradition;

8 research vs teaching;

9 scholarship vs administration;

10 pure research vs applied research;

11 town vs gown;

12 the values of collegiality and the scholarly community vs the individualistic orientation of scholars;

13 scholarship as universal vs data imperialism and scientific colonialism.

Discussion

A major source of information in understanding universities is Bailey's recent study, *Morality and Expediency*. He writes, 'any organization or community will have values and standards which cannot all be reconciled with one another' (1977: 15). Regarding universities in particular, he refers to the three-way pull between scholarship, collegial responsibilities, and obligations to the wider society (1977: 14). Elsewhere (1980) he puts his finger on a unique feature of the university: it is the only type of bureaucracy in which its members openly claim disloyalty, because commitment to scholarship overrides commitment to the organization.

Except possibly for the sixth, the thirteen contradictions listed above are self-evident. The sixth concerns the contradiction between the capacity to understand the world and to engage in it, or simply between the thinker and the man of action. Alienation is said to be the intellectual's disease. What is special about anthropology, at least according to some commentators, such as Sontag (1970), is its capacity to overcome alienation. This it does through the adventure and action that are part of the field-work. Sontag made these comments with direct reference to Lévi-Strauss, who more than any other anthropologist has written sensitively about the anthropologist's estrangement from his own society. Moreover, Lévi-Strauss claims that to the extent that one is capable of understanding, one is incapable of acting upon the world, and vice-versa. Finally, there is supposedly a contradiction between the fact that scholars are trained for research and the fact that they spend most of their time teaching in order to make a living. Contrary to popular opinion, graduate students *have* been taught to teach. They have gone through a long apprenticeship and have selected role models from their own instructors. The real problem is not the quality of classroom performance. Rather, it concerns contradictory activities – research versus teaching. The overwhelming emphasis in graduate training is on research. Yet the recent PHD must adjust to the fact that most of his efforts, at least initially, must be devoted to teaching elementary anthropology. This is a difficult adjustment, and explains why recent doctoral graduates often botch up introductory courses and yet excite the best students, especially in senior or graduate classes.[1]

A similar analysis could be applied to a closely related phenomenon: academic conferences. Their manifest purpose is to provide a forum for the dissemination of new knowledge, knowledge on the frontier. Yet most conference papers are too low in quality to warrant publication, and rarely is the standard of criticism any higher. Why, then, do academic conferences abound? I suppose the quick answer is that conferences provide the hard-pressed academic with an opportunity to have a mini-holiday, to meet old friends, and perhaps even to negotiate a new appointment. An even more cynical response relates to academic mobility. The man or woman on the make, unless extremely gifted, cannot avoid the conference circuit. Yet as in the case of the university bureaucracy, the explanation is more complex. Conferences too are pulled in different directions by irreconcilable goals and values. The dissemination of knowledge, for example, runs counter to the solidarity and social-control functions of conferences. Solidarity is a variation on the value of collegiality in the university setting. As a result of the revolutionary nature of new knowledge, academic disciplines are constantly threatened from within. One of the mechanisms that counteract the inherent

1 Of course, some anthropologists prefer teaching over research, and others find the two activities mutually reinforcing. I suspect that one cannot teach effectively in anthropology unless one is periodically engaged in research; conversely, however, one probably could conduct meaningful research without the benefit of the classroom, as long as one was exposed to the critical reaction of fellow practitioners, as in a research institution.

divisive force is the academic conference; in Durkheimian terms, the annual conference, like the annual harvest ceremony, infuses an institution with increased integration. In addition, in an enterprise devoted to dispassionate investigation, the significance of face-to-face interaction and particularistic relationships may be all the more important. We write, we publish, but our products exist apart from us, impersonal and without character. But when an author sits next to us at the conference table, and perhaps later joins us for refreshments, his work is animated, personified. Face-to-face interaction also provides a partial antidote to another problem within the scholarly community. Academic life, despite tenure and a steady income, is inherently insecure. The measuring rod for scholarly excellence is woefully inadequate. Success cannot be quantified according to salary or material possessions, and the article or book that inspires one colleague may be ridiculed by another. The conference circuit provides one with an opportunity to build a following, or at least to confirm one's scholarly credentials among peers. The implication is that the contacts made at conferences have a deeper meaning than mere instrumentality.

Any discussion of solidarity impinges on social control, and this too is part of the raison d'être of conferences. The days in which a few leading scholars held the careers of junior academics in their hands have gone. Yet there remain means of achieving orthodoxy. Conferences, especially the large annual variety, are vehicles for exhibiting publicly the central values of a discipline, its preferred direction of inquiry, and the use to which its research findings are put. Obviously, this side of conferences contradicts the frontier image, and the impetus for it comes both from within and outside a discipline. Without such a thrust, the centre could not hold; thus, academics themselves have a vested interest in non-revolutionary knowledge. Moreover, as I shall argue at more length in the next chapter, people at the top, those with power and position, almost always have an interest in stability rather than change. This is especially true of the state, from which the funds to organize a conference often come. These remarks are intentionally brief, and I am aware that they do not deal adequately with the phenomenon at hand. For example, the conference also is of great importance to those scholars whose individual works have gone off on similar tangents. The interaction made possible at a conference fosters subgroup legitimation, and provides the confidence necessary to continue in an innovative direction. Yet this observation evokes the earlier statement regarding the value of face-to-face interaction for an endeavour that breeds insecurity; moreover, scholars who embark upon fresh approaches are more likely to meet in mini-conferences of their own, or parallel to the general forums – anti-con-

ferences, if you will. Bailey has provided us with an anthropological investigation of the university itself, but there is as yet no comparable study of the
academic conference. When it is tackled, either as a PHD topic or otherwise,
it will, I hope, be set in the context of a range of comparable phenomena
such as the businessman's and the politician's conventions.

Black Movement and Racism

1 White social scientists, as Hsu (1973) points out, claim a mandate to study
all peoples, regardless of race, but they resent non-whites studying white
society. Hsu also indicates that white scholars prefer that coloured scholars
stick to ethnography, and leave theory – that more demanding and prestigious exercise – to whites.

2 Blacks don't want to be treated differently, yet they argue that non-blacks
can't understand them. This provides a rationale for the previous contradiction, which should please white scholars with racist tendencies.

Can a white man or woman study blacks in any meaningful way, or contribute through scholarly efforts to the defeat of racism? When my research
interests turned increasingly toward racism, I decided to select projects in
which my white skin would be an advantage. One possibility was field-
work among whites in the Ivory Coast, a country in which the expatriate
population increased sharply after independence. The project that I eventually chose concerned ultra-right-wing, racial supremacist organizations in
Canada. Yet regardless of how well the research goes, I shall always be an
observer, not a victim. Can I appreciate what it means to be subjected to
racism? One might argue that as a white I am privy to a range of data shut
off from black scholars, such as the racial slurs and jokes that whites pass on
to each other from day to day. A black anthropologist might counter by
stating that he is quite aware of what goes on among whites. Perhaps in the
end the best thing for concerned whites to do is simply not to interfere, and
leave the investigation of racism to non-whites. Yet as Sawyer (1973) points
out, the black researcher in a black community is under tremendous strain,
torn in different directions according to different loyalties, personal and
academic.

3 Black social scientists argue that blacks have been emasculated by racist
white society. The lives of black people have been devastated. Their families are disintegrated, they are impoverished, their heads are spaced out. Yet
these same black social scientists condemn white scholars for referring to

these problems, for not stressing the positive features of black American society.

How can one argue that black society is sick (as a result of racism), and at the same time splendid? The reason is rather simple, and explains why blacks argue that whites can't understand them. Whites, even liberal whites, conduct studies of black communities or ghettos and discover that they are rife with strain, poverty, theft, broken marriages, and single-parent homes. Then by a neat shift in logic they sometimes conclude reluctantly that blacks are thieves, that they lack the stability necessary to stay married or hold a job, that they are intellectually inferior to whites. It is in this vein that black intellectuals have condemned the Moynihan Report on black families (see Billingsley 1973). The position of black social scientists is not difficult to grasp. It is bad enough to suffer in the various ways that have been described; but to accept the judgment of white scholars that their unfortunate plight is due to their fragmented family structure or their lack of educational attainment is just too much.

4 Social scientists, black and white, have studied black ghettoes over and over again, with the hope that their studies will result in improved conditions. Yet the residents of the ghettos resent these studies. Two questions arise: is research useless, or is it subversive? If it is the latter, there is even more reason to focus on élites and racist organizations such as the Ku Klux Klan, on the victimizers rather than the victims.

5 'Positive racism' is a banner flown wide and high by many contemporary racist organizations, such as the American and Canadian branches of the Ku Klux Klan, the Western Guard in Toronto, and sophisticated South African racists. They claim that they are not against any ethnic group or race; they are merely for the advancement of the white race. Quite apart from the probability that their private views are quite different from their public statements, positive racism is a contradiction in terms: racism of any kind is misanthropic, and can only be positive to racists themselves.

6 'Equal but separate' constitutes a new expression of racism in America. Certainly it differs in emphasis from the South African apartheid policy of separate but equal. But it remains racist, an adjustment to changes in federal laws enacted to confront discrimination. Equality in law can be granted to blacks, but after all, people are different, and they don't have to live together. Equal-but-separate is the official policy today of a surprisingly broad range

of people, from outright racists such as members of the Ku Klux Klan, to many liberal academics with whom I have talked, and, apparently, a not insignificant segment of whites in the United States (see Willhelm 1973). Whites, Willhelm points out, have the suburbs, blacks the cities and urban ghettos. The result is that black youth today probably have less personal contact with the white world than any previous generation in America. The process is facilitated by the doctrine of equality. Undereducated and under-trained, blacks can't compete with whites for jobs distributed on the basis of objective qualifications. As Willhelm (1973: 145) ironically observes, 'Why discriminate when one can eliminate the Negro into non-existence by prac-ticing equality?' (emphasis in original).

7 'Talk "black power" during the day, and sleep "white" at night': A source of anger among many blacks concerns those among their radical spokesmen who preach that black is beautiful but prefer white women, within or out-side a marital relationship. Usually when academics consider links between racism and sex, they focus on the stereotypes of the uninhibited black woman or the well-endowed black man. But there is another link that is even more important: the dynamics of sexual relations between whites and blacks. I first became aware of these dynamics several years ago in Nigeria, where the pressure from white women to keep their men from sleeping with black women was enormous. Whites who did so were ostracized and were subject to vicious gossip. Jean Guiart (personal communication), a French anthropologist with many years of field experience in New Caledo-nia and elsewhere, even claims that sexual competition, especially relating to the role of women, is the major cause of racism. Although Guiart's posi-tion may be too strong, one only has to read works such as *Sexual Racism* (Stember 1976) or the writings of Jahoda (1961) for confirmation of the importance of sexual competition in a racist context.

Not many years ago it was thought that interracial marriage might be the answer. That is not often suggested as a solution to racial problems today. It is much more probable that young blacks will be critical of an older black married to a white woman. Many such white women, concerned and ideal-istic, could not understand why black women despised them. Usually black men married white women (who were often called white trash); only rarely were black women united with white men. Clearly, wealth and status were often involved. Those black men who became qualified professionals, or at least attained wealth, scored high on at least one status dimension, which made them attractive as marital partners for white women. White women who married less-educated black men with lower incomes were rare. When such marriages did take place, they were treated as curiosities; this occurred, for example, in a famous case in Nigeria involving a gifted artist. Significantly, even the idealistic young people who join the volunteer organization, the Canadian University Service Overseas, an equivalent of the American Peace Corps and the British VSO, are more likely to marry Thais than Africans.

Before moving on, I must say something about mulattos. Racists in North America used to say that the only blacks who ever contributed anything important to society or improved themselves were partly white. Just as many racists, including several of those whom I have interviewed in my study of white supremacist groups in Canada, claim that the 'mongrel' is the most despicable human being of all; their view is that 'mongrelization' ruins both races. Why the contradiction? Obviously two different values are in competition. One concerns the fundamental superiority of 'white blood.' The other concerns the belief that whites and blacks constitute two different species, that it is natural to keep them separate and disastrous to do otherwise.

8 Reverse racism manifests itself in two major ways: whites who claim everything black is good, and blacks who are prejudiced against whites – the hate that hate produced. Only those lacking all sympathy could condemn outright the first type, for at least a step in the right direction has been made. However, within this type there is a prominent and not very admirable subtype: whites who have an abstract appreciation for non-whites, but who are uncomfortable when confronted with the real thing. Happy is the field-worker who reaches the stage where he can choose to like some people and dislike others, as he would in his private life, and accept similar reactions from others toward him.

The other expression of reverse racism concerns black prejudice against whites. In my experience, many whites find such prejudice hard to understand, and some are not a little pleased: it indicates that blacks are just as bad as whites, and that perhaps racism is innate.

Several other contradictions concerning racism and the black movement can be described. For example, in Toronto some West Indian residents resent further West Indian immigration. The reason? It makes them more visible as a minority, with the possibility that racial attacks on them will increase. In the same city, the tension between blacks and Jews is high. Their interests appear to be contradictory. Blacks often accuse Jews of siding with the power structure. The implication is that Jews have finally made it, and their long history of involvement in organizations to improve the lot of blacks, such as the NAACP, is said to be just that – history.

Olowo

Governmental and private investigations of religious sects in the United States, sparked by the tragedy of Jonestown in 1978, were doomed from the start to be ineffective. Sects contain contradictions that defy resolution. For example, if freedom from religious persecution exists, on what basis can sects be prosecuted? Who is to say one sect is 'genuine' and another not? At what point does religious instruction turn into brainwashing? On what basis is de-programming of individual believers justified? Is de-programming a violation of the right of freedom of worship?

The contradictions implicit in these questions also existed in Olowo, along with many others. Olowo was a 'community.' Private enterprise had been abandoned and the family unit disrupted. Men lived on one side of the village, women on the other; children were raised by adults other than their own parents. Collective work and sharing were basic values, and were directly related to their pursuit of immortality. Only by living completely communally, so the Holy Apostles believed, would they achieve everlasting life. Yet there was a highly centralized authority structure: the village was ruled by an *oba* and several others who enjoyed correspondingly high status. Furthermore, despite the belief that immortality was imminent, the Apostles planned for the future; they built an industrial complex and hoarded their profits.

There were other contradictions, such as the demand by ordinary members of the community for more material goods and payment for work, and their significantly greater impoverishment when private enterprise eventually was introduced and the élite became wealthy. My main example, however, concerns the enormous strain in Olowo associated with marriage and adultery. Despite Olowo's economic success, conflict was widespread. The major source concerned the regulation of sexual affairs. One of the strongest norms in the community was marital fidelity and sexual abstinence for unmarried people. Olowo members impressed upon visitors that no man coveted another's wife. Yet adultery was widespread. Out of 130 cases of conflict in Olowo that I analysed, 57 concerned adultery (Barrett 1982). Punishment was severe: usually those found guilty were flogged with small sticks, often until blood began to flow.

In order to explain why the regulation of sexual affairs was the source of so much strain, two contradictions intrinsic to Olowo must be considered. These are illustrated in the accompanying diagram.

Contradiction 1

A family

vs   } = Marital experimentation = eventual conflict

B community

Contradiction 2

A religion and communalism   = Free love

vs   vs   = Immediate conflict

B centralized authority   = polygyny
and high status

The first contradiction is between the family and the community. This dilemma is extremely pronounced in closed societies, because the family rivals the community for a person's identity and loyalty. This contradiction partly explains why there was so much experimentation with marriage and sexual arrangements in Olowo: polygyny, monogamy, a complete ban on marriage and free love, monogamy again, free love again, a return to polygyny, and an arrangement called 'testing' which allowed high-status men to determine whether the wives of other men were fertile.

However, this contradiction does not explain why such experimentation caused widespread conflict. Only after a generation or so had passed did the situation change. By then the village's esoteric beliefs and practices clashed with those of the outside world, owing to secularization. In order to explain the extraordinary degree of conflict generated by adultery in Olowo, we must consider the contradiction between religion and communalism on the one hand and centralized authority and status on the other. Olowo people believed that only if they lived completely communally would their basic goal of immortality be reached. This meant not only that all economic goods had to be held in common, but also that marriage must be banned entirely. At the same time, Olowo had a highly centralized authority structure. An accepted norm in the village was that wealth should be distributed on an egalitarian basis; but an equally strong norm was that those in positions of high authority should be rewarded accordingly. Because material rewards were ruled out, this left non-material ones, such as status and deference. Status was reflected in salutations, such as the title of *oba*. Other members of the élite were known as *wole* (prophet). Ordinary people expressed their deference by genuflecting in front of the élite.

These rewards, however, were modest, and my argument is that a logical consequence of the link between centralized authority and the demand for high status was polygyny. It was the one reward that could clearly symbolize and buttress the authority of the leaders, which was not economic in nature since the family was not an economic unit before the introduction of private enterprise in 1968. Polygyny was practiced in the surrounding Ilaje society, and the pressures toward this marital form probably accelerated with the process of secularization. It can now be readily understood why most new female recruits were given to high-status men, and how such a blatant system of inequality as 'testing' could be introduced with little opposition from ordinary members. Both polygyny and 'testing' merely attested to the élite's claims to high rewards.

The contradictory structural principles – a complete ban on marriage, and polygyny for high-status people – largely explain both the specific nature of experimentation with marriage and the family over the years, and the ensuing widespread conflict over adultery. In 1949, the free-love system for example, was a response to the belief that only by living completely communally would immortality be attained. But it conflicted with the norm that the leaders should be highly rewarded. The monogamous system that was practised for the remainder of the first oba's reign was a compromise. While it provided some degree of equality by ensuring that all adults had a spouse, it failed to satisfy the conditions dictated by either side of the contradiction. This may partly explain why adultery continued to occur among low-status people, despite the high value placed on marital fidelity and abstinence. The peculiar link between religious beliefs and communalism meant that free sexual access should have been legitimate. It also helps to explain why high-status people not only committed adultery, but were less severely punished: they supposedly deserved greater rewards. Faced with these contradictory principles, the oba had little alternative but to try to enforce his compromise by severely punishing the subjects who defied it.

The situation obviously was highly unstable. It was maintained partly by the severe flogging, and partly by the unusual personal powers of the first oba. When he died in 1963, the inherent contradiction that pulled monogamy in two directions – toward free love and polygyny – crystallized. The second oba's reaction was to ban marriage once again. But this solution responded to only one side of the contradiction, and could not last. The third oba's reaction was to introduce polygyny and to ensure that men of high authority and status had the most wives. Polygyny also was one-sided, since it ignored the link between religious goals and communal living. Yet it was successful, and for obvious reasons. By then Olowo was a generation old.

The emergence of polygyny reflected the process of secularization that eventually defeats almost all Utopias as their settings begin to penetrate them.

THE MACRO LEVEL

Everything seems pregnant with its contrary. Social systems contain the seeds of their own destruction. Force is the midwife of every old society pregnant with a new one. Revolutions are the locomotives of history.

These are Marxian aphorisms, and they suggest why Marx is the obvious figure in any discussion of contradictions at the macro level. Marx restricted contradiction to a specific stage in history: class society. The essence of a class is to be in opposition to another class. Each class, such as the bourgeoisie produces its own gravediggers – in this case the proletariat.

The pre-class stage of the Asiatic mode of production, at least according to one interpretation of Marx (see Avineri 1968), lacked contradictions and thus the internal dynamic to propel it on to a higher stage. When pre-history comes to an end – that is, when the communist stage is reached – there again will be no contradictions, for there will be no classes. This will make possible the withering-away of the state, an oppressive institution, leaving only the necessary administrative machinery to facilitate social interaction. This last statement, I realize, is open to debate, but so is the argument that the Asiatic mode of production belongs to the pre-class stage, and virtually everything else in Marx's writing. The secondary literature on Marx is enormous, and any discussion of it would sidetrack my aim, which is to round out the picture of contradiction at all levels of behaviour and beliefs by this brief look at the macro level.

Central to Marx's framework is the absolute necessity of opposition and contradiction. He was opposed to reformists who wanted to improve society by reducing poverty or raising housing standards. In his view, equal distribution of scarce goods and class equality was not the goal; he advocated nothing less than class abolition. The reformists merely suppressed the contradictions in society and retarded the inevitable unfolding of historical movement. Marx also was opposed to Utopian experiments, such as Owen's and Fourier's, which he called 'castles in the air' (Tucker 1972: 361). Utopian movements were reactionary rather than progressive, for they amounted to escaping from society rather than changing it. According to Marx, there are fundamental laws of historical change. The contradictions in each social formation cannot be artificially excised; indeed, it is the contradictions that fuel the engines of change. For example, Marx states that at one stage the proletariat fights not its enemies (the bourgeoisie) but the enemies of its enemies (the land-owners, the remainder of the feudal monarchy). The victory of the bourgeoisie is in every way advantageous to the proletariat. Without it, the eventual victory of the proletariat over the bourgeoisie could not materialize. Similarly, the spread of capitalism around the world is to be applauded, especially where societies have been stuck in the Asiatic mode of production; capitalism provides the dynamic necessary to catapult such societies on to the next stage.

Marx (Tucker 1972: 192) and Lenin (Selsam et al. 1973: 357) also state that countries like Germany and Russia suffered not so much from capitalism as from its lack of full development. The implication is not only that countries must pass through specific stages of history, but also that the dynamic of class opposition is essential.

The class-generated dynamic is usually expressed as the clash between the forces and the relations of production. The forces of production include the resources, equipment, and men that produce a society's material goods. The relations of production constitute technology plus the social relations that people such as owners of capital and workers enter into in economic pursuits. As the material forces of production change, the existing social relations of production become out of tune. The system cannot withstand the strain, and revolution may occur. This can be illustrated by a brief look at the contradictions within feudalism and capitalism.

During the feudal stage, the ruling class consisted of the Catholic Church, the nobility, and the military élite. Beneath them were the serfs on the land and the artisans in urban centres. The serfs held a portion of land for themselves, and consumed what they produced. The artisans sold or bartered their products, but they were less alienated from their labour than modern factory workers because they fashioned the products in their entirety and marketed them themselves. The feudal social formation began to crumble partly because of the tremendous expansion of markets, which was due in turn to the discovery of America and the development of trade routes with the East. At this point commerce developed, spurred on by colonization and the era of imperialism. Specialization in craft production began, and the individual artisan started to lose his autonomy. Feudal society developed an internal contradiction that it could not resolve; the new economic order – commerce on a large scale, leading eventually to manufacturing – created new social relations and the merchant class. This new class successfully challenged the feudal aristocracy, and emerged as the ruling class in the capitalist stage.

Marx considered capitalism to be the most despicable stage of all. In humanistic terms, the degree of alienation of man was greater than in any previous stage; the central condition of capitalism was the existence of a mass of individuals who had nothing ot offer but their own labour. In logical terms, capitalism was the worst because it contained more contradictions than any previous stage. One of these was the contradiction between capital and wage labour. Another was the contradiction between socialized production and capitalist appropriation. Godelier (1970) sees these as contradictions both within capitalism and between capitalism and the subsequent stage, socialism.

Under capitalism there is constant pressure to increase production. This is partly achieved by expanding markets and by improving machinery, but mainly by increasing the division of labour. As Marx stated in *The Communist Manifesto* (Tucker 1972: 338), 'The bourgeoisie cannot exist without constantly revolutionizing the instruments of production ... Conservation of the old modes of production in unaltered form was, on the contrary, the first condition of existence for all earlier industrial classes.' The result, Marx argued, was the increasing misery of the masses of workers. Even members of the bourgeoisie suffered. As Marx put it, one capitalist kills many others as the fever of competition rises.

Yet Marx believed that there was a rainbow behind the clouds. The bourgeoisie, by pushing more and more people into the category of workers, passed its own death sentence. It was only a matter of time before the proletariat would rise up and overthrow the bourgeoisie, setting up the dictatorship of the proletariat. Significant here is Marx's argument that the dictatorship of the proletariat, which would merely replace the dictatorship of the bourgeoisie, would mark the first time in history that the ruling class constituted a majority of the people. In each previous stage the size of the ruling class increased, but remained a minority until the overthrow of the bourgeoisie. Murphy (1971) has remarked that Marx, unlike Weber, was an optimist. His belief in progress may have distorted his prognosis for the future.

Two final remarks about Marx: in chapter 4 I demonstrated the pendulous nature of anthropological theory. This also, as Merton, Barber, and Lynd have pointed out, is characteristic of empirical behaviour. In this context, Marx's analysis of the periodic crises in capitalism is relevant. The up-and-down business cycles that occur as production reaches a point beyond the capacity of society to consume it, resulting in the artificial destruction of part of the productive forces and its products, parallel the oscillating nature of theory and behaviour. The second point concerns Schaff's discussion of the freedom of the individual in Marxism. With direct reference to existentialism, Schaff (1970: 150) defines freedom as the capacity to make choices between alternative courses of action. But choice is a burden to the individual, because values clash and some choices are no-win situations. In Schaff's words (1970: 152), 'a man must choose something, but cannot decide what. This is not only a matter of purely subjective factors: given a thorough knowledge of a system of values and the commands and prohibitions it involves, every choice inevitably entails the breaking of some rule and every attempt at doing good is inevitably coupled with doing evil. How shall one choose? Which good is better, which evil worse? There are no prescriptions' (emphasis in original). The significance of Schaff's words is clear: they pose a problem for Marxism almost identical to that which guides this chapter. They cannot be dismissed as existential rubbish beyond the concern of Marxism. As Schaff stresses, alienation and the burden of choice for the individual have not disappeared under socialism; these problems transcend any particular political system.

While Marxism provides the major example of contradictions at the macro level, one could also turn to Lévi-Strauss, although his contradictions concern properties of culture rather than social structure and interpersonal relationships, and are 'macro' only in the sense of their assumed universality. Lévi-Strauss counterposes nature to culture, raw to cooked, wild to tame, sacred to profane, life to death, left to right, normal to abnormal, and cold to hot, to give only a few examples. The dialectical method is also central to his analysis, and myths are unravelled as systems of transformations, oppositions, and inversions. Writers such as Durkheim who have focused on general binary oppositions, such as the sacred versus the profane, could be easily pressed into this framework. Leach (1974: 88) is probably correct in saying that the mind is not limited to binary operations. Yet the anthropological evidence for binary classification is immense, and as Needham suggests (1979: 32, 57, 59–60) it may be an elementary, universal mode of classification, a natural operation of the human mind. Even Parsons' pattern variables (1951: 67), a series of dilemmas present in various degrees in all social action, such as specific versus diffuse relations and self versus collectivity orientation, could be recast as binary oppositions. Whether that would salvage these analytic tools, which in their conventional usage obfuscate rather than illuminate behaviour, at least in the comparison of industrial and pre-industrial societies, is a different question.

CONCLUSION

In a previous chapter I showed that contradictions are embedded in our conceptual schemes. In the present chapter I have documented the presence of contradictions at all levels of behaviour and beliefs. One could, following Freud, make the framework wider and deal with the psychological state of ambivalence, which involves a struggle at the personality level between contradictory attachments to the same thing, such as the love–hate syndrome between spouses. To continue the reductionist stance, it would also be easy to document opposed personality types among renowned anthropologists. Frazer and Malinowski, for example, had polar-opposite temperaments. Frazer avoided all argument and debate, while Malinowski revelled in it.

Yet it is not necessary to move beyond the boundaries of anthropology to state my case. For those who remain unconvinced, let me provide some additional documentation. Simmel argued that social life always involves harmony and conflict, love and hatred, attraction and repulsion. There may be a tendency to write Simmel off erroneously as marginal to anthropology, but what about Boas, Spencer, and Firth? Boas wrote (1962: 202), 'One of the great difficulties of modern life is presented by the conflict of ideals; individualism against socialization; nationalism against internationalism; enjoyment of life against efficiency; rationalism against a sound emotionalism; tradition against the logic of facts.' Spencer (see Kardiner and Preble 1961: 42) saw man as driven by two opposed instincts: his inherent egoism and his altruism. The institutions of society are a product of the strain between these opposed instincts; they subordinate the individual to the group's need for survival. Firth (1964: ix), commenting on changes in anthropology, stated, 'Assumptions about the stability and integration of primitive societies have given way to a recognition of the force of contradiction in social principles and of conflict in roles.' Firth's capacity to recognize these changes is all the more remarkable when it is realized that he himself did not move beyond the economist's decision-making model, in which the actor chooses between values that are scarce but not contradictory.

According to Slater (1976: 535 and 577), the norms of any society amount to an inconsistent, contradictory hodgepodge. Lipset and Raab (1970: 20) suggest that the 'genius' of American society is that it has legitimized ambiguity: materialism versus idealism, conformity versus individualism, majority rule versus minority rights, high crime rate versus high church attendance. They go on to argue that extreme political groups such as the Ku Klux Klan specialize in Utopian attacks on these ambiguities, resulting in a false sense of harmony and consistency. While Lipset and Raab suggest that such paradoxes reflect man's universal condition, they argue that they are especially pronounced in American society. My contention is that life everywhere is contradictory.

The dominant theme of Hatch's work (1973) is that different anthropologists dealing with the same problems have come up with quite divergent interpretations. As Kardiner and Preble (1961: 98) pointed out, 'Spencer glorified isolation and made "individualism" the principle of life and all of nature – organic and inorganic. Durkheim, with the same inheritance, fought isolation and made "social solidarity" the principle of human life.' Given the degree to which contradiction is embedded in our conceptual schemes and social life itself, such contrasting interpretations are not surprising.

Many of the contradictions in the above lists are obviously culture-bound, but I would argue that comparable lists could be made for all cultures if the investigator's knowledge was sufficient. Despite the ubiquity of contradictions and the absence of meaningful criteria to use in choosing between them, people not only choose and act but do so in a consistent, patterned manner. While this is mainly a result of the mechanisms to conceal contradiction, which will be described in the next chapter, the setting itself is important. For example, there is probably more consistency among the choices people make within a particular culture than there is across cultures. Similarly, structural characteristics will impinge upon one's choice, so that when a man is a subordinate, his selection among contradictory values will be different from his selection when he is a superordinate; or a woman will favour one side of a contradiction when in a mother–child relationship and another when in the role of plant manager, worker, or lover. Finally, following Bailey (1977), it is probable that choices between alternative values and norms will vary according to the arena: public or private, front- or backstage. One implication is that the pattern and consistency to which I referred is confined to specific spheres. Because a particular actor is a combination of all the spheres in which he interacts, he is a contradictory creature. In other words, the pattern and consistency that we find in behaviour is a property of man's relation to his setting, and is not intrinsic to the actor's personality.

This brings us to a controversial issue: the nature and meaning of the self. The search for one's true identity, one's real self, becomes especially feverish at the adolescent stage. But as the saying goes, most of us seem to 'find ourselves' as we grow older. This confirms what people generally assume: that there is a real self. After all, we say things such as 'He is beside himself with anger' or 'She is not herself today.' Yet the conclusion that my analysis leads me to is that there is no real self, at least in the sociological sense. A similar view is expressed by Slater (1976: 579): 'Any group, then, is made up, on the one hand, of group functions to be performed and, on the other, of *pieces of people* performing them ... Every group, to an extent, violates the integrity of the individuals who participate in it' (emphasis in original). Bailey, writing about the masks people wear in the university setting (1977: 145), states that for his inquiry 'when all the masks have been stripped away, nothing is left.' He acutely observes that even the 'real person' that people search for beneath the mask is itself a mask, a way of presenting oneself to the world. This notion that the adolescent crisis of self-identity has no solution, that there is no real self, has been beautifully put by Lévi-Strauss (1978: 3–4): 'I never had, and still do not have, the perception of feeling my personal identity. I appear to myself as the place where something is going on, but there is no "I," no "me." Each of us is a kind of crossroads where things happen. The crossroads is purely passive; something happens there. A different thing, equally valid, happens elsewhere. There is no choice, it is just a matter of chance.'

Some people – decidedly few – exhibit rather openly the contradictions by which we all live. As a result, they often are thought to be superficial and perhaps undependable. They may also be more receptive to new ideas and more innovative than the rest of us. At the opposite pole we find the authoritarian personality. That kind of person, As Festinger pointed out (1957: 268), has an exceptionally low tolerance for ambiguity and inconsistency.

Most people, while less extreme than the authoritarian personality type, try to hide the contradictions that are part of their everyday lives. They do so partly by avoiding any changes in their lives that would require the making of decisions; hence the humdrum routine of most people's existences. This explains, I believe, why people are intrigued by those few who seem to live spontaneously, and why we often claim that we ourselves do things on the spur of the moment. It explains why people enthusiastically follow the adventures of the man or woman who risks life and limb to climb a mountain or trek through a jungle. It accounts at least in part for – let us state it – the allure of anthropology to the non-specialist. It explains why we are intrigued by people who change occupations and lifestyles in mid- or late career (changing spouses no longer captures the imagination) or why we are captivated by inconsistency in people: they have come dangerously close to exposing the hodgepodge of contradictions that we all must cover up. Finally, it accounts for the rise we get out of the incongruous, and its importance as a source of humour. For example, several years ago I sat across the table from an elegant lady well into her years and her wine, surrounded by at least one ambassador and several high-ranking university officials. This carefully coiffured lady had us in convulsions as she related the graphic details of her honeymoon at Niagara Falls many years before. Her often repeated line was that she only saw the ceiling. That lady was not playing by the rules: she was breaking the pattern into which we had expected her to behave, and by doing so was bringing us too close to disorder for comfort.

Let us return to where we began: the argument that all behaviour involves choice between contradictory values and norms, but that no meaningful criteria exist to guide our choices. The exception concerns those blatant products of inequality, such as racism or poverty, that emasculate large portions of mankind. The daily lives of most of us revolve around more mundane issues. Rarely are we gripped by grandeur, by earth-shaking events, either terrible or wonderful. When I consider the smaller issues that characterize our daily behaviour, discussions over course content or visiting speakers in a departmental meeting, arguments between spouses on how to bring up their children, or bombastic debates at the local pub, I arrive at one conclusion: rarely is there a single defensible answer to an argument; the best we can hope to do is to articulate with some humility and humour the polar positions.

8

Neutralizing Mechanisms

Social life is cluttered with contradictions, but it also is patterned and consistent, or at least appears that way. How can this be explained? Numerous mechanisms conceal and neutralize contradiction, and in this way add to the complexity of the social realm. The main mechanism is the role of the power élite. In order to elucidate its role, a fresh definition of power will be introduced: power as the imposition of stability. I shall begin by discussing several relevant mechanisms, and then turn to the power élite.

BASIC MECHANISMS

1 *Man's felt need for control, order, and predictability.* Although man is an achievement-oriented animal, he is also a seeker of stability and thus inherently conservative. That explains in part why contradictions get pushed to one side and myths of unambiguous moral positions and harmony become dominant. In chapter 5 I drew a parallel between the impulse for order and consistency in primitive thought and in anthropological theory. What is striking about anthropologists is their preoccupation with order, their uneasiness in the face of inconsistency and apparent chaos. Perhaps because most laymen do not consciously force their thoughts to dwell on the disorderly and the unknown, they are marginally less disturbed by them. But if there is a difference, it is only a matter of degree. As Festinger argues regarding cognitive dissonance (1957: 260), there is an incessant drive to reduce the dissonance, to achieve harmony, consistency, and congruity.

2 *Sheer habit and convention.* The weight of tradition to some extent nullifies the necessity for choice, and conceals from the actor the existence of contradictions. As is often said, norms or rules exist so that one doesn't

have to resolve every mundane issue over and over again. Lynd (1964: 55) remarks that daily living would be impossible if one had to 'stop each moment to scrutinize every word, concept, symbol or other institutionalized device.' Slater (1976: 580) has written, 'To be utterly unroutinized, so that every act and motion of every day involved a new decision, would be a burdensome freedom, indeed.' A similar argument was made long ago by Durkheim (1961). Discipline, he explained, gives order and meaning to life. Morality, which has all the properties of a social fact, has the function of creating order and conserving our energies by not making us solve the same old problems day after day. Morality, or the normative order, determines the pattern of conduct and limits individual arbitrariness.

Tradition and habitual thought and action also were central to Boas's framework, and Marx, in a quite different context, wrote, 'The tradition of all the dead generations weighs like a nightmare on the brain of the living' (Selsam et al., 1973). People cling to the old ways. This is partly why force and revolution are necessary, for only in that way will the muck of ages be removed from the minds of men. The other reason is obvious: power can be obtained in no other manner. It may be thought that Weber's emphasis on the increasing rationalization of the world puts him into a different camp. But it was Weber who also focused on tradition as one of the three main ideal types of authority, and pointed out that even in the most developed bureaucracies, the charismatic people at the top are not appointed officials. Giddens (1979: 217) has stressed the recursive nature of social life, the degree to which it is guided by habit. As he points out, to the degree that behaviour does rest upon habit and convention, it is relatively unmotivated; it is not the product of the actor's conscious choice. To the extent that behaviour does not involve choice, it avoids a confrontation with contradiction, at least from the actor's perspective.

3 *The illusion of simplicity.* Academics specialize in the art of abstraction and simplification. People in general need to employ these tools if they want to retain their sanity. The wide range of contradiction that faces them is unacceptable, and in its place a simplified image of the world is carried around in their heads. There is, for example, one 'real' religion, one 'proper' way to bring up children, and a 'true' side to every argument, debate, feud, or war. In this context, Lévi-Strauss's concept of conscious models is relevant: they simplify, falsify, and obscure the contradictions embedded in social life. As Murphy (1971: 110) neatly put it, 'The conscious model patches up the untidiness of society and produces the appearance of order.' Let me stress that the professional scholar is little different from the ordinary citizen in

this regard. Indeed, my belief is that a major flaw in anthropological investigations has been the illusion that society is simple, about which I shall say much more in the next chapter.

4 *Man as rationalizer.* There appears to be a universal process by which man accommodates chaos, unpredictable outcomes, failure, and the inability to match achievement with aspiration; that process is man's proclivity to rationalize, to rebuild experience along lines acceptable to him, or at least not totally unacceptable. For example, many ethnic groups in West Africa believe in 'repeater children' such as the Igbo *ogbanje*, who supposedly die and are born over and over again. This is an obvious way of rationalizing, and thus accommodating, the high infant-mortality rate. So powerful is the rationalizing process that we often find cases where that which has to be explained away becomes the preferred state of affairs; for example, the tendency of the poorest people to support conservative political parties, or of impoverished 'natives' to express gratitude for the benefits brought to them by the colonial regimes.

Relevant here is Evans-Pritchard's (1937) brilliant analysis of 'secondary elaborations.' This is a process, associated, for example, with the diviner's craft, in which failures are excused in such a way that the belief system itself is not undermined. Anthropologists seem to think that secondary elaboration is basically a characteristic of pre-industrial societies, but this is wrong. It occurs in all societies, and is conceptually similar to Festinger's theory of cognitive dissonance. Every intelligent salesperson must not only fear the client's dissonance that accompanies a major purchase – let us call it buyer's remorse – but also must take solace in the knowledge that the client will reason it all out: the old car, after all, was on its last legs; the new one is safe and reliable, just what was needed.

In a similar vein, Slater (1976: 590–1) asks, 'How many individuals have retained a fervent loyalty to fraternities simply out of an unwillingness to face the absurdity of their having undergone humiliation, ridicule, degradation, and discomfort for very little reason? How many have become doctors, lawyers, or professors rather than admit that tedious learning, boring information, and difficult examinations were a waste of time? How many wars have been expanded in order to impart meaning to the deaths of soldiers?' These are good questions, and remind me of others. For example, how many PHD candidates who despised their teachers, or at least were uninspired by them, speak glowingly of the same professors and departments after graduation? I personally know of several cases, involving (perhaps not accidentally) some of the most prestigious institutions in Britain and North

America. The reason for the shift in judgment is not difficult to fathom. One can't very well broadcast the light-weight quality of one's degree. The same tendency to fictionalize one's experience occurs in field-work. How often have frustrated anthropologists complained in private that they will never master the ridiculous language of tribe x, and yet reported the contrary in their publications?

5 *The role of ritual.* The purpose of ritual is to smooth over contradiction and to elevate acts into the realm of moral sanctity, to render them as ends not subject to evaluation. Geertz (1957) and Leach (1965) paint quite a different picture. Geertz describes a funeral in Java which was a source of considerable strain to the community involved. He goes on to explain that this strain was due to a lack of fit between cultural beliefs and social organization, and concluded that the failure to distinguish those two levels is at the root of the inability to cope with social change. Leach, beginning with an equation of myth and ritual, contends that these can be mechanisms of disruption, reflecting the strain in actual behaviour. By pointing out that rituals sometimes can generate conflict, these authors appear to have disproved my essentially Durkheimian position. But that is not the case. Rituals indeed can be disruptive, but that is their effect, not their raison d'être. My argument is that from the perspective of the actor, ritual is always *intended* to be positive. Whether or not the intent and the actual outcome are the same is quite a different matter, and can only be determined by a close examination of each case.

For example, every January the Holy Apostles of Olowo celebrated Founder's Day, which they referred to as Christmas. I had been told about Founder's Day shortly after beginning field-work in Olowo in 1969, although the celebration was still six months away. Members frequently described it as a marvellous occasion. Sometimes when I was with a fisherman or carpenter who was relaxing after a hard day's work, he would suddenly talk enthusiastically about the coming Founder's Day. About a month before the grand event, concrete plans were made. Houses were painted, boardwalks repaired, new clothes purchased for all members, and a grandstand erected on a field that had been cleared by hundreds of workers. The actual ceremony lasted two days. On the first day there was a sermon in the church, and a dance on the field at night to the live music of a famous Nigerian band. The major event on the following day was a march around the village by almost the entire population, all of whom were decked out in new clothes. The 1970 Founder's Day celebration was a definite success. While people were not especially gay – perhaps they had worked too hard to prepare for the event – they were pleased, and with good reason. The village glowed with prosperity, and everywhere there were signs of technical expertise. The ceremonies were well organized, and the Apostles' bond to a common cause was reaffirmed as they relived the harsh events that led to the establishment of Olowo in 1947. By 1972 private enterprise had partly replaced the communal system. The Founder's Day ceremony that year was a dull affair. Community funds to finance the ceremony were no longer available, and the leaders no longer could demand the same amount of unpaid labour. By 1974 private enterprise had almost totally replaced communalism, and the village had split into rich people and poor people. The celebration that year was a disaster. The display of wealth by the *oba* and other members of the élite clashed with the poverty of the majority of members. Most of the educated youth boycotted the ceremony in order to express their hostility. Rather than uniting the Apostles, the annual celebration had split the community into two hostile sections: those who supported the élite, and those opposed to its growing wealth.

Ritual and contradiction cannot consciously coexist. When ritual is prominent, contradiction will be deeply disguised; when it is not disguised, behaviour is by definition considered to be abnormal and treacherous. A good example concerns graduation ceremonies. University students taking part in them are supposed to be euphoric, or at least somewhat pleased, and often they are momentarily moved by the sacred occasion. But in the 1960s contradictions often forced their way to the forefront: university as the fulcrum of rational discourse and the advancement of man versus research funded by a military establishment bent on devastating Vietnam. Students often refused to play their part. They tore up their diplomas on the graduation stage. By such acts, ritual was denied.

6 *The role of ideology.* Ideology belongs to the cultural realm, and one of the most important characteristics of this realm is that it is orderly, tidy, and patterned. Ideology settles like a net over the chaos of actual behaviour, pulling it into some semblance of a recognizable shape. This mechanism is one of the resources at the disposal of the power élite, since it is more or less consciously employed to render the masses inert. It is usually considered the anthropologist's task to demonstrate patterns or correlations in apparent chaos. However, perhaps we should try to discover underlying patterns at the behavioural level and underlying chaos at the cultural level. In other words, one part of the anthropologist's job is to dismantle pattern, not demonstrate it.

7 *Systematic nature of society.* Parsons' view (1951) of society as composed of functionally interdependent subsystems has been shared by most anthropologists. Depending on one's politics, this either reflects the pervasive but unfortunate influence of structural functionalism, or reinforces Davis's argument (1959) that functional analysis and sociological analysis are one and the same thing. The Protestant ethic, for example, is said to be compatible with the spirit of capitalism. The nuclear family fits the requirements of an industrial society. Even in nations where development has not followed the Western model, such as Japan, functional interdependence is supposedly at work. For example, the Bushido ethic (see Bellah 1957) is a functional equivalent of the Protestant ethic, and the Japanese stem family is a microcosm of the polity, characterized by loyalty and obedience, all of which are necessary for an industrializing strategy organized by the state.

Yet there is another side to the story, an argument that the systemic nature of society has been greatly exaggerated. Fanfani (1967) contended that if Protestantism facilitated the emergence of capitalism in any way, it was by divorcing the two realms, so that capitalism would not be impeded. We now know that the long-accepted hypotheses that the extended family retards development and that the nuclear family must follow it are erroneous (see Barrett 1974: 96–106). The contradictory demands of individual status mobility and economic success versus family responsibility, of universal tolerance and compassion towards one's fellow man versus the dog-eat-dog syndrome of the marketplace, cast doubt on the neat interdependence of the institutions of society. The functionally interdependent subsystem is a first cousin of the over-socialized conception of man. All that can legitimately be claimed is that the subsystems of society are interrelated to such a degree that they provide at least a weak brake on the range of non-patterned behaviour and potential subsystem variability. As a result, the scope of man's contradictory nature is reduced.

POWER AS THE IMPOSITION OF STABILITY

We arrive now at what is probably the most important of the several mechanisms that neutralize contradiction and provide social life with a patterned appearance: the role of the power élite and the weight of the power structure on social relations.[1] The conventional definition of power, following

---

1 To mount this argument, it will be necessary at times to draw on the sociological literature, which is much richer than that of anthropology in terms of the analysis of power. This exposes a gap in anthropology that must be filled in the years ahead.

Weber, is the capacity of A to impose his will on B, even against B's resistance. Weber distinguished between power and authority, the latter being formal, institutionalized, or legitimate power. This notion of power usually connotes change: B is forced to act in a way he otherwise would not have done, to do something against his will, to modify his behaviour in accordance with A's wishes. On a grand scale Hitler had power in this respect, as did Napoleon, and Marx's revolutions are results of power struggles.

I do not deny that power often does bring about change; this book itself is an attempt to persuade other anthropologists to adopt a new conception of the discipline. However, there is another side to power that usually has been overlooked: its capacity to impose stability, to maintain the status quo. The reigning élite almost always has a vested interest in the status quo; it also has a monopoly over the instruments to secure stability, from outright force to ideologically induced consent. To go back to Weber, power can be redefined as the capacity of A to force B to act as he has always acted or to change his ways, even against his will. My focus will be on power as the imposition of stability, not only because this perspective has been neglected by anthropologists, but also because stability is as frequently the consequence of the exercise of power as is change, and possibly more so.

Two further distinctions are necessary: that between force and consent, and that between intentional and unintentional use of power. Force and consent are at the opposite poles of the resources available to the power élite to maintain its position of superiority. As Gramsci has indicated (Merrington 1968), force is resorted to as the principal means of social control only in times of crisis; usually force and consent operate in unison to assure the persistence of a social formation. Similarly, Lenin (Selsam et al. 1973: 363–4) referred to force and liberalism as two tactics used by the ruling class. Lenin observes that those tactics oscillate back and forth according to the requirements of the bourgeoisie, and argues that such oscillation has been peculiar to European countries since about 1850. Yet an almost perfect example of these two faces of social control was provided by my own research in Olowo (see Barrett 1979b). By the mid-1970s, this Nigerian Utopia had entered its third distinctive stage of stratification. The first was the communal era, lasting from 1948 to 1968. During that period there were only minimal differences in wealth, but a small number of men, led by the *oba*, ruled the community with an iron hand. The second stage corresponded with the appearance of private enterprise, roughly from 1968 to 1973. During that period significant differences in wealth emerged, and the higher a person's status before the introduction of private enterprise, the more probable it was that the person had become wealthy. This was a result of many factors, not least of which was the élite's control of the community treasury. The third stage began toward the end of 1973. Before then Olowo's élite had consisted of the elders (who as young men had founded the community and enjoyed the reputation of being the most gifted prophets) and what might be termed the new technocrats: the oba and his loyal supporters, most of whom were no older than forty and had been trained to run the village's industries. During the transition from communalism to capitalism, the oba had wooed the old élite with gifts such as electric fans and motorcycles. By 1974 the transition from communalism to private enterprise was virtually complete. In the process the new élite had successfully claimed most of the village's assets for itself, and the old élite was set adrift, no longer powerful and on the verge of poverty.

Corresponding to these three stages of stratification were three distinct phases of social control. During the communal period, normative control operated. Although the village was governed by a handful of powerful prophets, they supposedly expressed the collective will of the Apostles. The leaders were obeyed because they were able to communicate with God. Religious values, especially belief in immortality, were prominent, and disobedience and laziness were defined as sins. During the next stage, when private enterprise began to replace the communal system, repressive control emerged. Flogging became more widespread, an expulsion was not uncommon. Several new groups with functions strictly confined to social control were established. At the same time religion faded into the background. Services were held less frequently, and the previous signs of religious activity outside the church, such as hymn-singing along the boardwalks, all but disappeared. The third stage of social control followed the new élite's successful consolidation of its wealth. It was marked by a return to normative control. Flogging was reduced, expulsion no longer occurred, and religious activity enjoyed a new-found prominence. People were free to leave and re-enter the community as they wished, to choose their own line of work, to spend their money as they wanted. Olowo, in other words, had entered the era of liberalism, but by then it was too late for most of the Apostles, for the wealth had been cornered by the men at the top. It was not accidental that the repressive phase lasted only a short time. As Gramsci has observed, the resort to force is a sign of great weakness. To prolong it is dangerous. Much more effective is the show of liberal policies, the granting of concessions, and the parade of shared norms and values.

The distinction between the conscious, purposeful use of power and its unintentional, non-deliberate use is important. The intentional use of power to maintain a system of inequality is the more obvious of the two. A case in point is colonialism. The first rumblings of revolt in countries like Kenya and Ghana were smothered by the colonial armies. It may be objected that independence eventually was granted. True enough, but with it emerged neo-colonialism, which in the circumstances was a less expensive means to achieve (at least partly) the same objectives: raw materials, and markets for first world products. In some countries, such as the Ivory Coast, there has been little attempt to conceal the power and influence of the 'mother' country. Incredibly, the expatriate population, rather than decreasing after formal independence in 1960, more than doubled in the following decade (Amin 1967). Much has been made of the Ivory Coast's remarkable economic success, which has been achieved by its policies of private enterprise and its open-door policy to foreign investors and expertise. It is also the one West African country that has advocated dialogue with South Africa.

Any situation in which force is used reflects the intentional use of power, and examples ranging from Vietnam to the disruption of student protests are easy to come by. Perhaps a less apparent example concerns university departments. The trend in recent years, at least in North America, is to appoint as chairmen not the leading scholars, but instead persons who express the administration's will. Let me hasten to add that I personally know of some notable exceptions, especially among women. Motivated by factors not shared by men but created by them, the most gifted female scholars may be more willing to accept administrative duty than the males, although this willingness may be dwindling down along with the women's movement. At its best, the position of chairman is similar to that of the village headman. In recent years it has become even more difficult. The chairman today gets few perks, and often lacks the scholarly credentials to command respect as well as the formal capacity to impose his or her will, especially in those institutions still affected by the democratic reforms of the student rebellion; sometimes the chairman must bear the brunt of the anger of both faculty and students, while at the same time reassuring the dean. The fact that there appears to be no shortage of candidates eager for the job illustrates the seductive lure of power. As Wrong (1959) has observed about stratification, the differential rewards required to induce motivation need not be great.

Before moving on to the unintentional use of force, I must refer to a distinction made by Bachrach and Baratz between decisions and non-decisions. Their central argument (1962 and 1963) is that power is not restricted to situations in which decisions are made; power is not entirely reflected in the debates and confrontations between interest groups. This is because those in positions of authority with a vested interest in the status quo, or simply in advancing their own interests, are often able to restrict the scope of decision-making to issues that do not threaten them. For example, in a southern U.S. community, the issue of whether blacks should be allowed to attend a white school could almost indefinitely be kept off the agenda by the mayor.

As prevalent as the deliberate application of power may be both in terms of decision-making and preventing decision-making, it is not the only kind. Equally effective is the weight of the existing institutions of society. Independent of the actor's conscious volition, they press behaviour into a particular mode and reproduce the conditions that perpetuate them. While some support for this argument is provided by Godelier (1970: 350), one must look beyond the anthropological fold for similar views. In a paper that deserves wider circulation, Baldus (1975: 180) defined power as 'the capacity to maintain and produce a given pattern of structured social inequality over time.' Lukes (1974: 38) adopts a similar position, relating power to 'the sheer weight of institutions' independent of the activity or conscious will of leaders. Lukes is particularly concerned to point out the limitations of the approach of Bachrach and Baratz, to whom power is voluntaristic rather than structural. Giddens (1979) agrees with Lukes's criticism of Bachrach and Baratz for failing to move beyond the boundaries of motivation: non-decisions, those that are excluded from the arena of discourse and debate, are as intentional and purposeful as decisions. Giddens also criticizes Lukes for failing to achieve what he advocated: a structural approach to power, in which a social system is sustained by the weight of its institutions. What is required, according to Giddens (1979: 91) is a combination of two perspectives: the subjective view of power, stressing A's capacity to modify B's actions, and the structural view, stressing the capability of a social system to reproduce itself via the mobilization of bias, habit, and tradition.

There are many similarities between my approach to power and Giddens's approach, and he points out some of the ways in which ideology contributes to the maintenance of stability. One is to portray sectional interests as universal interests (Giddens 1979: 193). A strike-free labour force, for example, might be passed off by the bourgeoisie as a requisite for a country's survival or for the prosperity of everyone, workers included. A second effect of ideology is the denial of contradictions. As Giddens (1979: 194) states, 'It is normally in the interests of dominant groups if the existence of contradictions is denied or their real locus is obscured.' He refers to a third achievement of ideology as the naturalization of the present (1979: 195). Simply put, the status quo is portrayed as immutable, as God's way, rooted in nature, for the obvious benefit of dominant groups.

It may be thought that Weber anticipated this line of analysis with his emphasis on traditional authority. Not only does this type of formal power reinforce the status quo, but it is largely unintentional, the result of immemorial custom. However, traditional authority is somewhat of an anomaly in Weber's work. His general emphasis was on social change. Charismatic and legal–rational authority were intrinsically connected to the transformation of society, and commanded most of Weber's attention. Moreover, all sociologically meaningful behaviour for Weber is intentional: A takes into account the behaviour of B and modifies his conduct accordingly; subjectively meaningful social interaction has causal consequences. The notion of the sheer weight of institutions on the actor, independent of his motivation, is foreign to Weber's social-action program, although not necessarily to his macro-institutional comparative investigations.

Weber may not fit into this approach to power and inequality, but surely Marx does. After all, it is to Marx that we turn to understand the manner in which ideology reflects and reinforces existing social relations of inequality. Religion is the opiate of the people; the legal institution is mistaken for an a priori reality rather than a reflex of underlying economic relations; both the capitalist and the worker think that wages are payment for work, but part of that work is unpaid, and in Marxian terms constitutes the secret of capitalism: surplus value; the ideas of the ruling class are the ruling ideas; the class that is the dominant material force is also the dominant intellectual force; or, following Gramsci (see Merrington 1968), intellectuals are experts in legitimation – they render the ruling class's position of superiority acceptable to the rest of society. The implication is that Marx did indeed provide the foundation for explaining how existing social relations of inequality are maintained. Yet his dominant concern, like Weber's, was social change. It was Marx who said that no social order ever disappears before all its potential productive forces have been developed. But he also stated that the new relations of production take seed and grow in the womb of the old social formation. Recall that every social system contains the seeds of its own destruction, or the clash between the forces and relations of production. That, and not stability, is the essence of Marxism. Once more, Marx's problem may have been his optimism, the influence of the pervasive nineteenth-century notion of progress. Writing in the last quarter of the twentieth century, I am much more impressed by the tenacity of systems of inequality, by the capacity of societies to deny change. The revolutionary force of ascending classes is nipped in the bud. Today the basic contradiction does not seem to be between the nascent class of workers and the owners of the means of production, but between the developed and underdeveloped countries, between the First (plus the Second?) and the Third Worlds. This is a clash between white and black society, and thus involves racism. For historical reasons, anthropology more than any other discipline is caught up by this dilemma, which is at once the source of its current plight and its potential revitalization, providing that it rises to the challenge.

My analysis of power as the imposition of stability places me close to Parsons and other functionalists in some senses. For example, I agree that long-term equilibrium runs do characterize social systems. But this is not because of any propensity of the social system toward consistency, or any underlying need for consensus and harmony. Instead, it is a result of differential power, both in its deliberate application and in the sheer 'bias of mobilization' that is part and parcel of any institutional framework. Surely there cannot be many sociologists who still accept Parsons' view that power is a resource for the general good, resulting in stability and cohesion and explaining why compliance and consensus are freely offered by the masses.

I must also stress, especially in light of my argument, that I accept the existence of two fundamental types of change: revolutionary and gradual piecemeal change, or qualitative versus quantitative change. Qualitative change implies the transformation of an entire system. This would seem to be a clear definition; for example, surely the replacement of feudalism by capitalism was a revolutionary change. Yet some writers, such as Marcuse (1971: 177), argue that revolutions can occur in which one system of domination simply replaces another; that is not qualitative change. Furthermore, perhaps because the superstructure in advanced developed societies is so elaborate, or maybe owing simply to the enormous range of instruments of force and influence – armaments, military police, welfare agencies – we are stuck with what we have; revolution is a luxury of the past. The other type of change, gradual piecemeal change, always occurs, for society is never static. The recognition of this in no way detracts from the argument that a major consequence of differential power is the imposition of stability, the maintenance of the status quo. Piecemeal change is absorbed by the power structure without posing a threat to it. For example, it is sometimes contended that Western international conglomerates that operate and invest in South Africa are instruments of social change that will bring about the end of apartheid by granting blacks better wages and living conditions. That argument is baseless. Any changes brought about by such improvements are readily absorbed by the power structure of South Africa. Indeed, such concessions probably will prolong, not abbreviate, apartheid.

MOCK CHANGE

A subtle variation on the theme of the imposition of stability can be called 'mock change.' 'Change' here carries with it the connotation of progress and improvement. Mock change takes two principal forms. In one, what has the appearance of change is not change at all; groups that were dominant before the change remain dominant after it. The other type concerns programs set up to improve conditions and to redress grievances, but which in reality never were meant to be effective. What they are is clear: safety valves that siphon off strain and buy time for those who benefit from oppression and suffering. There is a close parallel between salvage theory, as discussed in chapter 4, and mock change. Both are 'mock', one in the realm of theory and the other in the realm of behaviour.

One example of the first type of mock change was the transformation of Olowo from a communal to a private-enterprise society. The impetus for this change came from the mass of followers in Olowo, not from the leaders of the community. People had begun to complain that they worked too hard without sufficient personal reward. They demanded more luxuries and more choice in how they lived. Faced with these demands, the third *oba* decided that a radical change had to be made, one that would result in the renewed work-motivation of the Apostles. This led to the introduction of private enterprise. Ironically, it was the élite rather than ordinary members who benefited mostly from the change. High-status members became wealthy, while other members sank into impoverishment as previous community benefits such as free clothing and food were withdrawn.

Corsica provides a second example. For most of its known history, Corsica has been controlled by external powers, including the Greeks, the Vandals, the Moors, the Genoese, and now the French. Independence movements have almost been incessant, and continue today. But following each successful attempt to throw out an alien power, a new foreign power has taken its place. Paoli, the hero of Corsican independence, succeeded in winning the support of the British in his efforts to oust the French partly through the intercession of Boswell. Britain then briefly took over the island for itself. The era of Genoese rule from the thirteenth to the eighteenth centuries was extremely harsh, and it may be argued that Corsicans enjoy a better life as citizens in a French département. Nevertheless, Corsica remains ruled by an outside power, and in that respect nothing has changed for several centuries. It seems that foreign domination is usually facilitated by the implicit cooperation of the indigenous élite. It may be significant that many of the names of the most prominent families in Corsica three or four centuries ago are the names that dominate the social, economic, and political spheres today.

Olowo and Corsica reflect the first type of mock change. An example of the second type concerns Canadian native people. In a wide-ranging paper, Mortimore (1978) argues that the normal process of bureaucracies is to maintain themselves at the expense of their clients. He describes the techniques used by the Canadian government to keep native peoples under control. One of the main techniques is to tranquillize them: requests to the government are answered in incomprehensible jargon; troublemakers are cooled out by denying them privileges guaranteed by law and making them return time after time before they are allowed to see a government official. Governmental programs set up to instil a sense of independence and self-reliance among native peoples are discontinued just when it appears that they might be successful (Mortimore, personal communication 1980). The government makes a show of consulting with native peoples, thus putting them momentarily off guard, but introduces legislation exactly the opposite of what was requested by native peoples.

Similar examples of 'consultation' and 'ameliorative programs' are easy to come by. A few years ago, the Ontario government established the Ontario Human Rights Commission. While its mandate covers all human-rights issues, in recent years the commission has had to grapple particularly with growing racism in Toronto and other centres. Yet the reaction of many spokesmen for minority ethnic groups is that the commission is a smoke-screen, a mechanism that tranquillizes the population by appearing to be tackling racism and other issues. People point out that their complaints take forever to be heard, and that little is done in the end to redress the complainant's grievance. Recently one of the most effective and outspoken members of the commission was removed, which confirmed the suspicion of many that the commission was so much window-dressing.

Unions are another example. Engels remarked that trade unions formed an aristocracy within the working class (Selsam et al. 1973: 370). Gramsci (Merrington 1968: 158) described unions as part of capitalist society, not as opposition to it. Similarly, Lenin observed that every imperialist country has its bourgeois labour party (Selsam et al. 1973: 373). Like unions, the labour parties may appear to side with the producer, the working man, but in reality they form an integral part of the capitalist system and contribute to its sustenance.

Finally, we turn to an example that reflects both types of mock change: racism and the black movement in America. Nowhere is there a better example of change without change, as reflected in the following quotation from Piven and Cloward (1979: 184): 'No group in American society has been as subjected to the extremes of economic exploitation as blacks. Each change in their relationship to the economic system has mainly represented a shift from one form of extreme economic subjugation to another: from slaves to cash tenants and sharecroppers; from cash tenants and sharecroppers to the lowest stratum in an emerging southern rural free labor system; and finally, to the status of an urban proletariat characterized by low wages and high unemployment. In effect, the black poor have progressed from slave labor to cheap labor to (for many) no labor at all.' Marx commented that slavery itself was a great step forward, for people were kept as workers rather than killed, and some readers might see a shadow of progress in the changing relations of blacks to the means of production. If so, it is marginal progress only.

The other type of mock change is also closely connected to blacks. Several years ago a great deal of money and publicity was poured into a program in the United States to reduce unemployment among black youth. Yet recent studies have shown that during the last decade, black employment has decreased, not increased. The occupational status of blacks in the second half of the twentieth century is the same as it was at the beginning of the century. Since 1950, the absolute income gap between white and black American men has actually doubled (see Reich 1971: 108). A similar (and widening) gap exists with respect to higher education (see Prager 1972: 142). Piven and Cloward (1975: 4) argue that the failure of welfare programs aimed at blacks was not due to poor management or other such reasons; it was a result of deliberate policy. The welfare bureaucracies, they claim, were intended to help the powerful, not the poor. Like Mortimore, they conclude that public bureaucracies chiefly strive to assure their own stability and growth.

Piven and Cloward (1972) tried to explain why welfare oscillates between expansion and contraction. They found that relief-giving agencies supported U.S. economic and political institutions. When mass unemployment leads to turmoil, relief programs are expanded to nip rebellion in the bud and restore order. When harmony is achieved, welfare programs are reduced; those who remain on the rolls are insulted and degraded, so that people who have any kind of job at all, no matter what the wages, will count themselves lucky. Marx had foreseen the up-and-down business cycles in capitalism, the periods of expansion and periods of inflation and shortage. The welfare program, as Piven and Cloward have indicated, is one of the solutions that lubricates this cycle. With little imagination, other examples could be given.

Those knowledgeable about the women's movement tell me that in terms of mock-change programs it is a perfect parallel to the black movement. Aid programs to Third World countries also fit into this analysis. Who now believes that governmental loans and aid benefit the poor in Third World countries rather than their new bourgeoisie and the donor countries themselves? Incredibly, as O'Connor has reported (1970: 119), in 1963 Liberia spent 94 per cent of its annual revenues simply to repay foreign loans. The point, I believe, has been made: if governments and bureaucracies are good at anything, it is tranquillizing people with a dosage of apparent improvements.

CONCLUSION

Man is achievement-oriented,[2] a striver who seeks progress and thus is prone to change; yet he has a basic need for order, stability, and predictability. A large part of the anthropologist's task is to understand the consequences of this tension, and especially how it is manipulated by actors seeking to dominate others. For if there is one single mechanism that cannot be ignored in attempting to understand how behaviour, rent with contradictions, is given order and pattern, it is the ubiquitous play of power. Power can be exercised consciously or unconsciously, deliberately or non-deliberately, can be latent or manifest, can involve change or stability, and can range from force to legitimate authority and from repression to concession.

Although the main mechanisms that neutralize and conceal the contradictory nature of social life have been described, several others play a less direct and pronounced role. For example, Malinowski indicated how magic is resorted to in times of strain or when the outcome of actions is not pre-

2 One can make this basic assumption about mankind without being ethnocentric if a distinction is drawn between achievement motivation and achievement orientation. The former is a psychological property, the latter a sociological one. McClelland's need-to-achieve thesis (1961) was addressed to achievement motivation; I have little sympathy with it, because it *is* ethnocentric: actors with high levels of need to achieve supposedly will become economic entrepreneurs, regardless of the society. But as Kahl (1964–5) and Scanzoni (1967) pointed out several years ago, achievement orientation is culturally diverse: achievement goals will vary from culture to culture. I would argue that even the Hindu emphasis on duty and obedience in this world, which results in a static society, does not constitute an exception. Hindus act in accordance with these values in order to realize a higher form of reincarnation in the next life; they are, in other words, achievement-oriented. What is significant is the cultural idiom. Of course, a different question is whether Hindus actually behave in accordance with these values. For a suggestion that they do not, see Bailey (1969: 182).

dictable, such as in offshore fishing or planting the annual yam crop. In these situations, magic generates a sense of control. The anthropological literature is rich in examples of mechanisms around the world that neutralize strain and make social life possible: the incest taboo and the exchange of consanguines for affines, resulting in social solidarity; widespread grandparent terminology, to capitalize on the harmonious relations between alternate generations; godparents, an important means of extending familial obligations in Mediterranean communities and elsewhere; institutionalized best-friendships, such as those based on the ceremonial exchange of umbilical cords between potentially hostile groups among the Adamanese; institutionalized joking relationships; humour in general to nip deviance and strain in the bud; Sunday-afternoon drinking and fighting in central Europe, an institutionalized outlet for aggression and hostility described by Malinowski (1941: 532); Hallowe'en, Carnival, Guy Fawkes Day, and other periodic celebrations of unlicensed behaviour which act as safety valves; myths of common origin; the Igbo chalk bowl, permitting strangers to safely visit or pass through foreign Igbo territory without fear of attack; artificial kinship and rituals (*prostavacka* and *babari*) In Yugoslavia (see Balikci 1965); geographical mobility and physical isolation to avoid fighting between hostile groups such as the Tamil and Singhalese (see Malinowski 1941); social distance generated by wide stratification; witchcraft as a rationalization for misfortune and a mechanism to recast hostilities between people to a non-material level; the exchange and solidarity produced by the Trobriand *kula* ring; recognized equivalence between blood and money, so that feuds can be terminated without taking further lives; the use of non-lethal weapons when fighting occurs within a social group, and lethal weapons when fighting different social groups (see Evans-Pritchard on the Nuer, 1940: 151, and Peters on the Bedouin, 1967: 269); and the use of external conflict to create internal solidarity, such as a staged battle between Olowo and its neighbours, cleverly organized by the third *oba* to bring his subjects into line during the transition from communalism to capitalism.

To the extent that these several mechanisms contribute to social solidarity and harmonious, recurrent relationships, they also conceal and neutralize contradiction. Yet as the Olowo example of external conflict suggests, not everyone benefits to the same degree; harmony is the dream of every person occupying one of the best seats in the house.

The implication is that the majority of people must suffer from stability, excepting (at least theoretically) instances where Marx's dictatorship of the proletariat has been attained. This is probably correct in terms of man's motivation to achieve, to strive for better things. But it is not necessarily so in terms of his need for order and regularity. This latter need, significantly, is partly fulfilled by the élite's capacity to impose stability. Yet the need itself may be fostered by the power élite in order to realize its own ends. To the extent that this is correct, stability is detrimental for the majority of people in terms of both their achievement drive and their search for security. Once more we are led to the view of complex social life. We also can appreciate the advantages that accrue to people in the upper echelons of a stable society. They enjoy a double benefit: like other people, they have security; unlike others, they also have wealth and power.

9

The Illusion of Simplicity

DEFINING COMPLEXITY

The interplay between the contradictory nature of social life and the mechanisms that conceal it indicates the vast complexity in the midst of which our lives unfold. Curiously, laymen and undergraduates first introduced to the discipline may be less surprised by this image of a complex world than my fellow anthropologists. Both laymen and practising anthropologists are exposed to the mystifying mechanisms described in the previous chapter. But anthropologists are subject to an additional influence: they spend their lives trying to prove that order exists. This partly accounts for their tendency to over-simplify the cultural realm. This mistake is not restricted to anthropologists or to their analysis of primitive society. It is probably intrinsically related to the attempt to establish a positivistic science of society.[1] Some of

---

1 Certainly I do not mean to suggest that anthropology has been any less successful than other social sciences. The reputation enjoyed by anthropology regarding the relative quality of its data has been well-deserved. What I do want to argue is that all social sciences have underestimated the degree of complexity of society. By conceptualizing social life as complex and contradictory, a new challenge has been laid down. Even the sophisticated and imaginative scholars – Verdon (1981) is an example – among those who take a position directly opposed to the one in this book, and argue that we can move beyond Radcliffe-Brown and attain nomothetic, scientific status, are perfectly aware of the complexity of social life and the difficulty in gathering valid data. They attempt to conceptualize the anthropological domain in a manner that pushes the fortuitous and the infinitely variable to one side, that slips through the shale and hits bedrock below. However, by locating the fortuitous and infinitely variable outside the parameters of the discipline, some of the central features of social life are excluded from investigation. Moreover, the consistent argument in this study is that there is no bedrock, and just when one thinks it has been located, an earthquake shifts it elsewhere, or it crumbles before one's eyes, like the naïve positivist's hallowed image of society.

the most trenchant critiques of sociology by members of that discipline, such as Phillips's essay (1971), have been inspired by the vision of a more complex world. The view of primitive society as simple was fostered by early evolutionism in order to support the theory of progressively complex stages, and by Radcliffe-Brown's focus on isolated social systems, splendidly free from external complicating influences.[2]

Many years ago Lynd (1964: 57) wrote, 'All cultures, even those of the so-called "simpler," "primitive" peoples, are more complex than we are wont to conceive them to be.' Similar criticisms have been made by anthropologists. Van Gennep (see Honigmann 1976: 165) remarked that primitive society was not clearly as simple as the evolutionists had claimed. In a devastating attack on the equation of simplicity and primitive culture, Bascom (1948) documented the tremendous complexity of West African cultures, citing the elaborate political structures of the Ashanti, Yoruba, and Benin kingdoms; the myriad kinship systems, including thirteen forms of marriage among the Dahomey; the more than 400 deities of the Yoruba, who also possess over 5,000 folktales and countless myths, riddles, proverbs, and praise names. A few years later, Leach's influential study entitled *Political Systems of Highland Burma* appeared, where the idea of simple society was again attacked. Leach claimed (1965: 290–1) that the tribes described by anthropologists were 'ethnographic fictions.' In other words, 'tribes' were artificially created or bounded off by anthropologists in order to give the appearance of order and discreteness upon which analysis depended. With criticisms such as these, one would think that the notion of simple societies would have been dropped like a hot potato. Yet it persisted even after anthropologists had made the major adjustment within the discipline following the Second World War and the end of formal colonialism – the emerging emphasis on development studies. Rather than speaking of 'primitive' and 'advanced,' or 'underdeveloped' and 'developed' societies, many anthropologists advocated a more 'neutral' dichotomy: simple and complex societies.

From the emic viewpoint, it is improbable that primitive society – or preindustrial, peasant, or colonial society, since these terms more accurately describe the peoples among whom most research has been done – was more simple than modern, industrial society. Both are complex to the actors who

2 Radcliffe-Brown also contributed to the illusion of simplicity by promoting the view that indigenous society was stable and healthy, consisting of organic harmony. Referring to this viewpoint as a 'fantasy,' Langham (1981: 265–6) makes clear the degree to which Australian social organization studied by Radcliffe-Brown was disintegrating before his eyes; his ethnographic subjects were dying out as the image of harmony was born.

live in them. Even from the etic viewpoint, it is not correct to say that pre-industrial society is any less complex, as is marvellously illustrated by Bascom. To understand this point, a distinction must be drawn between two definitions of complexity. The conventional one concerns role or structural differentiation. According to this definition, a society with both Protestantism and Catholicism, and perhaps Judaism and Islam as well, is considered more complex than a society with only one religious belief system, such as the pre-colonial Yoruba. To put it differently, a society in which the roles of hardware-man and undertaker have differentiated is more complex than one in which they have not.

The other definition concerns role or structural diffuseness. Here the focus is on a single institution and the degree of complexity within it, rather than on two or more roles or institutions. For example, Yoruba religion boasts hundreds of major and minor deities; beliefs and behaviour defined as 'religious' are extremely broad, ranging from ideas of a central deity to localized and personal deities, henotheism, divination, ancestor worship, herbalism, magic, witchcraft and sorcery, and ritual in general. My argument is that it is as legitimate to describe Yoruba society as complex, with its multifunctional and diffuse religious institution, as it is to attach that label to societies with more than one religious institution. From this perspective I also contend that institutional overlap, or the lack of differentiation between the family and the economy, for example, reflects complexity. In fact, what might actually be meant by complexity with regard to contemporary industrial society is alienation, contradiction, and powerlessness – not owing to role differentiation and institutional segregation but instead to the nature of the societal type. As Marx has argued, capitalist society contains more contradictions than any previous historical stage. Up-and-down business cycles, periodic inflation, class antagonisms – all these have their effect. On top of it all, we must consider the emergence of the state. Had the state not emerged, it might make sense to talk about the increasing complexity of society, at least as conventionally defined. But the state is the new unifier, as pervasive and effective as kinship ever was in the pre-industrial society. In a sense, the state is the ultimate example of what Durkheim meant by the argument that new structures must emerge to bridge the results of structural differentiation. It is also partly what causes alienation. In contrast to Durkheim's theory, recent writers such as Chambliss and Seidman (1971) and Sheleff (1975) contend that the movement in history is from restitutive to repressive control as bureaucratization increases. The state is one expression – the most significant – of the bureaucratic trend.

My second definition of complexity goes against the grain of most anthropological work, and for those who are reluctant to accept it I shall swing my attack back to the conventional approach. Even in the sense of role differentiation and role specialization, it is doubtful that primitive societies were simple. For example, Udy (1959) showed that the bulk of non-industrial societies in his sample met the criteria of bureaucratic and technological complexity. At this point two questions arise. First, how much role differentiation must occur before a society can be described as complex? This appears to be a matter of arbitrary judgment involving the economic realm in particular, which leads directly to the second question. On what basis does that realm determine which society is complex and which is not? Even if primitive economic systems had been simple in the degree of role specialization, which was not the case, other spheres, such as kinship and religion, were extremely complex. It would seem that whereas most social anthropologists have until recently rejected the Marxian framework which assigns causal primacy to techno-economic factors, they have implicitly accepted it in order to support the assumption that modern societies are more complex. This is an interesting case in which selective distortion has been used when it has been profitable to do so.

The assumption that modern industrial societies are more complex than pre-industrial societies can be attacked from a different direction. Most of us refer to structural and value convergence or role equivalence on a worldwide scale these days. At that level of generality, society appears to be becoming less differentiated and complex than before; we are witnessing the emergence of monoculture. It is quite possible that monoculture may not be as new as is generally thought. In the distant past, before the neolithic era, cultural similarities among the world's population may also have been high at specific periods. We put so much emphasis on the trend today toward the emergence of a universal culture because we live in an era dominated until recently by cultural diversity, or exceptionally sharp but sometimes overlapping differences among modes of production and social formations in various parts of the world. These differences were generated by comprehensible historical circumstances, related primarily to the uneven spread of capitalism and localized technological advances. Paradoxically, as time goes by, the same factors smooth over the differences in cultures and point us in the direction of monoculture.

Anthropologists, of all people, should have appreciated the complexity of pre-industrial colonial societies. Perhaps they have failed to do so in order to legitimate their generalizations about them. On the basis of a few months of field-work, anthropologists have been prepared to generalize about an entire culture, even if their research was confined to a single village. This was possible because they defined their subject matter as simple, which may reflect the limited knowledge that they had about these societies rather than the so-called homogeneity of primitive culture. If these same anthropologists were charged with explaining their own Western societies, they would be much more reluctant to generalize, supposedly because of the complexity of those societies. Bailey, whose data on India were unusually rich, was prepared to generalize across tribe, caste, and nation, and even to apply the field-work techniques of anthropology to India's parliamentary institution. Yet when he examined the modern university in Western society, he kept his analysis much more confined.

Not everyone would agree with these comments. Leaf (1979: 285), for example, congratulates Bailey for recognizing that village India was composed of multiple political structures, and hence was exceedingly complex. Silverman (1974–5: 115) observed that whereas Bailey appreciated the complexity of Indian culture, he suffered from the illusion that continental Europe was easy to understand, and grossly over-simplified it after a brief spell of field-work. Certainly Bailey did recognize the complexity of Indian society, but this did not stop him from making fairly hefty generalizations. As regards his European phase of research, I know for a fact, having been a student at the University of Sussex at the time, that Bailey and his students who worked in European communities did not find it easy going; nor did they think it was. Their usual reaction was to stress the difficulty of field-work in Europe as compared with Africa or India. If Bailey's European research program is to be criticized, it is for reasons other than those listed by Silverman. What was remarkable and sometimes maddening about this program was the implicit assumption of immense cultural variation. Not only could villages in different countries only be superficially compared, but the same was true of those within a single country, right next door to each other. Perhaps it was this assumption of the uniqueness of each and every community and the fantastic degree of complexity of European rural society that dissuaded Bailey's students from placing their work more firmly within the larger political and economic context of the state.

THE EMERGING SYNTHESIS

The story I have been relating in this book has been unfolding since the time of Comte, because the attempt to establish a positivistic science of society produced both believers and sceptics. In the United States at the turn of the century it was Boas who led the charge against a facile science of man. Boas was not against such a science on principle. He merely believed that the complexity of culture was so stupendous and our techniques to explore it so puny that the possibility of the discovery of laws was remote. Faced with the false claims of evolutionism, Boas's criticisms of the reigning school and the comparative method were appropriate and sensible. They do not reflect an anti-scientific stance; if anything, the standards for field-work that Boas set for the discipline were too rigorous.

This is an important point, because most of the writers who have succeeded in denting the armour of positivism have been committed to a nomothetic science of man. Malinowski contributed to the attack by insisting that what people said and what they did were two different things. Perhaps this was a cynical viewpoint, but it also was much more in tune with reality than were the structural dopes in Radcliffe-Brown's vision. Yet Radcliffe-Brown, like Durkheim before him, flirted with an incipient dialectic. The groundwork for a different approach to the analysis of social life was prefigured in the conflict model of Gluckman, who never questioned the scientific status of the discipline, and in the emphasis Evans-Pritchard gave to history and moral systems. The career of the concept of 'social structure' in British social anthropology also reflects underlying doubt. Is social structure empirically real or is it in the mind of the investigator? How can one reconcile changing, non-repetitive events with the static nature of structure? Out of these concerns emerged distinctions such as social structure and actual structure, social structure and structural form, social structure and social organization, and, finally, the fictitious structures announced by Leach, and Lévi-Strauss's invisible but none the less ontologically real structures underlying observable behaviour.

The changing orientation of anthropology was facilitated by the innovative work of Barth, with his emphasis on choice, change, reciprocity, and feedback; his generative models, however, were far too ambitious. Had they been attainable, anthropology would be the envy of biologists and chemists. Along the way to a new synthesis there have inevitably been false starts. Included here is network analysis, the claims for which are out of proportion to what in reality is a modest advance in technique. Included also is socio-linguistics, which sidestepped the essential limitations of positivism by wrongly assuming that one part of social life – mentality – was equal to all of social life. Here too we must put structuralism, for despite its onslaught against empiricism, it too has emerged as a form of mentalism, or, as Murphy states, a frozen dialectic.

The inability to prop up structural functionalism even with the aid of Gluckman's brand of conflict, the pseudo-scientism of American formal analysis, the seductive yet suspect structuralism of Lévi-Strauss, and the growing recognition of anthropology as a child of imperialism – all of this produced simultaneously a demand for relevance and a doubt about positivism that would not go away. Of course, it also produced the opposite reaction as well, as reflected in the not-so-new evolutionism of Steward and White, and more recently in socio-biology. But the urge for relevance and the doubt remained, and into the breach stepped another generation of anthropologists armed with Marx, with his concern for dynamic analysis, the intricate relation between the system and the acting agent, and power and oppression. Lest we have forgot, there also was Kuhn's fresh analysis of the history of science, which made it possible for anthropologists to be sceptical about the prospects of cumulative advance and rigorous verification procedures without creating an inseparable gulf between their discipline and the hard sciences.

BASIC ELEMENTS

The basic elements of the emerging synthesis are as follows.

1 *Norm versus act, culture versus social organization.* While causal primacy may be assigned either to norm or act, it is usually assumed that they overlap and tend toward homology. Yet, as Murphy argues, it is much more fruitful to regard them as dialectically related.

2 *Mind versus matter, or mind versus action.* Again, we turn to Murphy, who conceives of mind and matter (action, social relations, mode of production), as necessary oppositions out of which culture as a totality is produced (1971: 185–6 and 240). While the mind undoubtedly is one of the conditions that play upon culture, in my view it would be a mistake to make it a central focus of the discipline to the extent recommended by Murphy and Lévi-Strauss; to do so would be to detract from our basic concern, the non-reductionist explanation of the socio-cultural realm.

3 *Group versus individual, or system versus actor.* This amounts to a revival of one of Marx's central concerns, the relation between man and society. This also was Weber's concern, and Durkheim's too in his anti-positivistic moods. As Marx argued, man creates his own history, but not in a vacuum, for the weight of the past and existing institutions constrain him. Compatible with this element of the new synthesis is the distinction Giddens draws between agency and system, and his argument that both are

required in any analysis; the implication is that a common front may be emerging in both anthropology and sociology.

4 *An emphasis on choice, manipulation, power, contradiction, complexity, and dynamic rather than static analysis.* This brings together the enduring cricitisms of structural functionalism and the recent excursions into dialectics by people such as Murphy, informed at all times but not trapped by Marxism.

5 *A tolerance for disorder and open-ended conceptual schemes.* The tendency to systematize and the attraction of logical closure are enormous; yet as Davis (1971: 340) found when he attempted to erect a systematic scheme to explain and sum up his remarkable analysis of interesting and boring theories, the spark went out of his argument. He concluded that one has to choose between being systematic or interesting, for it is very difficult to be both (1971: 341). It is for that reason that I have talked in terms of an emerging synthesis rather than a new model; the latter suggests a closed system of logically interdependent variables, but the new synthesis is a set of assumptions that orient the investigator.

6 *The explanation of major expressions of inequality in the contemporary world, especially in urban settings.* None of the writers from whom I have drawn in order to mount my arguments for a new theoretical direction has expressed a similar emphasis, but as I argue in chapter 10, it is fundamental to the revitalization of the discipline.

7 *The recognition that while we must strive for rigorous science, we always fall short of the mark.* Deceptive rigour is characteristic of disciplines seduced by the allure of science but devoid of its essential qualities. This explains why sociologists often concentrate on complex, sophisticated data analysis while neglecting the quality of the data themselves. The result is an illusion of precision.

LEACH, MURPHY, AND BAILEY

Although numerous anthropologists over the years have contributed to the emerging synthesis, sometimes unintentionally, three contemporary figures have made the difference; Leach, Murphy, and Bailey. Stressing choice, contradiction, and power, Leach (1965) argued that while our models are always equilibrium models, real life is a disorderly, continuous flux. He also argued that the actor's ideal model, like the observer's, is a fiction. Neither of them corresponds to the dynamic complexity of behaviour on the ground. In the best of his three monographs on India, Bailey (1960) too stressed choice, power, complexity, and contradiction. He considered structure, the focus of theory, to be inherently static, and opted instead for a descriptive account of dynamic behaviour. As Leaf (1979: 285) has pointed out, both Leach and Bailey sighted the target but failed to pull the trigger. Both saw clearly the complex, contradictory world. Leach took refuge behind the fictitious equilibrium models, while Bailey abandoned theory for description. What we need to do is stick with the dynamic, contradictory realm of behaviour and work it over theoretically.

Enter Murphy. In what must be the most innovative synthesis of anthropological theory in several decades, Murphy moulded a dialectical approach that empirically oriented social scientists could live with. In an exhilarating rout that left Parsons in tatters, he fashioned the works of Marx, Simmel, Lévi-Strauss, Leach, Freud, and at times Durkheim and Radcliffe-Brown into a new instrument. He accepted the disorderly nature of behaviour, but rather than escaping to the safer waters of abstract theory where the disorder could be ignored, he plunged ahead and related it to social life, clarifying in the process the perennial bugbears of norm and act, mind and matter. Early in his book (1971: 4) Murphy sketched out the basis of his theory: 'It is not the dialectics of Marx, for it combines elements of phenomenology and an increased concern for subjective states. It takes off from the base laid by structural-functionalism, but goes beyond the empirical structures derived from actual observation to infrastructures that are logical products of the investigator's mind and transformations and negations of the apparent reality.' Later (1971: 117) he states that his 'dialectical approach is simple in the extreme, for it requires only that the analyst of society question everything that he sees and hears, examine phenomena fully and from every angle, seek and evaluate the contradiction of any proposition, and consider every category from the viewpoint of its noncontents as well as its positive attributes. It requires us to also look for paradox as much as complementarity, for opposition as much as accommodation. It portrays a universe of dissonance underlying apparent order and seeks deeper orders beyond the dissonance ... It enjoins us to query the obvious and given truths of both our culture and our science.'

Honigmann (1976: 355–6) has argued that Murphy exaggerated the degree of contradiction in social life, but he did not suggest a different line of criticism that many, perhaps most, anthropologists would follow. Boiled down to its basics, Murphy's theory amounts to a scepticism, to a set of sensitizing assumptions rather than a model, that alerts the investigator to the complexities of social life. I think Murphy is right, but it is questionable whether his loose approach can ever gain ground in the discipline. The proclivity for systematization is overwhelming, even if it leads to distortion. Evidence of this perhaps inescapable academic disease is reflected in Murphy's own book. It is divided into three parts: the positive, the negative, and the (overall) structure; or, if you will, thesis, antithesis, and synthesis. Yet in terms of the material included in each part, it is doubtful whether the labels are appropriate, except in an aesthetic sense, invoking the concern with dialectics. Murphy is not the only culprit. Rarely do I write anything of any length without organizing it into three sections, as in the first draft of this book. So much for the earlier denial of the fundamental operations of the human brain!

Murphy may have succeeded in showing us how to approach complex and contradictory social life theoretically, but for anthropologists the litmus test always is the field-work situation. This takes us back to Bailey, for in his post-Indian writings, especially his recent study of university politics, his early interests in choice and contradiction have flowered, and he meets them head-on with a sophisticated theoretical approach rather than relinquishing theory to the infertile notion of static social structure.

Stratagems and Spoils, published in 1969, offers us a model of behaviour that stresses its fluid, dynamic character and man's innovative and manipulative nature. Although the book elegantly documents the chaos of behaviour, Bailey's purpose is the conventional one of demonstrating that underlying it all is at least a shadow of pattern. One gets the impression that he deplores disorder (1969: xiii), and one cannot help but wonder whether the regularity that he does discover is partly wish-fulfilment. Stratagems and Spoils is conceptually compatible with the later study of university politics, but there are differences. A major one is the central position given to contradiction in Morality and Expediency. A minor one might well be labelled a contradiction in itself: the earlier work, which strives to demonstrate order in the face of apparent chaos, is not itself well organized; the more recent work, which is more comfortable with the image of a chaotic world, moves smoothly and cogently. It also is more sophisticated than the earlier study, because Bailey does not seem to have the same urge to explain disorder and contradiction away or to imply that they are repugnant and perhaps not essential features of mankind.

In Morality and Expediency Bailey stresses the wide range of conflicting principles that confront the actor, and argues that there is no rational way of choosing among them (note, however, that 'rational' is used inconsistently in his study, sometimes to refer to the application of logic in a means–end scheme, and at other times to refer to action, pragmatism, and compromise). Bailey asks, how then does anything get done? The answer appears to be that compromise rules the day backstage, where principles can be relaxed or even abandoned. Bailey's argument that nothing gets done unless one moves backstage can be challenged, fot it implies that something must be done, that there are good decisions, that organizations do a progressively better job. I don't think this position can be defended. When decisions are taken – that is, when things *are* done – people are often letting us know that they are around; they are making a political statement. In most cases the decisions are devoid of meaningful ends. For example, every year in university departments with which I have been associated, a committee has played around with the curriculum; changes are always advocated, but the rationale behind them is usually suspect. In my department last year a course title was changed from 'Cross-Cultural Methodology' to the even vaguer 'Patterns of Culture'; if the future runs true to form, within a few years another committee will change it back to the old title. This kind of activity is comparable to making a neat bed in a hospital: such performance is easier to measure than bedside manner. Both the nurse and the academic must give signs that something has been done. In both cases a political statement is being made.

Morality and Expediency focuses on man's unprincipled side, on 'institutionalized façades, make-believe and pretence, lies and hypocrisy,' on what 'every public figure pretends does not exist' (1977: 2). To a somewhat lesser degree, that thesis was the focus of *Stratagems and Spoils* and the two books that emerged from Bailey's European phase of field-work (1971 and 1973). As in the case of Lévi-Strauss's *Totemism* and *The Savage Mind*, Bailey's *Stratagems and Spoils* is best regarded as a pivotal point in the development of his ideas. It bridges the triumphant structural analyses of his Indian monographs and his sophisticated symbolic-interactionist approach to university politics. As Bailey himself has stressed (1977: 2), it is exceptionally difficult to investigate the unprincipled side in a culture other than one's own. This partly explains, I think, why his earlier attempts to do so, and to guide his students, in European peasant communities have prompted criticisms such as Silverman's.

Bailey's distinction between public and private arenas, between the front and the back of the stage (and even *under* the stage), leads him to a useful analysis – at times a brilliant analysis. As in *Stratagems and Spoils*, he again shows the explanatory pay-off of introducing more subtlety into our analysis rather than using crude terms such as 'norm' and 'role.' For example, his 'masks' seem to stand mid-way between the concepts of personality and role. Although there is much to praise in Bailey's work, it is not without flaws. A major defect in *Morality and Expediency* seems to be an under-lying assumption of equality among the actors. Certainly that is not true of the world outside the university; nor is it true within it. Bailey (1977: 182) suggests that 'some opposition must come from those with vested interests, who see their life made worse by innovations which might benefit others. Probably that is the normal source of opposition to new procedures and new values.' He adds, 'we seem to have in our human essence a timidity which makes us think that known procedures, which may be uncomfortable and inefficient but are not disastrous, are to be preferred before new ways which may be an improvement but may equally, since we have never put them to test, bring disaster.' Both statements suggest two of the major mechanisms that I have argued contribute to stability in the face of contradiction: the role of differential power and the felt need for security. Yet neither occupies a central position in Bailey's analysis.

Elsewhere Bailey (1980) has advocated that we replace the term 'power' (and its linked concept, 'authority') with 'influence.' Influence is a cover term connoting force at one end and rational argument at another, with manipulation somewhere in between. As far as authority is concerned, I agree with Bailey. Too often it is forgotten that so-called legitimate or insti-tutionalized power is largely ideology, which expresses class interests; as long as authority is defined in terms of legitimacy, the concept probably should be avoided, for its ideological character is usually ignored. I have a very different reaction to Bailey's effort to do away with the concept of power. 'Influence' does not bite deeply enough; it is too closely related to persuasion. In this book I am trying to *influence* (persuade) readers to look at anthropological theory in a special light. Here the concept is apt, for I cannot force the reader to adopt my views, nor do I have the authority, in an ideological sense, of a Leach or a Firth, or indeed of a Bailey.

In Bailey's work there is a tendency to ignore or at least minimize dif-ferential power. His actors certainly strive to outdo one another, but the exercise is often a game in which the chances for victory are up for grabs. Yet as Coser (1976: 152) insists, power always involves asymmetrical rela-tions, always concerns inequality. Bailey's problem, I believe, is one to which all genuine field-workers in anthropology and those who operate within the symbolic-interactionist framework in sociology are susceptible. Field-workers are prone to minimizing power differences or to accepting Dahl-like (1961) pluralism. One will always find decisions being made and people striving to influence others. Is it this that turns off many anthropologists from the structural approach to power advocated by Marxists? We confront once again the old enemy: the macro–micro dilemma. Perhaps the more gifted one is as a field-worker, the less capable one is of appreciating power in all its dimensions.

Another problem concerns Bailey's emphasis on compromise. His argument is that people embrace contradictory values for which there is no rational resolution. If life is to go on, principles must be relaxed and we must become practical men; this is what happens behind the stage. I do not argue against this line of theory; it seems to ring true. The problem, however, is the underlying assumption that the middle ground reached by compromise is somehow superior to the polar positions, perhaps in the sense of being neutral territory. In my view there is no neutral territory. Every position along a continuum is value-laden. As Weber remarked long ago, the middle position, that happy academic solution to sticky problems, is no more neutral than either extreme. Sankoff (1973) falls into this error in her attempt to erect an index of excellence for evaluating scholarly work: one should not repeat what everyone knows, yet one also should not be too innovative. To the extent that Bailey's 'compromise' is said to constitute a solution to contradictory values rather than an appearance of a solution, it suffers in the same manner.

Anthropologists will have no difficulty recognizing the conceptual oppositions around which my analysis has proceeded, such as relative versus comparative, static versus dynamic, act versus norm, and agent versus structure. But the general reaction probably will be that before analysis can proceed, these oppositions must be resolved. Few anthropologists would build them directly into their analytic schemes. Frank (1975), for example, refers to such oppositions as 'false disjunctions.' For very different reasons, Sahlins (1976) shares Frank's reaction against oppositions. His argument centres on the distinction between meaningful (i.e., cultural) and practical reason, or normative and instrumental action, or anthropological versus Marxian analysis. What make man unique, Sahlins argues, is his capacity for meaningful interaction. Sahlins is opposed to any scheme that detracts from the overriding significance of culture. Thus, he is highly critical of Malinowski's manipulative, pragmatic Trobrianders, and of ecological approaches that assign to culture a mere adaptive function; in both cases, culture has been cannibalized. Sahlins's major conclusion (1976: 207) is that 'the practical interest of men in production is symbolically constituted.' This is a hymn in praise of man's symbolic capacity, of culture; and Sahlins's argument that material forces are themselves animated and directed by the cultural idiom rather than existing separately and containing the key to all other aspects of society is persuasive. Yet the end product of his analysis is disappointing. Culture becomes a monolithic entity, an all-embracing scheme, which in its generality articulates well with social life but lacks the specificity and dynamic capacity exhibited in the works of Bailey and Murphy. Sahlins grapples with an old issue: whether belief or action, meaningful or practical reason, and superstructure or infrastructure should be assigned causal primacy. His solution is to collapse the oppositions. In my view, the question of causal primacy is a false one, and thus its solution is equally wrong. It is much more fruitful to accept the opposed positions and to analyse their consequences.

Of course, another author who has eulogized man's symbolic capacity is Victor Turner, and his work has a peculiar significance to this study. As in the case of other 'two-headed' anthropologists, there have actually been two Turners: the man who so ably explored structural contradiction, conflict, and struggle in *Schism and Continuity* (1957), and the man who then turned his attention to ritual and symbolism in subsequent works (1967, 1969, 1974). The early Turner analysed Ndembu society in terms of a basic contradiction between the opposed principles of matrilineal descent and virilocal marriage. This and other contradictions are concealed by layers of ritual and symbol, much in the way that I depicted the basic mechanisms that neutralize contradiction. Ritual does not simply express the social structure; rather, it compensates for the flaws in it, such as the contradiction between familial and lineal organization. In an analysis resembling Bailey's, Turner (1957: 124) remarks, 'norms and their supporting values can only *appear* to be consistent, since they must cover the presence of contradictions within the structure itself' (emphasis in original). He goes on to state that norms expressing contradictory principles exist side by side, and throughout the study he stresses the constant struggle among manipulative actors in an arena of opposition and change.

Whereas ritual is something less than an equal partner in the make-up of social life in Turner's early work, it emerges as the dominant actor in his later work. Ritual symbols become the centre-piece. In Turner's words (1974: 55), 'Symbols instigate social action.' They have ontological rather than epiphenomenonal status (1974: 57). Yet by giving ritual symbol the centre of the stage and attributing independent causal status to it, the clash between symbol, structure, and contradiction has been lost, and with it explanatory power. To argue such is merely to confirm the improbable causal primacy of, or homology between, belief and act. Instead, both are necessary oppositions in a dialectical framework. That was the manner in which ritual symbol was treated by the early Turner, but not by the later Turner.

This explains why symbolic anthropology, including the otherwise equally imaginative works of Douglas (1966, 1970, 1975), occupies a minor place in this study. Without the clash between symbol and structure, or the working out of basic contradictions among the shifting, often irreconcilable norms that guide and rationalize behaviour by actors who strive to better their positions in a constantly changing world, dialectical anthropology cannot thrive.

Let us conclude by considering the light that my approach throws on contentious arguments in anthropology, such as Foster's 'image of the limited good' (1965). Foster's article has lent itself to polar-opposite interpretations. Some commentators have read into it the argument that social-structural factors are crucial for changes in peasant societies. Others have taken it as evidence of the overwhelming importance of cultural and psychological factors, such as the assumed conservatism of peasants. These conflicting interpretations are not accidental, for both positions exist ambiguously in Foster's work. Foster states that what is most necessary to promote development is to somehow replace the peasant's conception of limited good with the image of an open society in which individual initiative will not threaten the stability of the community. But he also contends that this can only be done by changing the social conditions that have produced this cognitive orientation. Foster is correct to include both psychological and structural factors. Yet left as they are, ambiguity is inevitable. The solution is to conceive of them in a dialectical relationship.

The famous controversy between Redfield (1930) and Lewis (1951) also is illuminated by this procedure. It is now accepted that Redfield documented the ideal or formal belief system of Tepoztlan, whereas Lewis showed us the actual system, what really went on beneath the surface of the cultural mask. If one has to choose, I suppose most anthropologists would favour Lewis's interpretation, for the very program of scholarly investigation involves probing beneath the surface of the obvious. Yet choice in this matter is not necessary. It is much more useful to embrace both the ideal and the actual system of beliefs and behaviour and to consider their dialectical interaction. As Murphy put it (1971: 218), values may not be congruent with action, but at the same time they never are irrelevant to it. Values inform behaviour, but in the course of acting people choose, modify, and distort values, resulting in the ever-dynamic flow of social life.

One last example: Lenski's (1954) theory of status inconsistency. This was an interesting idea that helped to explain some of the strain between individuals who stood high on one scale, such as profession, but low on another, such as race. Yet it failed to develop into a central theory in the discipline.

The reason, I believe, is that its potential dynamic quality was never fully exploited. By the simple adjustment of portraying inconsistent status criteria as dialectically opposed, a much more powerful tool of analysis is created. For example, one could speculate that if the incredible happened, and blacks took over the medical profession, there might be a momentary elevation in the status of all blacks, then an increased tendency to divide blacks by class criteria so that those within medicine could be considered 'unrepresentative,' and eventually a sharp drop in the status of medical practice itself. As it stands, Lenski's work is capable of encompassing such a dynamic analysis.

10

Reflections on Our Future

Is the discipline that brought us knowledge of the *kula* ring and the mother's brother slated for extinction? Has the labour of Morgan and Malinowski been for naught? These are the ringing questions that have disoriented anthropology for the past decade, reflecting its unique crisis. In recent years all the social sciences have been faced with the false promises of positivism, the accusation of ideological bias, and the demand for relevance and significance. But anthropology has been affected most deeply. This is because it has been confronted by an additional problem: the very disappearance of its subject matter, the specialized study of 'other cultures,' primitive or otherwise. Anthropology's noble past, its primary concentration on 'simple' societies, is history. Its future, if there is to be one, will be as much in the urban sectors of industrialized societies as in the new nations of the Third World. Its practitioners, if there are to be any, must prove as adept at studying the middle classes of their own societies as they have been in making sense of double descent in West Africa and shifting cultivation in Asia.

The resounding question, of course, is whether such a fundamental transition can be made. How much disjunction can a discipline endure without disintegrating? Will our research tools continue to work in the new research settings? Do we in fact have a separate place in the post-colonial world, or is it our fate to be devoured by other disciplines, notably sociology? It is my strong conviction that we can not only survive but can indeed thrive, that we do have the capacity to contribute in an important and unique way to the scholarly investigation of post-colonial society. However, adjusting the focus of the discipline to urban industrial society is only one step. At least two others are necessary. The second amounts to a moral commitment; the discipline must be built around the investigation of the major consequences of differential power and inequality with the goal of changing and improving society; in other words, it must focus on the outstanding social problems of our age. The third step is theoretical. Throughout part 2 of this book I have conceptualized social life as complex and contradictory. If anthropology is to win a place for itself in the contemporary world, it must prove itself capable of coping with a complex universe. This can be achieved, I suggest, by developing the dialectical perspective, which sparkles in the company of contradiction and illuminates the most attractive features of positivism, phenomenology, and structuralism.

REBIRTH STEP 1: URBAN-INDUSTRIAL SOCIETY

The easy way to make the adjustment to industrial society is to concentrate on the rural sector, where face-to-face relationships continue to prevail, as well as on those pockets of 'anthropological' behaviour such as street corners, motorcycle gangs, or religious sects. Yet to do so would be a mistake. Important as such topics are, they nevertheless lie on the periphery of industrial society. If anthropology is to thrive it must demonstrate its capacity to investigate the very core of society. The bizarre, the esoteric, and the ephemeral must take second place to mainstream behaviour. Of particular importance is the urban realm. As Keesing (1976: 516) has put it: 'Cities are where the action is, where the future apparently lies if there is to be one. Anthropology must be there, though it will continue to be in the hinterlands as well.' Willis (1972: 147) has stated the case even more forcefully. In his view, if anthropology is to be rebuilt, it will be done in the urban setting, where white anthropologists must show their ability to get along with coloured peoples who are 'angry, literate and politicized.'

Perhaps what is needed in order to establish anthropology firmly in urban industrial society is a master focus comparable to kinship. Such a potential focus does exist. As I wrote in chapter 9, the contemporary equivalent of kinship is bureaucracy. The modern state is as pervasive and effective as kinship ever was in pre-industrial society. My suggestion is that a renewed anthropology be built around the study of all levels of bureaucracy, whether or not in the investigator's own society. This only means taking Weber seriously, and Marx too, to the extent that we deal with inequality, differential power, ideology, and alienation.

The suggestion that we can profitably work in our own backyards is not without controversy. Frank (1968: 413) flatly states that anthropologists should restrict their field-work to their own societies in order to sever the links from the era of exploitation. The opposite view has been expressed by Fried (1972: 237–8), who argues that such a restriction would cripple, if not kill, anthropology because it would relinquish the discipline's cross-cultural perspective. The quick answer to Fried is that in most nation-states there are a wide variety of cultures, and in this sense comparative work could continue. But on the whole, I accept Frank's position only as a temporary tactic made necessary by historical circumstances: the overwhelming connection of anthropology to pre-industrial, colonial society. Once this link is broken, it should make no difference where research is conducted. As a step in that direction, perhaps anthropologists should be expected to carry out at least two major projects, one at home and one abroad. Anthropology, despite its image, has been cross-cultural only in the sense of being non-Western. The inclusion of Western, urban industrial societies within the discipline's spectrum might finally allow it to attain its universalistic goals.

OBJECTIONS

Among the many possible objections to this new focus, three stand out. The most important is the criticism that anthropology will simply become a part of sociology. It has long been recognized that social anthropology and sociology share the same conceptual territory, and thus a common theoretical foundation. As Goody (1969: 10) has written, 'a sociological "theory" which is distinct from a "theory" of social anthropology is conceivable only to the extent that zoological theory differs for sheep and goats: the base must be common for both.' The disciplines have maintained their individual identities by virtue of the fact that one has specialized in non-Western cultures and the other in the industrialized societies of the Western world. It would appear that a reorientation of anthropology to urban industrial society would threaten the discipline's separate identity. This fear is groundless. To understand why, a distinction must be made between logical and sociological properties of the two disciplines, which echoes the debate between Popper and Kuhn regarding the philosophy of science in general. From a logical perspective there is little that separates social anthropology and sociology. The preference for research with different societal types and a different array of techniques does not adequately distinguish between them. The two disciplines do indeed occupy the same conceptual territory and thus a common theoretical base. The implication is that the disciplines should have been joined long ago, as prominent writers such as Radcliffe-Brown advocated. Yet this did not occur, and the main reason is clear. A scholarly discipline is a sociological phenomenon. It is composed of roles and statuses, values and norms, habits and traditions, and motives and contradictions characteristic of the social world in general. Logic may dictate a particular path to follow, but social institutions never march solely to the melodies of logic. As Hughes (1958: 99) has remarked, the division of labour among academics can be explained more in terms of social movements than logic. Largely because of its unique characteristics, which have emerged owing to the accident of experience and habit and tradition as much as to rational considerations, anthropology will remain a distinctive discipline in its new research setting. The special characteristics of anthropology are holism, comparative (especially cross-cultural) analysis, participant observation, reliance on key informants, and the emic point of view. Added to this must be the elusive element of culture, which despite its vagueness reflects an analytic dimension that usually marks the anthropological enterprise. Certainly there always have been some participant observational studies in sociology (notably by the renowned Chicago school, led by Everett Hughes), and anthropology has no patent on comparative analysis. Yet no other discipline embraces this same set of characteristics to the same degree. In sociological (if not logical) terms, anthropology is unique.

There are several additional reasons why anthropology will remain autonomous in its new research setting. One is its relationship to the other branches of general anthropology. Although the unity of general anthropology has been more dream than reality, it cannot help setting social anthropology somewhat apart from the other social sciences. This may be especially true in the future if the recent signs of co-operation between social anthropologists and archaeologists continue (see Keesing 1976: 76); certainly there is no comparable influence on sociology. A second reason for the continued separation concerns my portrayal in chapter 4 of the dialectical relationship between sociology and anthropology. The two disciplines, as I argued, are locked in a contradictory system. The oppositions contained within the theoretical perspective of the one discipline are worked out or expressed in the other. In this limited sense, the disciplines feed on each other; their very separation is mutually beneficial. This partly explains why all past efforts to combine social anthropology and sociology have failed, and why they will continue to be separate in the future. A third reason again concerns logic, or the lack of it. In as much as there was no logical basis in the past for identifying anthropology with pre-industrial society, there are no logical barriers today to prevent a focus on urban industrial society. Fourth, drawing upon an analogy with biology, one would expect that if anthropology does succeed in adapting successfully to sociology's turf, the two disciplines will actually grow further apart. The explanation is related to the biological concepts of 'sympatry' and 'allopatry.' Species that are found in a similar geographical area are termed 'sympatric,' those in a different area 'allopatric.' As Odum (1971: 240) states, 'differences in closely related species are often accentuated (i.e., diverge) in sympatry and weakened (i.e., converge) in allopatry.' We can expect, then, that the minor differences between the two disciplines will become somewhat exaggerated in the years ahead. Finally, while there are today several styles of sociology, the quantitative-minded practitioners appear to run the show. Perhaps they will eventually realize their ambitions to turn their discipline into mathematical sociology. Should those ambitions materialize, the scholarly investigation of the central forces of contemporary society will become a wide-open field.

While it is probable that anthropology can remain autonomous even if a large part of its research is conducted in urban industrial societies (including the investigator's own), I am not arguing that it will have no links with sociology. I would advocate a constant interaction between the two, including borrowing concepts and theories when required, as I did regarding power in chapter 8. Anthropology no longer is a 'novice' discipline. We are mature enough to work closely with sociology without being threatened. Academic disciplines long rooted in urban industrial society have always tended to be imperialistic. Some political scientists, stressing the ubiquity of power and the philosophical roots of their discipline, might claim that they have the master social science. Economists, defining not simply economic but all social relationships as choice among scarce values, could claim that status for themselves. Geographers could argue that they rather than sociologists are the true synthesizers, especially when considering those sociologists who accept Parsons's restriction of their field to the institutionalization of value orientations. Psychologists might contend that all the social sciences rest on a psychological base and hence are branches of that discipline. The point, of course, is that there is nothing new to the argument that one discipline will or should absorb another. To the extent that political science can remain autonomous from sociology, so too can anthropology. The threat will be no greater. Of course, it could be argued that we would all be better off, given the common conceptual base, if social anthropology and sociology were combined. However, that reverts to logical as opposed to sociological considerations. In recent years, there has even been some suggestion that the existing disciplinary boundaries should be rethought (Chomsky 1972: 1). That idea too may have merit. But if this rethinking was to occur, it would not simply be a matter of losing anthropology. All the social sciences, including sociology, would be transformed.

In arguing that anthropology will not wither away if it moves into urban industrial society, I am not suggesting that there will be no changes. Almost certainly anthropologists must add to their skills a knowledge of quantitative analysis and computerized data processing. This will be necessary not only because we shall have to learn to take advantage of the available primary documentation that exists in a literate, bureaucratized social system (which increasingly describes Third World nations), but also so that we can decipher the analyses provided by sociology and other cognate disciplines. And there is a further reason: the Western world has entered the computer age. If anthropology hopes to cope with the very core of urban industrial society, there must emerge an anthropology of computerized society itself. To do so, we must practice what we have always preached: learn the language of the natives.

Despite the necessity of mastering quantitative techniques, our basic approach must continue to be participant observation. Anthropology's strength has always been its field-work orientation, and I doubt whether the discipline can persist without it. As anthropologists do gain a foothold in urban industrial society, we can expect a number of negative reactions from other social scientists, because they will be threatened by us. Participant observation, a technique that was allowed to be appropriate for pre-industrial society, will be dismissed by some as 'journalistic' in industrial society. This will be a mistake, for no other tool is as well suited for the task of penetrating below the surface level of rationalized behaviour and unravelling the contradictions therein. Furthermore, contrary to what the textbooks say, the choice of technique is not solely dependent on the problem. In most cases, observational studies will at least enrich a study, even one concerning units as large as the state or as complex as the modern university. As Hall observed many years ago (1946: 31), a sociological truism is that the analysis of the informal structure is more revealing than the analysis of the formal structure. With this in mind, Bailey's study of the underside of university politics takes on wider methodological significance. Rather than becoming irrelevant amateurs, poised upon the periphery of modern society, anthropologists can bring to the analysis of contemporary institutions a fresh capacity for tapping the informal side of life.

Field-work in general may be dismissed as amateur activity fit only for the poorly trained and theoretically impoverished. But that dismissal will merely reflect a misunderstanding that has been around for a long time: the assumption that theoretical work demands unusual intellect, while field-work requires only competence. Yet the range of potentially significant variables that confront the ethnographer is enormous. Simply to make sense of a minor incident such as a squabble between a man and his junior wife involves a constant juggling and revision of dozens of intricately related factors. It is, in short, a genuine theoretical exercise, and anyone who doubts it is advised to study the classical works of Goodenough (1956b) and Fischer (1958). The tendency to underrate field-work probably has something to do with the fact that it is 'dirty work,' where one must muck in with actual social life, while theory is 'clean work.' In addition to the analytic demands of field-work, there also are the personal ones – constant good humour, real or feigned interest and humility, sensitivity, charm, role-playing, and deception. The demands and the strain are considerable, and perhaps some anthropologists are secretly relieved that less emphasis is today placed on the field-work enterprise. Yet if we are successful in breathing new life into anthropological theory, it will be due in no small measure to our continuing capacity to produce sound ethnography.

A second possible objection to the redirection of the discipline toward urban industrial society, with no preference given to research conducted in other cultures or in one's own, is that we shall have lost our capacity to combat ethnocentrism. Yet this aspect of traditional anthropology has always been exaggerated and superficial. The message of ethnocentrism is not a profound or complex intellectual one. An undergraduate degree in anthropology is not required in order to understand the point of view, and residence in another country may sharpen one's prejudices rather than dull them; indeed, one of the surprises in my research among white supremacists was that so many of them had travelled widely. During my first visit to Nigeria several years ago, I became aware that if there was any correlation between the length of residence of an expatriate and the degree of knowledge and understanding of that country, it probably was a negative one. In other words, the 'old hands' among the foreign missionaries, teachers, traders, and aid specialists often were the worst informants. This will surprise few experienced anthropologists, but Willis (1972: 136) suggests that the field-work process itself, especially if a hit-and-miss affair, can confirm cultural bias. Despite Voget's claim (1975: 590) that anthropology has been internationalized, the fact remains that most of our anthropological interpretations have been filtered through the conceptual lens of the Western world.

The so-called advantage of studying other cultures in order to foster objectivity and insight has been greatly overrated. Some people appear to have the capacity (not necessarily innate) for objectivity, insight, and imagination, and others do not; that capacity will be realized whether the research is carried out at home or abroad. Hymes (1972: 32) has pointed out that many historians and philosophers have gained relativistic objectivity without ever having done field-work in other cultures, and Sahlins (1976: 75) has hinted that the anthropologist's 'etic' is his own society's 'emic.' In a perceptive paper, Heilman (1980) challenges the old anthropological notion that one must work abroad in order to attain objectivity. Heilman, a Jew, undertook investigations of the orthodox Jewish community in the United States. The usual problem that confronts field-workers as strangers or outsiders is a tendency to 'go native.' But as Heilman points out, natives like himself who try to carry out an objective analysis may 'go stranger.'

Stranger-value in field-work is deeply ingrained in the discipline, and most anthropologists can readily parade their pet stories to support it. I have one myself. It concerns an African colleague in a North American university. During a heated departmental meeting, in which deep hostility between the college dean and the academic vice-president was being aired in public, the African colleague transformed the atmosphere from rancour to hilarity with a somewhat elliptical remark: they are mates to the same man. For a moment or so there was complete silence, and then gradually we understood what he meant: the two administrators were 'co-wives' of the president of the university, and hence their continuous bickering and vying for attention. I doubt whether anyone else present at that meeting, including those anthropologists who had worked in polygynous societies, would have thought of this interpretation, which was so apt. But my African colleague was capable of comparable insights with regard to his own society, in which most of his field-work had been conducted. This itself was not accidental, for the rule that we must work in other cultures is set aside for 'natives' who wish to become anthropologists. These budding scholars are sent back to investigate their own societies, which seems to confirm Hsu's (1973) argument that white anthropologists don't like non-whites to study white society. A native anthropology (see Jones 1982), along with the anthropology of women, devoted to developing their unique perspectives, are two important potential sources of revitalization in the discipline. But a native anthropology that is subservient to the aims of anthropology in general and reduced to collecting data to promote established theoretical positions is a co-opted anthropology.

A third possible objection concerns those prominent anthropological twins, the exotic and the bizarre. The reasons for choosing a particular occupation are complex, but in the case of anthropology there appear to be two distinct avenues: some us are attracted for intellectual reasons; others are lured by the prospect of adventure, of exotic experience. It would be interesting to know whether the first type eventually turns into the second, and vice-versa. While that may occasionally happen, the usual result of the process of graduate training is to tone down the polar types and turn out homogenized products.

Such have been the changes in anthropological field-work already, with fewer and fewer students heading for Bongo-Bongo, that it may be thought that we already have abandoned the notorious twins. Yet pick up almost any textbook and images of the exotic will tumble out of the pages – indeed, usually from the dust jacket or cover itself! Tune into introductory anthropology courses, especially successful ones, and you will be enchanted by tales of quaint customs. The emphasis on the exotic, nevertheless, is totally indefensible. One reason is that the discipline's attempt to free itself from ethnocentrism and its attraction to the exotic are inconsistent. People and customs are exotic because they are different. All too readily what we regard as 'different' can imperceptibly fade into 'inferior.' Another reason is that the 'exotic' by definition is an alien's concept. People in the Third World countries do not consider their customs to be any more exotic than Westerners do their own; conversely, Western customs look as exotic to outsiders as non-Western customs do to an American or British citizen. My African colleague who lumped the dean and the vice-president into the category of co-wives used to turn the tables by lecturing on 'exotic' North American society. Not only can an argument be made to excise the concept of 'exotic' from the anthropological literature, but it might also be said that to the extent that anthropologists present their subjects as exotic, they have failed to understand them in emic terms. This statement must be qualified because of the tendency to exaggerate the degree to which one's 'people' are exotic and unique in order to impress one's colleagues. What is curious about anthropology is that it searches for order, regularity, and consistency – an aim shared by all disciplines – while it simultaneously seeks out the unique, the inconsistent, and the aberrant.

Frank (1975) dismisses the anthropologist's attraction to the exotic in scathing terms, and Bailey achieves the same effect in his sober analysis of university politics. Willis defines field-work as a kind of tourism (1972: 142), and condemns anthropology in general as a form of recreation for white people, especially in undergraduate classes. The time has come, it would seem, to give up our pursuit of the exotic. But we don't have to relinquish the bizarre. Bailey's dons may not be exotic, but they certainly are peculiar. Yet they are no more so than a society in which many of its old people live together, separated from younger people, especially children, not only in the warm regions of the southern United States, but increasingly in northern areas. And they are certainly no more bizarre than the white supremacists whom I have studied. Indeed, although I selected that project largely in order to focus on a major social problem – racism – the organizations involved are so extreme that they fall outside the core of Canadian society.

What brings them back in, however, and saves the project from oblivion, are their connections to the economic and political institutions of society, but that is a subject for a different book. Finally, as Nader (1972: 301–2) has written, 'For many students today, the experience of working in an international industrial complex would be more bizarre than anything a student anthropologist could find in a Mexican village, or in New Guinea for that matter. We anthropologists have studied the cultures of the world only to find in the end that ours is one of the most bizarre.' Perhaps Miner's (1956) 'Body Ritual among the Nacirema' never was meant as a joke.

REBIRTH STEP 2: SOCIAL PROBLEMS AND INEQUALITY

In my view there are no uninteresting problems, and the discipline should be as broad as the imaginations of its practitioners can stretch it, with room for the leisurely inspection of issues totally devoid of practical application. However, if there is not substantial concentration on social problems and inequality, something is lacking. The term 'social problems' as I use it has little in common with the manner in which it is often employed by sociologists. I do not mean a range of issues such as illegitimate birth, teenage gangs, or vandalism. It would be difficult to imagine anything less intellectually profitable for a discipline than a primary focus such as one of those, especially if it is not realized that a social problem is what is defined as a social problem. This is voyeurism, slumming at its worst. By social problems I mean something both broader and more precise. To focus on social problems means to investigate the major expressions of differential power and inequality. From my viewpoint, it is not a question of choosing between theoretical or social problems, or between pure and applied research. All social problems have theoretical import if they are defined as above. All theoretical problems, if they are not trite, have social significance. Moreover, in a pre- or non-paradigmatic discipline, the distinction favoured in the hard sciences between pure and applied research is not legitimate. All research is value-laden, but social-science research is doubly so because of the nature of the subject matter: the fact that we are part of what we investigate, human society. We cannot make a clear-cut distinction between theory and reform, between sheer knowledge for its own sake and social commentary. In anthropology pure research does not exist.

To expect anthropology to focus on the major expressions of inequality is to request a fundamental shift in the direction of the discipline, for it has rarely done so in the past. Anthropology was the discipline that dealt with colonial societies, and thus should have pioneered the analysis of colonialism. Yet it failed to meet the challenge. By virtue of its cross-cultural involvement, anthropology should also have taken the lead in the analysis and confrontation of racism. Later I shall describe this issue as one of the fundamental failures of the discipline; for the moment it must suffice to state that physical anthropology, especially the pre-Second World War variety, actually contributed to racism by its assumptions about phenotypical distinctions; and socio-cultural anthropology, for the most part, turned a blind eye to racism. The same criticisms hold for other issues, such as sexism. Whether anthropology has been more sexist than other social sciences is debatable, but it certainly has lagged behind in its analyses of sexism; only in the past decade has significant anthropology of women emerged, as reflected in the works of Boserup (1970), Friedl (1975), Reiter (1975), and Etienne and Leacock (1980).[1] This may partly have been a result of the less developed consciousness regarding sexual exploitation in 'anthropological' as opposed to 'sociological' societies, reflecting the Marxian-influenced theoretical interpretation that the degree of gender inequality is more pronounced in industrial than in pre-industrial society. When one recalls the great figures in anthropology, it may be thought that we have had a better record of equal opportunity than other disciplines. Yet scholars such as Mead and Benedict are merely exceptions that prove the rule. As Kuper (1975: 155) points out, although British anthropology could boast such outstanding women as Audrey Richards, none became head of a university department.

Nor is it sufficient to focus simply on major social problems and expressions of inequality. There must also be moral involvement. The discipline must be committed to the improvement of people's relationships with each other, which in a fundamental sense means the severe reduction of inequality, brought about by significant social change. It may be objected that to do so would be to relinquish the objective nature of anthropological inquiry. Yet the discipline, even when it had pretences to nomothetic status, never managed to achieve value-neutrality. What passed for objectivity was implicit support for the status quo, such as that provided by structural functionalism for colonialism. The conservative nature of anthropology had obvious causes. Most field-work was conducted under the aegis of colonial administrators, themselves often trained in anthropology, with funds provided by the colonial office. Moreover, approval from some sort of local authority, whether a chief, headman, or district officer, was usually required.

1 For competent surveys of the anthropology of women, see especially the review essays by Lamphere (1977) and Rapp (1979).

Both factors weighted the anthropologist's interpretation on the side of the governing élite. The very fact that most research focused on the poor and powerless also contributed to a conservative orientation. The lives of poor people were essentially recursive and reactive. The dynamic mainsprings of society were located elsewhere, where the power lay, but rarely did anthropologists venture there. Finally, as Lévi-Strauss has written, anthropologists have been conservatives abroad but critics at home. This may mean that the conservative bias in the discipline will eventually end. As fieldwork is partially redirected toward the investigator's own society, there may be a critical awakening.

The social sciences have always been pulled in two directions: toward humane understanding and social improvement, and toward scientific inquiry. If we go too far in the first direction, we become insufferably moralistic, without the benefit of the philosopher's cutting edge of logic. If we go too far in the other direction, we become technicians at best, a parody of science, handcuffed by our own false pretences. This, I believe, is what Evans-Pritchard meant when he remarked (1968: 53) that 'positivism leads very easily to a misguided ethics, anaemic scientific humanism or – Saint Simon and Comte are cases in point – ersatz religion.' One of the great pioneers of American sociology, A.W. Small, foundered on these shoals, but the course he tried to steer is the same one that makes sense today: scientific inquiry tempered by moral concern. Despite the seemingly overwhelming evidence in recent years that value-neutrality is an unattainable goal, there will be some among us who remain unconvinced. Even those scholars, however, will have to embrace the focus on the major consequences of differential power, because therein lie the fundamental forces of society, and hence its potential explanation. For those who are prepared to commit their work to the reduction of inequality and human suffering, the job will not be easy. As Ernest Becker (1971: 70) put it so forcefully, 'a society which is willing to apply social science in the active process of changing its vested-interest institutions has never yet been seen on the face of the planet.'

RACISM AND THE FAILURE OF ANTHROPOLOGY

Any list of major social problems in the contemporary world must include war and nuclear armament, welfare and poverty, sexism and racism, profiled against a common background of bureaucracy and élites. An anthropology of the future must range from the detailed ethnography of an apartment block to the wider workings of the United Nations. While theoretical growth will be to no small extent dependent on the quality of our ethnography, there will remain room for the general and the speculative, such as the essay that illuminates the relationships between industrialized and Third World nations. One encouraging sign is that successful studies of several of these subjects have already been completed, including the edited volume on warfare by Fried, Harris, and Murphy (1967), Wadel's (1973) sensitive analysis of welfare, and the growing literature on the anthropology of women. While any of these topics could serve to illustrate my argument, I shall deal here with the subject of my own recent research – racism.

The social anthropology of racism can be summed up in few words: it has been a dismal failure. This failure has been due largely to the gross inadequacy of our theory. In the last part of the nineteenth century, anthropology was locked in a raging battle between biology and culture. Victory went to culture, which has been celebrated ever since as the hallmark of human existence. For reasons too obvious to dwell upon, we applaud the victory and rejoice in the flexibility of human social organization while reaffirming the basic mental identity of the world's variegated population, the realization that there are no superior societies, and the principles that the fundamental nature and capacity of the human brain is everywhere the same. But along the way we have failed to appreciate the degree to which racism continues to shape relationships among people. Was the battle against biology too decisively won, causing us to cast out everything connected to race, including its social dimension, racism? Or, paradoxically, could it be that anthropology never really succeeded in disentangling racism from its biological connotation? To assume that racism evaporates with the victory of culture over heredity suggests such an interpretation.

What is interesting, given the paucity in recent decades of sophisticated works on racism by social and cultural anthropologists, is that most of the leading anthropologists prior to the Second World War had focused on race and racism. Certainly this was true of the physical anthropologists. Race, as Montagu (1963: 1) has pointed out, was the physical anthropologist's key concept. Until the middle of the present century, most physical anthropologists defined race in terms of observable physical characteristics rather than genes and chromosomes. Among the criteria used to determine a person's race (see Harris 1971: 89), the following stood out: colouration of skin, hair, and eyes; hair type; amount of hair on the body, face, and head; thickness of nose and lips; shape of face and head; body mass and stature; epicanthic fold, or skin flaps over eyes; and darkened area of skin at the base of the spine (the so-called mongoloid spot). Working either in the laboratory or in the field with a colour chart, anthropologists established numerous classifications of human populations, reflecting a tradition in taxonomy embarked upon by Linnaeus (1735). Some of these posited several dozen races, others only two or three, but the most famous has been the classification into Caucasoid, Mongoloid, Negroid, and sometimes Australoid. Social and cultural anthropologists now find themselves in the curious position of having to use the term 'sociological' rather than 'anthropological' type, because the latter refers to a biological entity.

Boas led the way toward a more enlightened anthropology with his popular work *Anthropology and Modern Life* (1962) and with *The Mind of Primitive Man* (1963), *Race, Language and Culture* (1940), and 'Changes in the Bodily Form of Descendants of Immigrants' (1910). However, anthropologists continued to pursue a flawed analysis, despite their opposition to racism, because of the tenacity of the phenotypical concept. Firth (1956), for example, denied any correlation between brain size and mental capacity, and argued that racial purity is not a scientific description, but instead a concept of political propaganda. Yet the same man could argue that the Zulu form a distinct racial group. Race, for Firth, was a biological concept based on the notion of phenotype. Guided by liberal views similar to Firth's, Kroeber argued that there was no scientific evidence to show that one race was more intelligent than another, or less susceptible to disease. He also referred to the potential significance of genes and chromosomes rather than phenotypes (1963: 115). But he dismissed this potentially new approach as 'a pure wish-fulfillment proposal,' and used the conventional criteria – hair type, prognathism, skin colour, and amount of body hair – as well as the terms Caucasoid, Negroid, and Mongoloid. As Bohannan (1963: 192) has humorously observed, in terms of explanatory power it makes just as much sense to use a beverage classification: milky white, chocolat chaud, café au lait, and weak tea.

Not until after the Second World War and the atrocities of Nazi Germany did a significant reaction against the physical anthropologist's use of phenotype begin to build. Even before that, Montagu had laid bare the fallacies in the approach with the first edition of *Man's Most Dangerous Myth* (1942). His condemnation (1964: 63) of anthropology was blunt: 'race is, to a large extent, the special creation of the anthropologist.' That this has been unfortunate he leaves no doubt (1963: vi and 3), for race is described as an idea that propped up 'a thoroughly exploitive period in the development of Western man' and as a completely erroneous and meaningless scientific concept. Montagu's continuing work, along with the UNESCO conferences on race of 1950 and 1952 (to which he contributed) and the later conference of 1964, did much to shift the emphasis from phenotype to genotype. While ambiguity remained with regard to the biologist's definition of race, the Moscow

Declaration, as the 1964 conference became known, made it clear that the groups that had been called races by physical anthropologists were not distinguishable in biological terms. Within human biology and physical anthropology the emphasis swung to analysis in terms of genes and chromosomes, something Kroeber doubted was possible, and to the recognition of the part played by genetic drift and mutation. Some biologists and physical anthropologists went even further and argued that race is not a meaningful biological concept even in the genetic sense (see Montagu 1963: 3; 1964: xi; Ehrlich and Holm 1964; Brace 1964). The result of this revolution in physical anthropology – for that is what it amounted to – was to deliver racism into the hands of the proper authorities, the social and cultural anthropologists, although they were poorly prepared to receive it.

The record of sociology in the scholarly investigation of racism has been almost as dismal as that of anthropology. This is despite the fact that the leading figures in early American sociology, such as Small, Sumner, Thomas, Park, and Cooley, like their contemporaries in anthropology, devoted much of their energy to the analysis of race relations. Once more, the primary source of the problem was the failure to develop an adequate body of theory. What differs is the explanation of the impoverished state of theory in each discipline. It was not the battle between biology and culture that rendered sociology deaf to the cries of racial prejudice and blind to institutionalized racism. Instead, it was the remarkable influence of the European social theorists, particularly Marx, Weber, and Durkheim, that deflected that discipline from its former course. The central theme behind the works of those early giants, as Blauner (1972: 3) points out, was the sharp difference between pre-industrial and industrial society. The underlying assumption was that as society industrializes, race and ethnicity become increasingly irrelevant as determinants of social action and explanations of behaviour. Once again, paradox rules the day, for the emerging theoretical sophistication of sociology was accompanied by a growing incapacity to capture a fundamental feature of the world it examined. Because the same European theorists also informed the basic categories of social anthropology, that discipline's capacity to understand racism was doubly thwarted.

In view of my emphasis on the fundamental role of the European theorists in laying the foundations of anthropology, their negative impact on the development of an adequate body of theory of racism warrants further comment. Durkheim, like his contemporaries in American anthropology, took pains to reject race in the physical anthropological sense as a meaningful influence on social facts; for example, in the first part of *Suicide* hereditary factors are among those entertained but quickly dismissed as possible causes of suicide. But Durkheim did not fill the void by conceiving of racism itself as a social fact. Weber, too, was sceptical of the physical anthropological position, but as Manasse (1947) points out, he was somewhat more sensitive than Durkheim to racism as a social reality, partly because of his direct observation of racial tension during his visit to America in 1904. Marx's position on racism is more complex. He wrote extensively about the American Civil War and slavery, and even compared the attitude of English working men toward Irishmen to that of poor whites in America toward 'niggers' (Selsam et al. 1973: 136). But what is significant is his interpretation. The prejudices of the English working man toward the Irish, Marx argued, served to consolidate the interests of the ruling class and to emasculate both the Irish and the English working classes. In other words, racism was epiphenomenal to class rather than a reality in itself. Much of the contemporary literature on racism continues the argument about the merits of the Marxian interpretation. Nikolinakos (1973), for example, drawing inspiration from Marx, sketches the emergence of racism as a mechanism to justify the exploitation of indigenous peoples, and makes the acute observation that the capitalist countries that did not inherit a racial problem will create it themselves, for racism is essential to capitalist exploitation. According to Nikolinakos, racism operates not only between black and white, but black and black and white and white. In his view, tribal conflict between Igbo, Hausa, and Yoruba in Nigeria and strain between Italian and Spanish workers in France and Germany are as much racial conflicts as those between black and white in South Africa or the United States. In his words (1973: 369), 'Colour is thus accidental as criterion for discrimination.' Yet such an argument would appear to render the concept of racism meaningless, for any form of exploitation would constitute racism, such as the exploitation of women by men, or children by adults, or indeed women by women or children by children. In contrast, Willis (1972) observes that while racism permeates the world, it has been especially pronounced toward black peoples. Africans, he states, have rarely been regarded by whites as 'noble savages.'

The independent causal status of racism is also at the heart of conflicting interpretations of the South African case. Wolpe (1975, 1976, and undated), for example, with Marx as his guide, skilfully marshals evidence to show that changes in the South African class structure, particularly changes involving the African petit bourgeoisie, have taken place despite apartheid because of economic necessity. In contrast, Sivanandan (1973: 385) argues that 'any talk of working-class alliances across colour lines and a class strategy to overthrow the system is so much pie in the sky.' Later (1973: 385) he remarks that 'what the South African experience indicates is that a total racist ideology could produce the same sort of social relations in colour and not class terms as the capitalist mode of production. For the intents and purposes of overthrowing an exploitative system, marxist theory must adjust itself to the fact that there is in South Africa only one reified class of proles, and they are all black.' I lean toward Willis and Sivanandan; otherwise, the racial factor is obfuscated and its sociological significance underestimated in order to promote a rival variable. In my opinion no other framework can equal Marx's when it comes to the analysis of class and power. The writings of Nikolinakos and Wolpe, however, represent clear examples of what can go wrong when one pushes Marxian class analysis too far.[2]

In summary, both anthropology and sociology have failed to develop a sophisticated body of theory addressed to racism and race relations. But as always, merely focusing on a problem is not enough; the perspective is equally important. In an outspoken statement, Willis (1972) contends that both Tylor and Morgan contributed to scientific racism; in order to argue the evolutionary line and to show that Europeans were at the head of development, primitives had to be shown to be inferior. Drawing on the writings of Stocking (1968), Willis goes on to state that Boas himself may have harboured colour prejudice. Boas believed that coloured peoples were 'less sensitive to suffering, more cruel, and less forgiving than white people' (Willis 1972: 125). Perhaps the sharpest criticism of all made by Willis is that Boas's scientific anti-racism was only indirectly and secondarily concerned with coloured peoples. Its real purpose, Willis claims (1972: 139), was to confront the endemic anti-Semitism of the time, to allow Boas and other Jews to dominate American anthropology. Lest the reader wrongly dismiss Willis's powerful arguments as the rantings of an angry man, I quickly turn to a highly respected member of the club, Morton Fried. Fried (1972: 61) too points out the racism in Boas's work, such as his argument that owing to the greater size of the brains of peoples of Asia, America, and Europe, they are superior mentally to the smaller-brained peoples of Africa, Australia, and Melanesia. Fried, in fact, goes beyond Willis to level his attack against the giant of modern anthropology, Lévi-Strauss. In Fried's view (1972: 63), Lévi-Strauss's commitment to the study of primitives, who provide the natural laboratory of anthropology, borders on racism, however unintentionally.

---

2 While a more exhaustive review of the current state of the literature addressed to racism is beyond the scope of this study, I have included some of the basic references in the bibliography. Of particular significance has been the attempt to move beyond Marx without eschewing a radical and revolutionary perspective, such as the internal colonial theory (see Blauner 1972 and Prager 1972).

Long ago Boas happily observed that men like Morgan, Tylor, Bastian, and Spencer could conduct their investigations without taking race into account. It was culture, not race, that was important, for underneath the veneer of culture all men expressed a basic psychic unity. Boas's satisfaction is understandable from the point of view of race as a biological entity. In that sense, the extrication of race from cultural analysis *was* dead on the mark. That is not so in the case of a social phenomenon – racism. Willis (1972: 141) may have overstated his case when he claimed that anthropologists have so little to say about their field-work experience because it is in essence a racist experience. Yet racism is a pervasive force in society today. Indeed, Rex has written (1970: 161), 'For the next few centuries the problems which will preoccupy men politically more than any other will be problems which they subjectively define as problems of race.' The revitalization of anthropology rests partly upon its willingness to grapple with these problems.

OBJECTIONS

There appear to be few serious objections to the argument that a major portion of anthropological research should concentrate on urban industrial society. But the suggestion that we should focus on social problems, especially with a commitment to resolving them, contains many possible flaws.

1 *Scholarship is our first priority.* Knowledge for its own sake must be the anthropologist's dominant motive. Otherwise one might as well become a politician, social worker, administrator, or revolutionary. This is Bailey's message (1977: 4–5): '*The real satisfaction comes from perceiving a pattern where none was known before.* Whether or not the pattern will help people survive an illness or get more to eat or be slightly less objectionable to their fellows is an entirely secondary consideration. Knowledge, new knowledge, the satisfaction of intellectual curiousity is its own reward' (emphasis in original). Lévi-Strauss (1974: 386) has a similar message: 'Action within one's own society precludes understanding of other societies, but a thirst for universal understanding involves renouncing all possibility of reform.' Turning to Fried (1972: 247), we find the conclusion that 'a basic incompatibility exists between the roles of anthropologist and revolutionary. No one can carry out both simultaneously without betraying one or the other.'

These arguments are persuasive, and all point in the same direction: one can't be a scholar and an activist at the same time. Yet the situation is not so clear-cut as it may appear. Recall Lévi-Strauss's description of anthropologists as conservatives abroad and subversives at home; this suggests not only that at least in one sphere the scholar can actively engage in transforming society, but also that the scholarly stance is a political one, whether in the field or at home base. Nor can we leave Fried's conclusion as it stands. Can one be both an anthropologist and a revolutionary? No, claims Fried, and intuitively he seems to be right: the scholarly mind is inimical to action. But can one be an anthropologist and support the status quo? Yes! The great majority of anthropologists do so, and are rarely accused of mixing scholarship and politics. It would seem, then, that the viewpoint that scholarship is our first priority is somewhat more complex than writers such as Bailey assume. Indeed, what is really meant by the statement that scholarship is its own reward? When we unpack this claim, we discover more often than not that one undertakes scholarly investigation and writes (shades of Orwell) for the sheer fame it may bring, or for the power that comes with a victorious argument, or for promotion from assistant to associate professor, or for the respect (if not the love) of fellow academics, or (in the case of textbooks) for financial gain. In other words, the motivation of the anthropologist is not so different from that of the entrepreneur or the hotshot athlete: it is the rules and setting that are different.

2 *Social problems, like other social phenomena, are complex and contradictory, and while anthropology can provide the actor with a highly informed viewpoint, rarely can it offer a solution to the problem or a basis for choosing between alternative viewpoints, except the general rule that we line up with the impoverished and powerless.* In other words, the applied anthropologist has to draw upon 'extra-anthropological' factors to be effective. Like the question whether insiders or outsiders are better equipped to undertake field-work, the question whether social scientists are more qualified than ordinary citizens to decide how society should operate has never been adequately answered.

3 *Some problems, such as the social, political, and economic deprivation of native peoples in North America, appear to have no feasible solution, peaceful or otherwise.* Native peoples are tranquillized by government bureaucracies, seduced by mock-change programs; and it cannot be seriously imagined that even the threat of violence will result in more than a temporary, piecemeal accommodation to the interests of rebellious groups.

4 *Social problems come and go.* Today inner-city slums may catch the imagination, tomorrow it may be the suburbs. Of course, the very notion of social problems is not a straightforward one. Social problems are those situa-

tions that are defined as problems, and it is crucial to determine who does the defining. For example, begging on the streets of Lagos or London may be a social problem from the perspective of governmental officials, but it is a mode of survival for the individuals involved.

5 *If a social problem is really severe, it may be immoral to devote one's time and funds to studying it rather than using those resources to relieve the suffering of individuals concerned.* For example, studies of the Sahel drought area in Africa may have fallen into this category, at least until the people affected were removed from imminent death. It may also be argued that research at present among North American native peoples is immoral; given their plight, scholarly inquiry may be an unaffordable luxury, and indeed many anthropologists now spend half their time defending native peoples from the heavy hand of government rather than in research per se. What we have, thus, is another contradiction: the more severe the social problem, the less it should be studied.

6 *The very idea of applied research may be misleading.* Earlier I argued that the distinction between pure and applied research is not applicable to anthropology. I define applied research as the process of using one's knowledge to formulate policy and make decisions that directly affect people. I do not consider research to be 'applied' simply because it focuses on a social problem. Very few anthropologists have ever been involved in applied work. In fact, there have been only three distinct phases of applied work in the history of anthropology. The most significant was the era of colonialism. While writers such as Kuper (1975) downplay the contribution of anthropologists to colonial rule, and while some of the anthropologists who were involved may argue that without them the colonized people would have been treated less rationally and more unjustly, others must have been embarassed by the fact that they helped the colonial regimes to function more effectively.

The second phase of applied work occurred during the First World War and the Second World War. Anthropologists appear to have readily offered their services to the home cause, providing background material on peoples in strategic locations, composing handbooks such as Benedict's *The Chrysanthemum and the Sword* (1946), and becoming colonial officers, such as Nadel and Audrey Richards, or intelligence officers, such as Leach (see Kuper 1975: 150). Evans-Pritchard (see Hatch 1973: 240) left Oxford to serve with the Sudan Defence Force during the early part of the Second World

War, and in 1942 joined the British Military Administration of Cyrenaica in North Africa as a political officer. While there is no reason to believe that the nationalistic fervour of anthropologists was greater than that of the average citizen, not everyone condoned their activities. Boas, for example, denounced as spies anthropologists who during the First World War carried out intelligence work under the guise of anthropological research. His denunciation prompted an official rebuke from the American Anthropological Association (Honigmann 1976: 195). The unauthorized military use of anthropological investigations was quite a different thing. Few cases are more reprehensible than the one described by Keesing (1976: 541), in which the American government, without permission of the author, translated a French anthropologist's study of a Vietnamese mountain people into English, distributed it to the U.S. Special Forces, and tortured to death one of the anthropologist's key informants in the course of extracting information from him.[3]

The third phase is recent: the drift of anthropologists, sociologists, and other social scientists to governmental bureaucracies. An extremely valuable study would be one that compared the work of anthropologists for the colonial governments of yesteryear with that of anthropologists for governments today. My impression is that the work of the latter is considered insignificant by the governments and largely ignored, or else the scholars are involved in tasks so superficial that their training is wasted, and they end up with an inferiority complex, racked by doubts that they are professionals at all. I suppose a fourth type of applied work could be identified: the efforts by some anthropologists to do research for specific interest groups. Research carried out within the government bureaucracy and that done for an interest group such as an Indian band are polar opposites in one respect. The first is window-dressing; at the most, the scholar is a broker, showing how the wishes of people can be accommodated to the government's policies. The second undertaking is committed to change, to bringing about an improvement for some sector of the society. But what they have in common, with one notable exception, is even more striking: their unfortunate ineffectiveness regardless of their skill and sincerity. The exception concerns land-claims research, which has probably had more practical effect than any other type of project since the end of the colonial era.

3 Relevant here as well is the infamous Project Camelot, a social science counter-insurgency project in Chile organized by the American Department of Defense (see Horowitz 1967).

7 *There is the disturbing possibility that to study a social problem is to make it worse.* It cannot be accidental that anthropologists have traditionally done their field-work in the most impoverished parts of the world, and have studied the deprived – for example, slum-dwellers – when they turn to so-called complex societies. Nor can the funding of this research by governments and corporations have been totally altruistic. To study a group is to expose it and to show how it can be controlled.

8 *A mere focus on social problems is not enough.* What is crucial is the theoretical perspective. From one perspective, the blame for poverty can be levelled at the poor themselves. From another, it can be traced to the dynamics of the capitalist system. Consider, for example, the functionalist explanations of poverty and racial conflict by Gans (1972) and Himes (1966). Drawing on the work of Merton, Gans identifies fifteen functions of poverty. The paper is lucid, the ideas imaginative, and the argument apparently novel, for poverty is usually regarded as negative, something to be overcome in any society. Gans claims that he has shown that functional analysis can be not only ideologically neutral but also radical. Yet a close inspection of the paper denies that claim. The argument only makes sense if seen from the perspective of the affluent. Gans recognizes this limitation, and states clearly that what may be functional to one sector of society may be dysfunctional to another. Yet he obfuscates the issue by speaking of the functions of poverty for 'a number of groups' (1972: 284), or 'many groups' (1972: 287), while in each case he means one specific group: the affluent. Why doesn't he come out and say 'the affluent'? To do so would render the argument superficial and reactionary; that is precisely the effect of the banal conclusion (1972: 287) *'that poverty persists not only because it satisfies a number of functions but also because many of the functional alternatives to poverty would be quite dysfunctional for the more affluent members of society'* (emphasis in original). This is hardly a surprise. Only if Gans had been able to show that poverty is functional for the poor would the paper be significant.

Some sociologists have informed me that 'The Positive Functions of Poverty' was intended as satire. Certainly there are no clues in the paper to give this impression, and writers such as Ritzer (1975: 52–6) in his well-known sociological theory text have taken it as serious commentary. If it is not satire, the argument is not only wrong, it is vicious. If it is satire, Jonathan Swift had nothing on Gans.

Whereas Gans draws on the equilibrium model, Himes bases his analysis of the functions of racial conflict on the pseudo-equilibrium model of Coser's conflict theory. Himes begins by excluding the following types of racial conflict: aggressive or exploitive actions of dominant groups or individuals toward minorities, covert individual antagonisms or compensatory affective and reflexive aggression, and spontaneous, non-rationalized violent racial conflict. By doing so, he has defined out of existence the central types of racial conflict. Conveniently, Himes, like Gans, does not deal with the dysfunctions of racism, and he refers (1966: 8) to 'the ultimate societal values' and the criss-crossing threads of racial conflict that sew society together. Anthropologists familiar with the works of Gluckman, Fortes, Colson, and others will recognize a familiar theme.

My purpose has not been to gratuitously attack Gans and Himes. Rather, it has been to point out the weaknesses in those functionalist approaches to classical social problems. Those papers were merely couched in the theoretical perspective dominant at the time, in which many of us were trained. In one sense, both papers are praiseworthy. They represent with admirable clarity the best that functional analysis had to offer. Paradoxically, the trouble with clear statements is that they bring about their own demise, for only with such statements do the hidden flaws become apparent.

Élites

These several criticisms suggest that a concern for social problems does not automatically confer upon them a solution, or offer anthropologists a glib platform for changing the world. We have a more modest role to play: to unravel the factors that create, conceal, and perpetuate inequality. In other words, we are in the business of demystifying the world. In this context it may be noted that some of the criticisms against focusing on outstanding social problems may disappear if the research thrust is transferred from the poor and powerless to élites, or from coloured peoples to white peoples, which amounts roughly to the same thing. Research on élites has not been extensive in the discipline, and little progress has been made beyond the earlier efforts of Lloyd on African élites (1966), although the lacunae have begun to be recognized in the recent literature; and at least one author (Marcus 1979) has advocated a focus on regional élites. Nader (1972) contends that we must start 'studying up.' That is, the research must switch from the powerless to the powerful, from the poor to the rich, from the colonized to the colonizers. Similarly, Carmichael (1971: 174) states that concerned white scholars should investigate the victimizers rather than the victims, and focus on the white-dominated institutions that generate racism. An identical position is adopted by Schwartz and Disch (1970: 63), who complain that whites almost always focus on blacks as if it is they who have the key to racial reform, but rarely examine white society itself. Research on élites is notoriously difficult. One reason is that unlike the poor and ethnic minorities they often enjoy a higher status than the researcher, and are not intimidated by him. In contrast, most of our research has been conducted in settings where people are so grateful for being treated as equals (at least temporarily) that they are prepared to bare their souls. On numerous occasions during my research in Nigeria, individuals remarked in wonder about my humility, despite my exalted status as PHD candidate. I found it all very pleasing. In Corsica, people seemed to have much less need of the researcher's approbation, and although the job was more difficult it was not remotely comparable to the obstacles that had to be overcome to conduct a successful interview with wealthy and powerful supporters of the white supremacists in Canada. Nevertheless, if anthropology is to be revived, it will have to meet the challenge of 'studying up' to a degree never before attained.

ETHICS AND SUBVERSION

I now turn to a problem that has been recognized as such only in recent years, although it can be expected to have an even higher profile in the future, especially if an anthropology of industrial society focusing on power and inequality does develop. The problem concerns the ethical factor in field-work. Ethics occupies a place in anthropology today comparable to that of social change during the structural-functional era: if the topic is discussed at all, it is usually relegated to the final chapter of a book, as it is here. While the issue of ethics has only recently become prominent in the discipline, it has of course always been implicit in our studies. Certainly it cannot seriously be contended that as a profession we suddenly have become more moral than our counterparts in the colonial era. What has happened is that we have lost our anonymity. No longer can we assume that our books and reports will not be read by the 'natives.' The absence of accountability that formerly characterized the anthropological enterprise no longer exists. But why should this change generate a greater sensitivity to ethical issues? The main reason has, I suspect, always been known but rarely admitted in public: field-work is a form of subversive activity. Before developing this contentious argument, let us look more closely at the ethical issue.

The problem of ethics is not a simple one. Contradictory goals operate within the university setting, and the same is true of research as an institutionalized pattern of activity. The field-worker must respond to at least three forces: scholarship, politics, and the personal worth of the actor. In the pursuit of pure knowledge, should one publish data that might be politically damaging to the group being studied, or a threat to an individual's personal worth? To echo Bailey (1977: 41) regarding the university setting, there are no rational criteria upon which a choice can be based. Indeed, to the extent that ethical issues are made simple and straightforward, they no longer remain ethical problems. To constitute an ethical issue, the problem must be complex and contradictory, devoid of facile solution. We should be equally wary, in other words, of both those who argue for scholarship at any price and those who would sacrifice scholarship at the altar of ethics.

The attraction of the latter solution to a discipline that still feels the sting of its erstwhile colonial connection is all too apparent. Yet one wonders if the advocates of such a solution appreciate the impact it would have on anthropology. It has always been the ethnographer's aim to probe beneath the surface, to push aside the obfuscating layer of conscious models and identify the unconscious ones, to depict the latent rather than the manifest functions and the informal and covert rather than the formal and overt. But it is precisely that realm of behaviour and belief that is marked out-of-bounds by an ethically conscious anthropology today. This is tantamount to stating that the more capable the field-worker, the less ethical the research, for only the gifted ethnographer really succeeds in discovering what was hitherto unknown.

Consent, Jorgensen (1971) states, lies at the heart of the ethical issue; not just consent at the point of entry, but consent throughout the career of a project, including consent to renewed requests for permission to continue as the aims of the research change. Nor, Jorgensen argues, does consent in regard to one topic give the field-worker the right to delve into other topics. But if consent must be sought for every phase of field-work, and for every topic examined, research as we know it would come to a sudden end. No longer would it be possible to produce 'an ethnography in the round,' and the anthropologist's time-honoured inductive procedure, permitting the analytic problems to emerge from the research exercise itself rather than attempting to spell them out beforehand, would no longer be feasible. Nor would we have the flexibility, often dictated by the realities of the field situation, of switching our research project entirely, especially when confronted by an unexpected gold-mine. If consent must constantly be obtained, if the conventional anthropological approach of 'deceptive candour' is to be disallowed, if we must be entirely 'up front' about what we are after, we might as well give the discipline a decent burial and find ourselves new occupations. For if we are completely candid, who is going to welcome us? Third World peoples in general and the residents of ethnic communities and the ghettos already are weary of our presence, suspicious of our aims, and justly sceptical about the benefits that our research may bring them. An ethnographer may genuinely want his research to be useful, but to obtain consent on that ground would be completely deceptive, judged by our past record. Consent from the power élite would be even more difficult to obtain, unless the ethnographer's purpose was to legitimate its position of privilege. Like it or not, if future anthropological research does hinge basically on consent, our results will be superficial and incomplete. In fact, historians in the next century who look back at our era would find our field-work products as limited as a structuralist would a single version of a myth.

Many sociologists, aware of the ethnographer's plight, seem to feel much more smug about their own situation. But that is mere self-deception. What distinguishes the sociologist from the anthropologist is the choice of weapons, not the target. The sociologist, armed with questionnaires and aided by research assistants, drops bombs from 10,000 feet. He only has a distant appreciation of their impact, but the damage is as devastating as the ethnographer's weaponry if the research has been competently conceived. Nevertheless, the anthropologist's involvement in the ethical issue is unusually deep, to an extent shared possibly only by psychiatry. Because we participate on a face-to-face level with our subjects and intrude into the backstage of their lives, field-work has an inescapable moral dimension. When done sensitively, anthropology can be the most humane of the sciences. When done crassly, it has the capacity to destroy.

Let us return to the charge that research is subversive. Although rarely stated explicitly, it is this factor that rides between the lines of most articles that focus on ethics. We study to learn, and possibly to help, but in the course of doing so we expose and implicitly criticize. We reveal the inner workings of a social system after peeling off the protective layer of rationalizations that conceals it. Only if this research activity does contain a subversive component does the demand for consent and the concern for ethics make sense. It is as if the more we learn, the greater the danger to the subject. To speculate further, it can even be suggested that the recent concern with the ethics of field-work is a variation on the old theme of objectivity. Paradoxically, ethics may be a euphemism for ethical neutrality. In former times, the status quo was partly reinforced by the norm that research should be free from value intrusion. In recent years both the possibility and potential benefits of value-neutrality have come under fire. Researchers are more willing to speak out on the side of the suffering; and there is the increasing realization that the élites too must come under scrutiny. Could it be that the emerging concern with ethics and the limits imposed by consent are the reverse of what they seem – an alternative means to sap the moral commitment of field-workers at the very moment it has started to blossom, especially in a discipline showing signs of 'studying up'? If this is so, morality in this context really means immorality.

In view of the moral challenge that has been set for anthropology in this book centring on the reduction of inequality, it would be curious indeed if I did not welcome a greater concern about ethical issues. However, the literature on the subject to date has been disappointing. The pleasant ring of platitudes is not going to solve the ethical problems inherent in field-work. Nor do we need pontification from on high. If there is a solution, it will have to be provided by those committed to field-work, not by armchair scholars. The path leading to a solution is the one that I have followed throughout this study: the concentration on differential power. As Ablon (1982: 39) has stated, 'We and others may work till doomsday with the impoverished and politically impotent but accomplish very little for general economic or social reform until middle and upper class populations are understood and moved to social and political action. Therefore, it can be argued that the mandate to work with these populations is our calling at this time.' If it is correct that research is subversive, there is even more reason for an ethically attuned anthropology to focus on the élite and wealthy rather than the weak and impoverished without undue concern about consent. It was, indeed, an appreciation of the potentially subversive nature of research that partly led me to study white supremacists rather than the victims of racism. Yet on reflection it seems to me that this too is only the appearance of a solution, that it cannot work. For it is improbable that a discipline can endure if the bulk of its research has the purpose of undermining the people who are investigated. It is too much to expect that the practitioners of a discipline could countenance such negativity. Just as people at large require the image of an orderly universe, anthropologists need the fiction that their scholarly efforts are, if not beneficial to mankind, then at least not harmful.

REBIRTH STEP 3: THE DIALECTICAL PERSPECTIVE

The main obstacles to a revitalized anthropology are not those in the way of adapting the discipline to urban industrial society or dealing with the outstanding social problems of the day. Instead they concern the nature of theoretical developments in the years ahead. Nor is it simply a matter of avoiding the potential dead-end orientations that were forecast at the end of chapter 4: a recast Durkheimian model and a hybrid of historical particularism and culture-and-personality. The real danger is that future theoretical work in the discipline will constitute a grand example of salvage theory. That is, the discipline may indeed be maintained, but in terms of explanatory value its continued existence will lack justification. That this possibility exists only reflects the deep vested interests to be found in any organized set of activities, including academic disciplines. In that sense, all human activity is conservative, and what should be least surprising is the effort of anthropologists to maintain their niche in the world of scholarship regardless of the price.

Contributing to this danger is the very adjustment of the discipline to a new ethnographic setting, with an increased sensitivity to the pivotal role of power. The usual pattern of such a major realignment in academic endeavours is not fresh analysis. Instead, tired old explanatory schemes are dusted off, and ancient arguments are rehashed. An upsurge of activity there may well be, but it is deceptive progress, producing little. This has been the fate of our close neighbour, sociology, as its subfield of rural studies has expanded in recent years. Rather than being a source of revitalization, rural sociology has all the earmarks of last decade's mainstream sociology, rediscovering its elementary principles. Had the practitioners of that discipline appreciated Leach's remarks about the fictitious nature of tribal boundaries, the infertile program of rural sociology may have been avoided; for in an even more obvious sense rural society in industrialized nations, where the state and bureaucratized behaviour reach everywhere, cannot be understood as a separate entity, one demanding a specialized body of theory. To some extent, a similar flaw has been characteristic of the anthropology of women. Once again (see Tiffany 1978), fresh data have been run through old perspectives, from structural functionalism to conflict theory. Perhaps this is an unavoidable phase in any fundamental shift of ethnographic and problem orientation. Occasionally social scientists do move beyond this phase, as in the case of the anthropology of women, and in the process ride an innovative crest that can refresh an entire discipline, making the trenchwork in the first phase worthwhile.

If we are to avoid salvage theory in the grand style, our theoretical perspective must be a match for the new world of research into which anthropology must march.[4] It will come as no surprise that I advocate dialectical

---

4 This is not to say that everything we learned in the past is useless. Not only can we have a Malinowskian analysis of baseball magic (Gmelch 1982) and a structuralist interpretation of Star Trek (Claus 1982), but we can also contribute some of our basic research conclusions, such as the fact that war is not natural (see Malinowski 1941) or that there are no superior societies. What we cannot do is transplant entire bodies of theory to contemporary society; that would constitute salvage theory, especially in light of the new demands imposed by a universe conceptualized as complex and contradictory.

anthropology. Nor is it accidental that the term 'perspective' rather than 'model' or 'theoretical system' has been used here. In his youthful, enthusiastic attempt to usher in the new archaeology, Binford (1962) argued for a systems model and deductive inquiry. But two decades later, as a more sophisticated and mature scholar, he (1982) pointedly denigrated the role to be played by theories or models. Instead, he realized that what was called for was an entirely new perspective, comparable in its many facets to a paradigmatic shift in Kuhnian terms, a shift that is much broader than a model or theory per se, allowing one to perceive the world through a new lens.

In similar fashion, I am arguing for a theoretical perspective, not simply a theory. Such a perspective, as defined at the beginning of chapter 2, includes conceptual territory, methodology, philosophy of the actor, and implicit or explicit assumptions about key factors. Perhaps the most crucial of these aspects is the conceptual territory of a discipline. That of dialectical anthropology has been carved out in the preceding chapters of part 2. There, social life was conceptualized as immensely complex and inherently contradictory; it was seen to be rendered more complex by the numerous mechanisms that conceal contradiction, including the ever-present play of power and the seductive illusion of simplicity. Recall that it is not the potential adaptation of the discipline to urban industrial society that ushers in a complex world; rather, it is the conceptualization of social life everywhere. The dialectical orientation includes the basic concepts of structural functionalism: structure, role, status, norm, and act. But it contains much more: power and conflict, contradiction and opposition are also part of the perspective. The perspective portrays social life as one of constant flux, arrested mainly by the mechanisms that produce stability for the benefit of the privileged. This perspective demands that we look for forces that break down behaviour as much as those that give it pattern, and for anti-structure as much as structure.[5] The positivist's world of hard fact is not rejected out of hand, but is meshed with phenomenological features: man's symbolic capacity, the subjective nature of social interaction, the part played by belief and norm. And both positivistic and phenomenological features are filtered through the structuralist's deeper level, fused to a Marxian world of contradiction and transformation.

Lévi-Strauss has his place in this theoretical orientation because of his appreciation of contradiction and dialectic. But his neat and elegant systems

---

5 Turner (1969, 1974: 272–3) redefines structure and anti-structure to mean outer circumference and inner generative centre. In contrast, my usage is more conventional: structure connotes pattern, anti-structure the obverse.

of contradictions do not belong here. The more appropriate image is that which was introduced in chapter 7: cluttered contradictions, ragged and uneven, messy and ill-fitting. Otherwise, dialectical anthropology will merely have shifted the locus of the orderly universe to the level lying below the surface of ongoing behaviour.

It will be apparent that I see less promise in Lévi-Straussian structuralism than Murphy does. It is not structuralism that will pave the way to success. Instead, it is the dialectical perspective influenced by structuralism. Nor will there be any convenient short-cuts to theoretical growth, such as reduced models. The models that are generated within the dialectical orientation will not occupy an order of reality independent of the empirical realm, nor will they be somehow more basic in the sense of encapsulating the entire scope of existential behaviour, itself regarded as a partially random and fortuitous expression of the underlying principles. More so than in Lévi-Strauss's approach, the models that we erect must work with, not move beyond, the surface realm of social action. I am suggesting that we return to the manner in which models were conceptualized in the days of Radcliffe-Brown before Lévi-Strauss's reductionist program made its impact. Models, in other words, should approximate in their logical form the contours of everyday life. The discrepancy in the structuralist procedure between model and behaviour must be eliminated. This will beckon back our former respect for ethnographic fact, and send packing the metaphysical undertones in the structuralist's 'order of orders.' The potential homology between model and behaviour is perhaps the closest that we can come to systematic theory and closure given a universe of flux and contradiction. Yet even there the rigorous nature of enquiry will be fragile. In a real sense, models dissolve in the process of becoming, because they can only be erected by selective distortion of limited sociological characteristics in a presumed static universe (which itself is untrue). Then there is the part played by the double or internal dialectic, which fuels all theories and propels them away from their ethnographic targets. In view of all this, an integral exercise in the dialectical perspective should be the periodic destruction of our models before they harden into ideologies. It is for this reason that theory and model play second fiddle to the more inclusive program of a discipline's general perspective.

Nor can we accept the mental infrastructures and the emphasis on the mind in Lévi-Strauss's version of structuralism, at least not to the same extent that Murphy does. I am not contending that the mind is irrelevant, that culture is not in some sense the product of mind and behaviour. It does not require much sophistication to realize that the human brain does play upon perception, conception, and behaviour itself. The very act of trying to shape this argument, indeed any activity (scholarly or otherwise), is dictated partly by the analytical and synthetic properties of our mental make-up. However, ours is not the task of neurophysiology. If anthropology is to thrive, it must address itself primarily to its distinctive subject matter: the socio-cultural realm. Reductionism has always dogged the steps of the discipline, and part of its attraction has been the promise of a key factor, a fundamental variable around which social life in general unfolds, such as the operations of the human mind. The dialectical perspective, in contrast, assumes that one-factor theories belong to the kindergarten stage of scholarly investigation, especially those theories that lie beyond the conceptual territory of the discipline.

I have already argued that our methodology must enter the computer age while we continue to forge ahead with participant observation. As always, our data will usually not be amenable to rigorous tests of reliability based on replication studies, but they will have a high degree of validity if we can regain the standards set by earlier ethnographers, which means reversing the trend toward shorter periods of field-work. Because of the lack of meaningful criteria of verification or disconfirmation, we shall remain in that grey area between art and science. Plausibility rather than proof will rule the day. To advocate such is merely to formalize what all good ethnographers have always done in practice.

The argument that we strive for but never attain rigorous scientific status is not an invitation to sloppiness. As Evans-Pritchard (1968: 53) remarked in his Marett Lecture, the research of those who have modelled anthropology on the natural science has been neither better than nor different from the work of those who have taken the opposite view. It is my contention that we must and can be much more rigorous than normally has been the case. The comparative method, for example, remains an extremely valuable methodological tool, but it should be used for purposes of control rather than illustration. The style of anthropological reporting must also be improved. Most monographs and journal articles are not guided by specific hypotheses, and it is often difficult to evaluate the importance of data as they are presented. Many writers are satisfied to highlight a few generalizations at the end that appear to grow out of the material. The deductive approach is not appropriate in the field. But at the writing-up stage there is no excuse for failing to present an explicit argument around which the material is organized. Such arguments, when imaginatively related to the relevant literature, probably constitute the most meaningful type of theorizing that we have in the discipline. If most published works in anthropology were organized in this way, there would be little justification for describing field-work as a refuge, a place to hide when the thinking gets heavy.

The actor in the dialectical perspective will be innovative, contradictory, manipulative and self-seeking rather than robot-like, and motive will be as important to the investigator as the system. But the active agent will be partially immobilized by the weight of the institutional framework, confounded by the dead-end avenues that he is urged to enter as he responds to the mechanisms that impose stability. The relationship between the individual and the institution will be regarded as the fulcrum of basic tensions and contradictions in a society, a battleground where the normative order is pressed into service by the power élite only to be twisted and restructured by those intended as its targets, who themselves more often than not are bent upon joining the ranks of the élite itself. Action will impinge upon value, and in the process both will be transformed, repeatedly generating new patterns of normative complexes that articulate the actor to the system and temporarily neutralize their disparate interests.

The actor of a future anthropology will be neither more nor less rational or emotional than in the past. Since long before the beginning of formal anthropological inquiry, the balance between the rational and the emotional has been a constant. An anthropology addressed partly to urban industrial society will not change anything. One of the fundamental truths is that the twentieth-century explosion of knowledge has not rendered us less emotional creatures. Several decades ago Boas (1955: 4) wrote that the advances in the knowledge of our objective world are quickly discarded as soon as we are faced with a crisis. This continues to be the case today. Finally, any consideration of the philosophy of the actor must deal with good and evil, for the theoretician's basic assumptions about the nature of mankind will guide his interpretation of social life. As psychological attributes, those terms fall outside the anthropological realm. I assume that all human activity contains a self-seeking and manipulative dimension, regardless of the class position of the actor. However, until this aspect is translated into sociological terms and institutionalized into the framework of society so that it becomes a variable rather than an constant, it remains merely a background condition of social life in general, a parameter informing all behaviour. To render good and evil relevant, they must become aspects of social life itself. In the dialectical perspective they are operationalized in terms of differential power. In a very real sense, anthropology is a witness to and a participant in a battle between institutionalized good and evil involving the haves and the have-nots, which is another way of describing the discipline's inescapable moral dimension.

That, in essence, is the dialectical perspective, and at the risk of over-simplification I shall sum up the program that it sets for anthropology in a few basic rules.

Negative

1 Whenever social stability endures, be alert to mechanisms that conceal and neutralize contradiction.

2 Whenever a systematic model gains wide support in the discipline, look for the operation of an internal dialectic, and be prepared to demolish the model.

3 Whenever our various models become repetitive, oscillating, and cyclical, search for the embedded conceptual contradictions.

4 Whenever objectivity and value-neutrality are promoted, be aware of the vested interests that are served.

5 Whenever an attempt is made to place the discipline on a nomothetic footing, recognize the sharply restricted and inadequate manner in which its territory is conceptualized.

Positive

1 Conceptualize social life as complex and contradictory.

2 Match models of social life to the manner in which it is conceptualized.

3 To enhance the critical perspective, search for opposition, contradiction, and anti-system in all apparent patterns of belief and behaviour.

4 Aim for objective, nomothetic inquiry and explicit rules of disconfirmation, but realize that these can only be approximated, never attained.

5 Treat the surface level of observable reality, including motives, beliefs, and perception, as the equal of the deep level, rather than as a mere expression or a realm of deception; in this way, positivism, phenomenology, and structuralism can be joined.

6 Build the theoretical enterprise around the basic issue of differential power and inequality.

7 Employ differential power and its potential for immorality as the fundamental criterion of choice among contradictions.

8 Define the discipline's scope as universal, embracing all societies, rather than as restricted to one sector of mankind.

Even if these rules are followed, it is improbable that anthropological knowledge will ever become cumulative in the classical (but perhaps mythical) scientific sense, or that the discipline will achieve nomothetic and paradigmatic status. Nevertheless, the unproductive oscillating rhythm of our theories may be slowed down if not terminated, and the analogy between theory and myth may be rendered obsolete, allowing us finally to move beyond the early pioneers. Such are the manifold promises of the dialectical perspective. In my view anthropology has not lost its élan vital. Life has just begun.

Bibliography

Ablon, J. 1982. 'Field Method in Working with Middle Class Americans.' In *Anthropology for the Eighties*, edited by J. Cole. New York: Free Press.

Althusser, L. 1969. *For Marx.* Translated by B. Brewster. London: Allen Lane, The Penguin Press.

Althusser, L., and Balibar, E. 1970. *Reading 'Capital.'* Translated by B. Brewster. London: New Left Books.

Amin, S. 1967. *Le Développement du Capitalisme en Côte d'ivoire.* Paris: Les Editions de Minuit.

Andreski, S. 1972. *Social Science as Sorcery.* London: André Deutsch.

Applebaum, R.P. 1979. 'Born-Again Functionalism? A Reconsideration of Althusser's Structuralism.' *Insurgent Sociologist* 9: 18–33.

Avineri, S., ed. 1969. *Karl Marx on Colonialism and Modernization.* New York: Anchor Books.

Ayoub, M. 1959. 'Parallel Cousin Marriage and Endogamy: A Study in Sociometry.' *Southwestern Journal of Anthropology* 15: 266–75.

Bachrach, P., and Baratz, M.S. 1962. 'Two Faces of Power.' *American Political Science Review* 56: 947–52.

– 1963. 'Decisions and Non-decisions: An Analytic Framework.' *American Political Science Review* 57: 632–42.

Bailey, F.G. 1960. *Tribe, Caste and Nation.* Manchester: Manchester University Press.

– 1966. 'The Peasant View of the Bad Life.' *The Advancement of Science* 23 (114). Reprinted in Joint Reprint Series 7, School of African and Asian Studies and the Institute of Development Studies, University of Sussex.

– 1969. *Stratagems and Spoils.* Oxford: Blackwell.

– ed. 1971. *Gifts and Poison.* Oxford: Blackwell.

– ed. 1973. *Debate and Compromise.* Oxford: Blackwell.

- 1977. *Morality and Expediency.* Oxford: Blackwell.
- 1980. 'The Exercise of Power in Complex Organizations.' Unpublished paper for Burg Wartenstein Symposium no. 84.
Baldus, B. 1975. 'The Study of Power: Suggestions for an Alternative.' *Canadian Journal of Sociology* 1: 179–201.
Balikci, A. 1965. 'Quarrels in a Balkan Village.' *American Anthropologist* 67: 1456–69.
Banton, M. 1966. 'Race as a Social Category.' *Race* 8: 1–16.
- 1967. *Race Relations.* London: Tavistock Publications.
- 1978. *The Idea of Race.* Boulder: Westview Press.
Banton, M., and Harwood, Jonathon. 1975. *The Race Concept.* New York: Praeger.
Barnes, J.A. 1966. 'Durkheim's Division of Labour in Society.' *Man* 1: 158–75.
Barrett, S.R. 1974. *Two Villages on Stilts.* New York: Chandler.
- 1977. *The Rise and Fall of an African Utopia.* Waterloo: Wilfred Laurier University Press.
- 1979a. 'Social Anthropologist: Marginal Academic?' *Canadian Review of Sociology and Anthropology* 16: 367–86.
- 1979b. 'From Communalism to Capitalism: Two Phases of Social Control in an African Utopia.' *Contemporary Crises* 3: 269–89.
- 1982. 'Sex and Conflict in an African Utopia.' *Journal of Comparative Family Studies* 13: 19–35.
Barth, F. 1954. 'Father's Brother's Daughter Marriage in Kurdistan.' *Southwestern Journal of Anthropology* 10: 164–71.
- 1966. 'Models of Social Organization.' *Royal Anthropological Institute, Occasional Paper* no. 23.
Bascom, W. 1948. 'West Africa and the Complexity of Primitive Cultures.' *American Anthropologist* 50: 18–22.
Becker, E. 1971. *The Lost Science of Man.* New York: G. Braziller.
Becker, G. 1957. *The Economics of Discrimination.* Chicago: University of Chicago Press.
Bellah, R. 1957. *Tokugawa Religion.* Glencoe: Free Press.
Benedict, R. 1932. 'Configurations of Culture in North America.' *American Anthropologist* 34: 1–27.
- 1946. *The Chrysanthemum and the Sword.* Boston: Houghton Mifflin.
- 1959 (orig. 1934). *Patterns of Culture.* Boston: Houghton Mifflin.
- 1960 (orig. 1945). *Race, Science and Politics.* New York: Viking Press.
Bennett, J.W. 1946. 'The Interpretation of Pueblo Culture: A Question of Values.' *Southwestern Journal of Anthropology* 2: 361–74.
Bernstein, J. 1979. *The Restructuring of Social and Political Theory.* London: Methuen.

Biddiss, M. 1965–7. 'Gobineau and the Origins of European Racism.' *Race* 7–8 255–70.

Binford, L. 1962. 'Archaeology as Anthropology.' *American Antiquity* 28: 217–5.

– ed. 1977. *For Theory Building in Archaeology.* New York: Academic Press.

Binford, L., and Sabloff, J. 1982. 'Paradigms, Systematics, and Archaeology.' *Journal of Anthropological Research* 38: 137–53.

Billingsley, A. 1973. 'Black Families and White Social Science.' In *The Death of White Sociology,* edited by Joyce A. Ladner. New York: Vintage Books.

Black-Michaud, J. 1975. *Cohesive Force: Feud in the Mediterranean and the Middle East.* New York: St Martin's Press.

Blanqui, M. 1841. *Rapport sur L'État économique et moral de la Corse en 1838.* Paris: W. Coquebert, Editeur.

Blauner, R. 1972. *Racial Oppression in America.* New York: Harper and Row.

Bloch, M., ed. 1975. *Marxist Analyses and Social Anthropology.* London: Malaby Press.

Boas, F. 1897. *The Social Organization and the Secret Societies of the Kwakiutl Indians.* Report of the U.S. National Museum, 1895, Washington.

– 1910. 'Changes in Bodily Form of Descendants of Immigrants.' Washington: Government Printing Office.

– 1940. *Race, Language and Culture.* New York: Macmillan.

– 1955 (orig. 1927). *Primitive Art.* New York: Dover Publications.

– 1962 (orig. 1928). *Anthropology and Modern Life.* New York: W.W. Norton and Co.

– 1963 (orig. 1911). *The Mind of Primitive Man.* New York: Collier Books.

Bohannan, P. 1963. *Social Anthropology.* New York: Holt, Rinehart and Winston.

Boissevain, J. 1974. *Friends of Friends.* Oxford: Blackwell.

Bologh, R. 1979. *Dialectical Phenomenology: Marx's Method.* London: Routledge and Kegan Paul.

Boserup, E. 1970. *Women's Role in Economic Development.* London: Allen and Unwin.

Bottomore, T. 1975. *Marxist Sociology.* London: Macmillan.

Bourguignon, E. 1979. *Psychological Anthropology.* New York: Holt, Rinehart and Winston.

Brace, C.L. 1964. 'A Non-racial Approach Towards the Understanding of Human Diversity.' In *The Concept of Race,* edited by Ashley Montagu. New York: The Free Press.

Burling, R. 1964. 'Cognition and Anthropological Analysis: God's Truth or Hocus-pocus?' *American Anthropologist* 66: 20–8.

Burridge, K.O.L. 1960. *Mambu.* London: Methuen.

– 1968. 'Lévi-Strauss and Myth.' In *The Structural Study of Myth and Totemism,* edited by Edmund Leach. Social Science Paperback, ASA Monograph 5.

Carmichael, S. 1971. 'Black Power.' In The Dialectics of Liberation, edited by David Cooper. New York: Penguin Books.

Carrington, D. 1971. Granite Island. London: Longman.

Caws, P. 1970. 'What is Structuralism?' In Claude Lévi-Strauss: The Anthropologist as Hero, edited by E.N. Hayes and T. Hayes. Cambridge: MIT Press.

Chambliss, W.J., and Seidman, R.B. 1971. Law Order and Power. Reading: Addison-Wesley.

Chomsky, N. 1972. Language and Mind. New York: Harcourt Brace Jovanovich.

Clammer, J. 1975. 'Economic Anthropology and the Sociology of Development: "Liberal" Anthropology and its French Critics.' In Beyond the Sociology of Development, edited by I. Oxaal, T. Barnet, and D. Booth. London and Boston: Routledge and Kegan Paul.

Clarke, S. 1978. 'The Origins of Lévi-Strauss's Structuralism.' Sociology 12: 405–39.

Claus, P. 'A Structuralist Appreciation of "Star Trek."' In Anthropology for the Eighties, edited by J. Cole. New York: Free Press.

Cloward, R., and Piven, F. 1975. The Politics of Turmoil: Poverty, Race and the Urban Crisis. New York: Vintage Books.

Cohen, P.C. 1969. 'Theories of Myth.' Man 4: 337–53.

Colman, A.M. 1972–3. '"Scientific" Racism and the Evidence on Race and Intelligence.' Race 14: 137–53.

Comas, J. 1961a. 'Scientific Racism Again?' Current Anthropology 2: 303–40.

– 1961b. 'Racial Myths.' In UNESCO, Race and Science. New York: Columbia University Press, pp. 13–55.

Coon, C.S. 1962. The Origin of Races. New York: Alfred A. Knopf.

Coser, L. 1964 (orig. 1956). The Functions of Social Conflict. Glencoe, Ill.: Free Press.

– 1976. 'The Notion of Power: Theoretical Developments.' In Sociological Theory, 4th ed., edited by L. Coser and B. Rosenberg. New York: Macmillan.

Coser, L., and Rosenberg, B., eds. 1976. Sociological Theory, 4th ed. New York: Macmillan.

Cox, O. 1948. Caste, Class and Race. Garden City: Doubleday.

Dahl, R.A. 1961. Who Governs? New Haven: Yale University Press.

Davis, K. 1959. 'The Myth of Functional Analysis as a Special Method in Sociology and Anthropology.' American Sociological Review 24: 757–72.

Davis, M. 1971. 'That's Interesting.' Philosophy of the Social Sciences 1: 309–44.

Dawkins, R. 1976. The Selfish Gene. New York: Oxford University Press.

De George, R., and De George, F., eds. 1976. The Structuralists from Marx to Lévi-Strauss. Garden City, NY: Anchor Books.

De Gramont, S. 1970. 'There Are No Superior Societies.' In *Claude Lévi-Strauss: The Anthropologist as Hero*, edited by E. Hayes and T. Hayes. Cambridge: MIT Press.

Dobzhansky, T. 1963. 'Possibility that Homo Sapiens Evolved Independently 5 Times Is Vanishingly Small.' *Current Anthropology* 4: 360–7.

Douglas, M. 1966. *Purity and Danger: An Analysis of Concepts of Pollution and Taboo*. London: Routledge and Kegan Paul.

– 1968. 'The Meaning of Myth.' In *The Structural Study of Myth and Totemism*, edited by Edmund Leach. Social Science Paperback, ASA Monograph 5.

– 1970. *Natural Symbols*. New York: Pantheon Books.

– 1975. *Implicit Meanings: Essays in Anthropology*. London: Routledge and Kegan Paul.

Durkheim, E. 1938 (orig. 1895). *The Rules of Sociological Method*. Chicago: University of Chicago Press.

– 1951 (orig. 1897). *Suicide*. Glencoe, Ill.: Free Press.

– 1961 (orig. 1925). *Moral Education*. Glencoe, Ill.: Free Press.

– 1968 (orig. 1912). *The Elementary Forms of the Religious Life*. London: George Allen and Unwin.

Durkheim, E., and Mauss, M. 1963 (orig. 1903). *Primitive Classification*. London: Cohen and West.

Eckberg, D., and Hill, L. 1979. 'The Paradigm Concept and Sociology: A Critical Review.' *American Sociological Review* 44: 925–37.

Effrat, A. 1972. 'Power to the Paradigms: An Editorial Introduction.' *Sociological Inquiry* 42: 3–33.

Eggan, F. 1968. 'One Hundred Years of Ethnology and Social Anthropology.' In *One Hundred Years of Anthropology*, edited by J.O. Brew. Cambridge: Harvard University Press.

Ehrlich, P., and Holm, R. 1964. 'A Biological View of Race.' In *The Concept of Race*, edited by Ashley Montagu. New York: The Free Press.

Ehrmann, J., ed. 1970. *Structuralism*. New York: Anchor Books.

Engels, F. 1940 (orig. 1876). *Dialectics of Nature*. New York: International Publishers.

Etienne, M., and Leacock, E., eds. 1980. *Women and Colonization: Anthropological Perspectives*. New York: Praeger.

Evans-Pritchard, E.E. 1937a. *Witchcraft, Oracles and Magic Among the Azande*. Oxford: Clarendon Press.

– 1937b. 'Anthropology and the Social Sciences.' Further Papers on the Social Sciences. J.E. Dugdale, ed. London.

– 1940. *The Nuer*. Oxford: Oxford University Press.

- 1951 *Kinship and Marriage among the Nuer*. Oxford: Clarendon Press.
- 1956. *Nuer Religion*. Oxford: Oxford University Press.
- 1968 (orig. 1950). 'Social Anthropology: Past and Present.' In *Theory in Anthropology*, edited by R. Manners and D. Kaplan. Chicago: Aldine Publishing.

Fanfani, A. 1967. 'Catholicism, Protestantism and Capitalism.' In *Protestantism and Capitalism*, edited by R. Green. Boston: D.C. Heath.

Fanon, F. 1968 (orig. 1961). *The Wretched of the Earth*. New York: Grove Press.

Festinger, L. 1957. *A Theory of Cognitive Dissonance*. Stanford: Stanford University Press.

Firth, R. 1951. 'Contemporary British Social Anthropology.' *American Anthropologist* 53: 474–89.

- 1956. *Human Types*. New York: Barnes and Noble.
- 1957 (orig. 1936). *We, the Tikopia*. London: George Allen and Unwin.
- 1964. *Elements of Social Organization*. Boston: Beacon Press.

Fischer, J. 1958. 'The Classification of Residence in Censuses.' *American Anthropologist* 60: 508–17.

Forde, C.D. 1934. *Habitat, Economy and Society*. London: Methuen.

Fortes, M. 1945. *The Dynamics of Clanship among the Tallensi*. London: Oxford University Press.

- 1949. *The Web of Kinship among the Tallensi*. London: Oxford University Press.

Fortes, M., and Evans-Pritchard, E., eds. 1940. *African Political Systems*. London: Oxford University Press.

Foster, G. 1965. 'Peasant Society and the Image of the Limited Good.' *American Anthropologist* 67: 293–310.

Fox, R. 1968. 'Totem and Taboo Reconsidered.' In *The Structural Study of Myth and Totemism* edited by Edmund Leach. Social Science Paperback, ASA Monograph 5.

Frake, C. 1964. 'Notes on Queries in Anthropology.' *American Anthropologist* 66: 132–45.

Frank, A.G. 1970. 'The Development of Underdevelopment.' In *Imperialism and Underdevelopment*, edited by Robert I. Rhodes. New York: Monthly Review Press.

- 1975. 'Anthropology = Ideology; Applied Anthropology = Politics.' *Race and Class* 17: 57–68.

Fried, M. 1972. *The Study of Anthropology*. New York: Thomas Y. Crowell.

Fried, M., Harris, M., and Murphy, R., eds. 1967. *War: The Anthropology of Armed Conflict and Aggression*. Garden City: The Natural History Press.

Friedl, E. 1975. *Women and Men: An Anthropologist's View*. New York: Holt, Rinehart and Winston.

Friedman, J. 1974. 'Marxism, Structuralism and Vulgar Materialism.' *Man* 9: 444–69.

Friedrichs, R. 1970. *A Sociology of Sociology.* New York: Free Press.
- 1972a. 'Dialectical Sociology: Toward a Resolution of the Current "Crisis" in Western Sociology.' *British Journal of Sociology* 13: 263–74.
- 1972b. 'Dialectical Sociology: An Exemplar for the 1970s.' *Social Forces* 50: 447–55.
Furnivall, J.S. 1967 (orig. 1939). *Netherlands India: a Study of Plural Economy.* London: Cambridge University Press.
Gans, H. 1972. 'The Positive Functions of Poverty.' *American Journal of Sociology* 78: 275–89.
Garfinkel, H. 1967. *Studies in Ethnomethodology.* Englewood Cliffs, NJ: Prentice-Hall.
Geertz, C. 1957. 'Ritual and Social Change: A Javanese Example.' *American Anthropologist* 59: 32–54.
- 1968. *Agricultural Involution: The Process of Ecological Change in Indonesia.* Berkeley: University of California Press.
Giddens, A. 1979. *Central Problems in Social Theory: Action, Structure and Contradiction in Social Analysis.* London: Macmillan.
Gluckman, M. 1963a (orig. 1956). *Custom and Conflict in Africa.* Oxford: Blackwell.
- 1963. *Order and Rebellion in Tribal Africa.* London: Cohen and West.
Gluckman, M., Mitchell, J.C., and Barnes, J. 1949. 'The Village Headman in British Central Africa.' *Africa* 19: 89–106.
Glucksmann, M. 1974. *Structural Analysis in Contemporary Social Thought.* London: Routledge and Kegan Paul.
Gmelch, G. 1982. 'Baseball Magic.' In *Anthropology for the Eighties,* edited by J. Cole. New York: Free Press.
Gobineau, J. 1915 (orig. 1853–55). *The Inequality of Human Races,* translated by Collins. New York: Putnam.
Goddard, d. 1975. 'Philosophy and Structuralism.' *Philosophy of Social Science* 5: 103–23.
Godelier, M. 1970. 'System, Structure and Contradiction in *Das Kapital.*' In *Structuralism: A Reader,* edited by Michael Lane. London: Jonathan Cape.
- 1972 (orig. 1966). *Rationality and Irrationality in Economics.* London.
- 1980. 'The Emergence and Development of Marxism in Anthropology in France.' In *Soviet and Western Anthropology,* edited by Ernest Gellner. New York: Columbia University Press.
Goodenough, W. 1956a. 'Componential Analysis and the Study of Meaning.' *Language* 32: 195–216.
- 1956b. 'Residence Rules.' *Southwestern Journal of Anthropology* 12: 22–37.

Goody, J. 1969. *Comparative Studies in Kinship*. London: Routledge and Kegan Paul.

Gouldner, A. 1970. *The Coming Crisis of Western Sociology*. London: Heinemann.

Habermas, J. 1970. *Towards a Rational Society*. Translated by J. Shapiro. London: Heinemann.

Hall, O. 1946. 'The Informal Organization of the Medical Profession.' *Canadian Journal of Economics and Political Science* 12: 30–44.

Hammel, E. 1972. 'The Myth of Structural Analysis: Lévi-Strauss and the Three Bears.' Reading: Addison-Wesley.

Harris, M. 1968. *The Rise of Anthropological Theory*. New York: Thomas Y. Crowell.

– 1971. *Culture, Man, and Nature*. New York: Thomas Y. Crowell.

– 1974. *Cows, Pigs, Wars and Witches*. New York: Vintage Books.

– 1978. *Cannibals and Kings*. New York: Random House.

Hatch, E. 1973. *Theories of Man and Culture*. New York: Columbia University Press.

Heilman, S. 1980. 'Jewish Sociologist: Native-as-Stranger.' *The American Sociologist* 15: 100–8.

Held, D. 1980. *Introduction to Critical Theory*. Berkeley and Los Angeles: University of California Press.

Henderson, R.N. 1972. *The King in Every Man*. New Haven: Yale University Press.

Himes, J. 1966. 'The Functions of Racial Conflict.' *Social Forces* 45.

Homans, G. 1961. *Social Behavior: Its Elementary Forms*. New York: Harcourt Brace Jovanovich.

Homans, G., and Schneider, D. 1955. *Marriage, Authority and Final Causes*. New York: Free Press.

Honigmann, J. 1976. *The Development of Anthropological Ideas*. Homewood, Ill.: The Dorsey Press.

Horowitz, I. 1964, ed. *The New Sociology*. New York and London: Oxford University Press.

– 1967. *The Rise and Fall of Project Camelot*. Cambridge: MIT Press.

Hsu, F. 1973. 'Prejudice and Its Intellectual Effect in American Anthropology: An Ethnographic Report.' *American Anthropologist* 75: 1–19.

Hughes, A. Stewart. 1958. *Consciousness and Society*. New York: Vintage Books.

Hughes, D., and Kallen, E. 1974. *The Anatomy of Racism: Canadian Dimensions*. Montreal: Harvest House.

Hughes, E.C. 1958. *Men and Their Work*. Glencoe, Ill.: Free Press.

– 1976. 'Dilemmas and Contradictions of Status.' In *Sociological Theory*, 4th ed., edited by Lewis Coser and Bernard Rosenberg. New York: Macmillan.

Hymes, D. 1972. 'The Use of Anthropology: Critical, Political, Personal.' In *Reinventing Anthropology*, edited by Dell Hymes. New York: Pantheon Books.

Jahoda, M. 1961. 'Race Relations and Mental Health.' In UNESCO, *Race and Science*. New York: Columbia University Press.

Jarvie, I.C. 1975. 'Epistle to the Anthropologists.' *American Anthropologist* 77: 253–66.

Jay, M. 1974. *The Dialectical Imagination*. London: Heinemann.

Jones, D. 1982. 'Towards a Native Anthropology.' In *Anthropology for the Eighties*, edited by J. Cole. New York: Free Press.

Jones, R. 1973. 'Proving Blacks Inferior: The Sociology of Knowledge.' In *The Death of White Sociology*, edited by Joyce A. Ladner. New York: Vintage Books.

Jorgensen, J. 1971. 'On Ethics and Anthropology.' *Current Anthropology* 12: 326–33.

Kahl, J. 1964–5. 'Some Measurements of Achievement Orientation.' *American Journal of Sociology* 70: 669–81.

Kaplan, D., and Manners, R. 1972. *Culture Theory*. Englewood Cliffs, NJ: Prentice-Hall.

Kardiner, A., and Preble, E. 1963. *They Studied Man*. New York: Mentor.

Keesing, F.M. 1961. 'Review of Burridge's *Mambu*.' *Man* 61: 148.

Keesing, R.M. 1976. *Cultural Anthropology: A Contemporary Perspective*. New York: Holt, Rinehart and Winston.

Khuri, F. 1970. 'Parallel Cousin Marriage Reconsidered: A Middle Eastern Practice that Nullifies the Effects of Marriage on the Intensity of Family Relationships.' *Man* 5: 597–618.

Kolakowski, L. 1971. 'Althusser's Marx.' *The Socialist Register*: 111–28.

Kroeber, A.L. 1963 (orig. 1923). *Anthropology: Biology and Race*. New York: Harcourt, Brace and World.

Kuhn, T.S. 1970 (orig. 1962). *The Structure of Scientific Revolutions*. 2nd ed. Chicago: University of Chicago Press.

– 1972. 'Reflections on My Critics.' In *Criticism and the Growth of Knowledge*, edited by I. Lakotos and A. Musgrave. Cambridge: Cambridge University Press.

Kuper, A. 1975 (orig. 1973). *Anthropologists and Anthropology*. London: Peregrine Books.

Kuper, Leo. 1974. *Race, Class and Power: Ideology and Revolutionary Change in Plural Societies*. London: Duckworth.

Lacan, J. 1970. 'The Insistence of the Letter in the Unconscious.' In *Structuralism*, edited by J. Ehrmann. New York: Anchor Books.

Lafaye, J. 1972. *Sartène de 1919 à 1939*. Mémoire de Maîtrise d'Histoire. Nice: Université de Nice.

Lakatos, I., and Musgrave, A., eds. 1972. *Criticism and the Growth of Knowledge.* Cambridge: Cambridge University Press.

Lamphere, L. 1977. 'Anthropology.' *Signs: Journal of Women in Culture and Society* 2: 612–27.

Lane, M., ed., 1970. *Structuralism: A Reader.* London: Jonathan Cape.

Langham, I. 1981. *The Building of British Social Anthropology.* Dordrecht, Holland: D. Reidel.

Leach, E.R. 1961. *Rethinking Anthropology.* London: Athlone Press.

– 1965 (orig. 1954). *Political Systems of Highland Burma.* Boston: Beacon Press

– 1973. 'Structuralism in Social Anthropology.' In *Structuralism: An Introduction,* edited by David Robey. Oxford: Clarendon Press.

– 1974. *Lévi-Strauss.* Fontana.

Leaf, M. 1979. *Man, Mind and Science: a History of Anthropology.* New York: Columbia University Press.

Leiris, M. 1961. 'Race and Culture.' In *Race and Science.* New York: Columbia University Press.

Lenski, G. 1954. 'Status Crystallization: A Non-Vertical Dimension of Social Status.' *American Sociological Review* 19: 405–13.

– 1966. *Power and Privilege.* New York: McGraw-Hill.

Lerner, D. 1958. *The Passing of Traditional Society.* New York: Free Press.

Le Vine, R. 1966. *Dreams and Deeds.* Chicago: University of Chicago Press.

Lévi-Strauss, C. 1945. 'French Sociology.' In *Twentieth Century Sociology,* edited by Georges Gurvitch and Wilbert E. Moore. New York: The Philosophical Library.

– 1963 (orig. 1962). *Totemism.* Boston: Beacon Press.

– 1966 (orig. 1962). *The Savage Mind.* London: Weidenfeld and Nicolson.

– 1967a (orig. 1958). *Structural Anthropology.* New York: Anchor Books.

– 1967b. *The Scope of Anthropology.* London: Jonathan Cape.

– 1968 (orig. 1958). 'The Story of Asdiwal.' In *The Structural Study of Myth and Totemism,* edited by Edmund Leach. Social Science Paperback, ASA Monograph 5.

– 1969 (orig. 1949). *The Elementary Structures of Kinship.* Boston: Beacon Press.

– 1974 (orig. 1955). *Tristes Tropiques.* New York: Atheneum.

– 1975 (orig. 1964). *The Raw and the Cooked.* Vol. 1. New York: Harper Colophon.

– 1978. *Myth and Meaning.* Toronto: University of Toronto Press.

Levy, M. 1952. *The Structure of Society.* Princeton: Princeton University Press.

Lévy-Bruhl, L. 1966 (orig. 1923). *Primitive Mentality.* Translated by L.A. Clare. Boston: Beacon Press.

Lewis, O. 1951. *Life in a Mexican Village.* Urbana: University of Illinois Press.

Linnaeus, C. 1735. *Systema naturae, sive Regna tria naturae systematice proposita per classes, ordines, genera species.* Lugduni Batarorum, apud T. Haak.

Lipset, S.M., and Raab, E. 1970. *The Politics of Unreason: Right-Wing Extremism in America, 1790–1970.* New York: Harper and Row.

Little, K. 1961. 'Race and Society.' In UNESCO, *Race and Science.* New York: Columbia University Press.

Lloyd, P.C., ed., 1966. *The New Elites of Tropical Africa.* New York and London: Oxford University Press.

Long, N. 1975. 'Structural Dependency, Modes of Production and Economic Brokerage in Rural Peru.' In *Beyond the Sociology of Development,* edited by I. Oxaal, T. Barnet, and D. Booth. London: Routledge and Kegan Paul.

Lowie, R.H. 1937. *The History of Ethnological Theory.* New York: Holt, Rinehart and Winston.

Lukacs, G. 1971 (orig. 1923). *History and Class Consciousness: Studies in Marxist Dialectics.* Translated by R. Livingstone. London: Merlin Press.

– 1973. *Marxism and Human Liberation.* Edited by E. San Juan. New York: Dell.

Lukes, S. 1974. *Power: A Radical View.* London: Macmillan.

Lynd, R.S. 1964 (orig. 1939). *Knowledge For What?* New York: Evergreen Press.

MacKinnon, N., and Summers, G. 1976. 'Homogenity and Role Consensus: a Multivariate Exploration in Role Analysis.' *Canadian Journal of Sociology* 1: 439–62.

Mair, L. 1972. *An Introduction to Social Anthropology.* Oxford: Clarendon Press.

Malinowski, B. 1922. *Argonauts of the Western Pacific.* New York: E.P. Dutton.

– 1941. 'An Anthropological Analysis of War.' *American Journal of Sociology* 46: 521–50.

– 1944. *A Scientific Theory of Culture and Other Essays.* New York: Galaxy Books.

Manasse, E. 1947. 'Max Weber on Race.' *Social Research* 14: 191–221.

Manners, R., and Kaplan, D. 1968. *Theory in Anthropology.* Chicago: Aldine.

Mannheim, K. 1949. *Ideology and Utopia.* New York: Harcourt, Brace.

Marcus, G.E. 1979. 'Ethnographic Research among Elites in the Kingdom of Tonga: Some Methodological Considerations.' *Anthropological Quarterly* 52: 135–51.

Marcuse, H. 1964. *One-Dimensional Man.* Boston: Beacon Press.

– 1971. 'Liberation from the Affluent Society.' In *The Dialectics of Liberation,* edited by David Cooper. New York: Penguin Books.

Marx, K. 1887. *Capital.* Vol. 1. Reprinted (n.d.). Moscow: Progress Publishers.

Marx, K., and Engels, F. 1888. *Manifesto of the Communist Party.* Reprinted 1952. Moscow: Progress Publishers.

Masterson, M. 1972. 'The Nature of a Paradigm.' In Criticism and the Growth of Knowledge, edited by I. Lakatos and A. Musgrave. Cambridge: Cambridge University Press.

Maybury-Lewis, D. 1970. 'Science or Bricolage?' In Claude Lévi-Strauss: The Anthropologist as Hero, edited by E. Hayes and T. Hayes. Cambridge: MIT Press.

McClelland, D. 1961. The Achieving Society. Princeton: Princeton University Press.

McCracken, G. 1982. 'Rank and Two Aspects of Dress in Elizabethan England.' Culture 2: 53–62.

McFeat, T. 1979. 'Anthropology Changing.' Transactions of The Royal Society of Canada, series IV, Vol. 17: 215–27.

Meillassoux, C. 1964. Anthropologie Économique des Gouro de Côte D'Ivoire. Paris: Mouton et Cie.

Memmi, A. 1967 (orig. 1957). The Colonizer and the Colonized. Translated by Howard Greenfeld. Boston: Beacon Press.

Merrington, J. 1968. 'Theory and Practice in Gramsci's Marxism.' Socialist Register: 145–76.

Merton, R.K. 1957 (orig. 1949). Social Theory and Social Structure. New York: Free Press.

Merton, R.K., and Barber, E. 1976. 'Sociological Ambivalence.' In Sociological Theory, 4th ed., edited by L. Coser and B. Rosenberg. New York: Macmillan.

Metzger, D., and Williams, G. 1966. 'Some Procedures and Results in the Study of Native Categories: Tzeltal "Firewood."' American Anthropologist 68: 389–407.

Midgley, M. 1980. 'Rival Fatalisms: The Hollowness of the Sociobiology Debate.' In Sociobiology Examined, edited by Ashley Montagu. Oxford: Oxford University Press.

Miner, H. 1956. 'Body Ritual among the Nacirema.' American Anthropologist 58: 503–7.

Mirkovic, D. 1980. Dialectic and Sociological Thought. St Catharines, Ont.: Diliton Publications.

Montagu, A. 1942. Man's Most Dangerous Myth: The Fallacy of Race. New York: World Publishing.

– 1963. Race, Science and Humanity. New York: Van Nostrand Reinhold.

– ed., 1964. The Concept of Race. New York: Free Press.

– ed., 1980. Sociobiology Examined. Oxford: Oxford University Press.

Mortimore, G. 1978. 'The Bureaucratic Put-Down: How and Why Organizations Control Their Clients.' Unpublished paper, Department of Anthropology and Sociology, University of British Columbia.

Murdock, G.P. 1949. Social Structure. New York: Macmillan.

– 1951. 'British Social Anthropology.' American Anthropologist 53: 465–73.

Murphy, R. 1971. The Dialectics of Social Life. New York: Basic Books.

– 1979. An Overture to Social Anthropology. Englewood Cliffs, NJ: Prentice-Hall.

Nadel, S.F. 1957. The Theory of Social Structure. New York: Free Press.

Nader, L. 1972. 'Up the Anthropologist – Perspectives Gained from Studying Up.' In Reinventing Anthropology, edited by Dell Hymes. New York: Pantheon Books.

Neal, Sr M.A. 1965. Values and Interests in Social Change. Englewood Cliffs, NJ: Prentice-Hall.

Needham, R. 1962. Structure and Sentiment. Chicago: University of Chicago Press.

– 1979. Symbolic Classification. Santa Monica: Goodyear Publishing.

Nettl, J.P., and Robertson, R. 1966. 'Industrialization, Development or Modernization.' British Journal of Sociology. 17: 274–91.

Nikolinakos, M. 1973. 'Notes on an Economic Theory of Racism.' Race 14: 365–81.

Nutini, H. 1970. 'Some Considerations on the Nature of Social Structure and Model Building: A Critique of Claude Lévi-Strauss and Edmund Leach.' In Claude Lévi-Strauss: The Anthropologist as Hero, edited by E. Hayes and T. Hayes. Cambridge: MIT Press.

O'Connor, J. 1970. 'The Meaning of Economic Imperialism.' In Imperialism and Underdevelopment: A Reader, edited by Robert Rhodes. New York: Monthly Review Press.

Odum, E. 1971. Fundamentals of Ecology. Toronto: W.B. Saunders.

Ottenberg, S. 1962. 'Ibo Receptivity to Change.' In Continuity and Change in African Cultures, edited by W.J. Bascom and M.J. Herskovits. Chicago: University of Chicago Press.

Parsons, T. 1951. The Social System. Glencoe, Ill.: Free Press.

– 1964 (orig. 1949). Essays in Sociological Theory. Glencoe, Ill.: Free Press.

– 1966. Societies: Evolutionary and Comparative Perspectives. Englewood Cliffs, NJ: Prentice-Hall.

– 1967. 'A Paradigm for the Analysis of Social Systems and Change.' In System, Change, and Conflict, edited by N.J. Demerath and R.A. Peterson. New York: Free Press.

Pelto, P. 1970. Anthropological Research. New York: Harper and Row.

Penniman, T.K. 1965. A Hundred Years of Anthropology. London: Gerald Duckworth and Co.

Peters, E. 1967. 'Some Structural Aspects of the Feud among the Camel-herding Bedouin of Cyrenaica.' Africa 37: 261–82.

Phillips, D. 1971. Knowledge From What? Chicago: Rand McNally.

– 1973–74. 'Paradigms, Falsification, and Sociology.' Acta Sociologica 16–17: 13–30.

Piaget, J. 1951. *Plays, Dreams and Imitation*. London: Routledge and Kegan Paul.
– 1970. *Structuralism*. New York: Basic Books.
Piven, F., and Cloward, R. 1972. *Regulating the Poor: the Functions of Public Welfare*. New York: Vintage Books.
– 1979. *Poor People's Movements*. New York: Vintage Books.
Polanyi, K. 1944. *The Great Transformation*. New York: Holt, Rinehart and Winston.
Pomponi, F. 1976. 'La Femme Corse: Approche Monographie et Démographie du Problème.' In *Femmes Corses et Femmes Mediterranéenes*, special edition of *Études Corses*, no. 6–7: 323–57.
Popper, K. 1974. 'The Myth of the Framework.' In *The Abdication of Philosophy: Philosophy and the Common Good*, edited by E. Freeman. La Salle, Ill.: Open Court Publishing.
Prager, J. 1972. 'White Racial Privilege and Social Change: An Examination of Theories of Racism.' *Berkeley Journal of Sociology* 17: 117–50.
Prattis, J.I. 1980. 'Synthesis, or a New Problematic in Economic Anthropology.' Department of Sociology and Anthropology, Departmental Working Paper 80–3. Ottawa: Carleton University.
Radcliffe-Brown, A.R. 1964 (orig. 1948). *A Natural Science of Society*. Glencoe, Ill.: Free Press.
– 1971 (orig. 1952). *Structure and Function in Primitive Society*. London: Cohen and West.
Radcliffe-Brown, A.R., and Forde, D., eds. 1964 (orig. 1950). *African Systems of Kinship and Marriage*. London: Oxford University Press.
Rapp, R. 1979. 'Anthropology.' *Signs: Journal of Women in Culture and Society* 4: 497–513.
Rapoport, A. 1966. *Two-Person Game Theory*. Ann Arbor: University of Michigan Press.
Redfield, R. 1930. *Tepoztlán, A Mexican Village*. Chicago: University of Chicago Press.
– 1955–6. 'Societies and Cultures as Natural Systems.' *Journal of the Royal Anthropological Institute* 85–6: 19–32.
Reich, M. 1971. 'The Economics of Racism,' In *Problems in Political Economy: An Urban Perspective*, edited by David Gordon. Lexington, Mass.: D.C. Heath.
Renfrew, D., Rowlands, M., and Segraves, B., eds. 1982. *Theory and Explanation in Archaeology*. London: Academic Press.
Rex, J. 1961. *Key Problems of Sociological Theory*. London: Routledge and Kegan Paul.
– 1970. *Race Relations in Sociological Theory*. New York: Schocken Books.
– 1973. *Race, Colonialism and The City*. London: Routledge and Kegan Paul.

Ritzer, G. 1975. *Sociology: A Multiple Paradigm Science*. Boston: Allyn and Bacon.

Runciman, W.G. 1970. *Sociology in Its Place*. Cambridge: Cambridge University Press.

Sahlins, M. 1960. 'Evolution: Specific and General.' In *Evolution and Culture*, edited by M. Sahlins and E. Service. Ann Arbor: University of Michigan Press.

- 1968. 'Culture and Environment: The Study of Cultural Ecology.' In *Theory in Anthropology*, edited by R. Manners and D. Kaplan. Chicago: Aldine.

- 1976. *Culture and Practical Reason*. Chicago: University of Chicago Press.

- 1977. *The Use and Abuse of Biology: an Anthropological Critique of Sociobiology*. Ann Arbor: University of Michigan Press.

Sankoff, G. 1973. 'The Ethnosemantics of Excellence.' Newsletter, *American Anthropologist*: 9–11.

Sawyer, E. 1973. 'Methodological Problems in Studying So-Called "Deviant" Communities.' In *The Death of White Sociology*, edited by Joyce Ladner. New York: Vintage Books.

Scanzoni, J. 1967. 'Socialization, n Achievement, and Achievement Values.' *American Sociological Review* 32: 449–56.

Schaff, A. 1970. *Marxism and the Human Individual*. New York: McGraw-Hill.

Scheffler, H.W. 1970. 'Structuralism in Anthropology.' In *Structuralism*, edited by J. Ehrmann. New York: Achor Books.

Scholte, B. 1970. 'Epistemic Paradigms: Some Problems in Cross-Cultural Research on Social Anthropological History and Theory.' In *Claude Lévi-Strauss: The Anthropologist as Hero*, edited by E. Hayes and T. Hayes. Cambridge: MIT Press.

Schuman, H. 1969. 'Sociological Racism.' *Trans-Action* 7: 44–8.

Schwartz, B., and Disch, R., eds. 1970. *White Racism*. New York: Dell.

Selsam, H., Goldway, D., and Martel, H., eds. 1973. *Dynamics of Social Change: A Reader in Marxist Social Science*. New York: International Publishers.

Sheleff, L. 1975. 'From Restitutive Law to Repressive Law: Durkheim's *The Division of Labor in Society* Re-visited.' *European Journal of Sociology* 16: 16–45.

Silverman, S. 1974–5. 'Bailey's Politics.' *Journal of Peasant Studies* 2: 111–20.

Sivanandan, A. 1973. 'Race, Class and Power: An Outline for Study.' *Race* 14: 383–91.

Slater, P. 1976. 'Social Bases of Personality.' In *Sociological Theory*, 4th ed., edited by L. Coser and B. Rosenberg. New York: Macmillan.

Smith, M.G. 1965. *The Plural Society in the British West Indies*. Berkeley: University of California Press.

Sontag, S. 1970. 'The Anthropologist as Hero.' In *Claude Lévi-Strauss: The Anthropologist as Hero*, edited by F. Hayes and T. Hayes. Cambridge: MIT Press.

Spencer, H. 1876. *Principles of Sociology*. New York: Appleton.

Stember, C.H. 1976. *Sexual Racism*. New York: Elsevier.

Steward, J. 1955. *Theory of Culture Change*. Urbana: University of Illinois Press.

Stocking, G. 1968. *Race, Culture, and Evolution*. New York: Free Press.

Terray, E. 1969. *Le Marxisme devant les Sociétés Primitives: Deux Études*. Paris: Maspero.

Thurow, L. 1969. *Poverty and Discrimination*. Washington: Brookings Institute Press.

Tiffany, S. 1978. 'Models and the Social Anthropology of Women: A Preliminary Assessment.' *Man* 13: 34–51.

Todorov, T. 1973. 'The Structural Analysis of Literature: the Tales of Henry James.' In *Structuralism*, edited by D. Robey. Oxford: Clarendon Press.

Tucker, R., ed. 1972. *The Marx–Engels Reader*. New York: W.W. Norton.

Tunteng, P.K. 1972–3. 'Racism and the Montreal Computer Incident of 1969.' *Race* 14: 229–40.

Turner, V. 1957. *Schism and Continuity in an African Society*. Manchester: University of Manchester Press.

– 1967. *The Forest of Symbols: Studies in Ndembu Ritual*. Ithaca, NY: Cornell University Press.

– 1969. *The Ritual Process: Structure and Anti-Structure*. Chicago: Aldine Publishing Company.

– 1974. *Drama, Fields, and Metaphors: Symbolic Action in Human Society*. Ithaca, NY: Cornell University Press.

Tyler, S., ed. 1969. *Cognitive Anthropology*. New York: Holt, Rinehart and Winston.

Tylor, E.B. 1874. *Primitive Culture*. Boston: Estes and Lauriat.

Udy, S. 1959. *The Organization of Work: A Comparative Analysis of Production among Nonindustrial Peoples*. New Haven: HRAF Press.

van den Berghe, P. 1965. *South Africa, A Study in Conflict*. Middletown, Conn.: Wesleyan University Press.

– 1967a. 'Dialectic and Functionalism: Toward a Synthesis.' In *System, Change, and Conflict*, edited by N.J. Demerath and R.A. Peterson. New York: Free Press.

– 1967b. *Race and Racism*. New York: John Wiley and Sons.

Vayda, A. 1961. 'Expansion and Warfare among Swidden Agriculturalists.' *American Anthropologist* 63: 346–58.

Verdon, M. 1981. 'Kinship, Marriage, and the Family: An Operational Approach.' *American Journal of Sociology* 86: 796–818.

Voget, F.W. 1975. *A History of Ethnology*. New York: Holt, Rinehart and Winston.

von Neuman, J., and Morgenstein, O. 1947. *Theory of Games and Economic Behavior*. Princeton: Princeton University Press.

261 Bibliography

Wadel, C. 1973. *Now Whose Fault Is That? The Struggle for Self-Esteem in the Face of Chronic Unemployment.* Newfoundland Social and Economic Studies, no. 11. St John's: Memorial University.

Wallace, A., and Atkins, J. 1960. 'The Meaning of Kinship Terms.' *American Anthropologist* 62: 58–80.

Ward, B. 1965. 'Varieties of the Conscious Model.' In *The Relevance of Models for Social Anthropology,* edited by M. Banton. London: Tavistock Publications.

Warner, W.L., and Srole, L. 1945. *The Social System of American Ethnic Groups.* New Haven: Yale University Press.

Weber, M. 1958. *The Protestant Ethic and the Spirit of Capitalism.* Translated by Talcott Parsons. New York: Charles Scribner's Sons.

Westhues, K. 1976. 'Class and Organization as Paradigms in Social Science.' *The American Sociologist* 11: 38–49.

White, L. 1949. *The Science of Culture.* New York: Grove Press.

Willhelm, S.M. 1973. 'Equality: America's Racist Ideology.' In *The Death of White Sociology,* edited by Joyce Ladner. New York: Vintage Books.

Willis, W.S. 1972. 'Skeletons in the Anthropological Closet.' In *Reinventing Anthropology,* edited by Dell Hymes. New York: Pantheon Books.

Wilson, E.O. 1975. *Sociobiology – The New Synthesis.* Cambridge: Harvard University Press.

Wolpe, H. 1975. 'The Theory of Internal Colonialism: the South African Case.' In *Beyond the Sociology of Development,* edited by I. Oxaal, T. Barnet, and D. Booth. London: Routledge and Kegan Paul.

– 1976. 'The Changing Class Structure of South Africa: The African Petit-Bourgeoisie.' Unpublished paper, Department of Sociology, University of Essex.

– Undated. 'Class, Race and the Occupational Structure in South Africa.' Unpublished paper presented at the ISA Research Committee on Urban Sociology Seminar, 'Race, Caste and Tribalism in the Urban Context,' at the 7th World Congress of Sociology.

Woodbury, R.B. 1977. 'On Book Reviewing.' *American Anthropologist* 79: 551–4.

Worsley, P. 1968. 'Groote Eylandt Totemism and Le Totémisme Aujourd'hui.' In *The Structural Study of Myth and Totemism,* edited by Edmund Leach. Social Science Paperback, ASA Monograph 5.

Wrong, D. 1959. 'The Functional Theory of Stratification: Some Neglected Considerations.' *American Sociological Review* 24: 772–82.

Zanden, J.W. 1960. 'The Klan Revival.' *American Journal of Sociology* 65: 456–62.

Zimmerman, R.L. 1970. 'Lévi-Strauss and the Primitive.' In *Claude Lévi-Strauss: The Anthropologist as Hero,* edited by E. Hayes and T. Hayes. Cambridge: MIT Press.

Zucherman, H., and Merton, R.K. 1971. 'Patterns of Evaluation in Science: Institutionalization, Structure and Functions of the Referee System' *Minerva* 9: 66–100.

Index

Ablon, J. 235
achievement orientation 85; among Igbo 20–1; and modernization 192
Althusser, L. 88–9, 137–8, 146; see also structuralism and salvage theory
ambivalence 156, 172–3; see also contradiction
Andreski, S. 31
anthropology: crisis in 6; social 15–16; cultural 17–19; two-headed 135–6; and colonialism 6–7, 51–2, 92, 221; and subversion 234–7; of women 221, 238; and sociology 94–7; and racism 222–34
anti-Semitism 237
applied anthropology 230–1
armchair anthropology 50–1

Bachrach, P., and Baratz, M.S. 185–6; see also power backward theory 93–4
Bailey, F.G. 36–8, 71–2, 145, 149–50, 153, 159, 174, 204–7, 219, 228, 235
Barnes, J.A. 73
Barth, F. 200
Bascom,W. 196
Bellah, R. 182
Binford, L. 53n, 239
Black-Michaud, J. 141n

Blauner, R. 225
Boas, F. 3, 8, 40–1, 173, 199–200, 224, 242
Boissevain, J. 46
bricolage 111–12
bureaucracy 212
Burridge, K. 146

change: qualitative and quantitative 188; mock 189–92
Chomsky, N. 215
comparative method 25–7, 241
componential analysis 43–44
conceptual contradictions 78–84, 145; see also contradiction
conceptual territory 19–20, 239
conflict model 32–5, 87
contradiction: and conceptual schemes 73–84; and behaviour 145–72; and conflict 146–50; definition of 146–50; cluttered 150, 240; and rules 151–3; and roles 155–6; and attributes 157; and universities 158–60; and conferences 160–2; and black movement 162–5; and Utopias 166–9; and Marxism 146, 169–72; disguised by mechanisms 177–94
contraries 146; see also contradiction
Corsica 138–41, 189

Coser, L. 33, 206
cultural ecology 46–8
cultural materialism 45–50, 67–8
culture and personality 41–4
cumulative knowledge 73

decisions and non-decisions 185; see
  also power
dialectic: internal 81, 106, 115; double
  81; unrecognized 94–7; hidden 116;
  perspective 237–44; see also contradiction
differential power 5, 211; see also
  power
Douglas, M. 209
Durkheim, É. 3–4, 22–4, 233–4; and
  racism 225–6

élites 233–4
Engels, F. 190
ethnics 234–7
ethnocentrism 217
ethnomethodology 14
Evans-Pritchard, E.E. 17, 179, 193, 200,
  222, 241

Festinger, L. 153, 177
Firth 16, 173
Forde, C.D. 26
Fortes, M. 16
Foster, G. 209
Frank, A.G. 207, 212, 219
Frankfurt school 13
French economic anthropology 89–92
Fried, M. 212–13, 227–8

Gans, H. 232–3
Geertz, C. 46, 180
Giddens, A. 12n, 186
Gluckman, M. 26, 33, 200
Godelier, M. 89, 137, 146, 186

Goody, J. 213

Harris, M. 4, 41, 49–50
Hatch, E. 26n, 173
Heilman, S. 218
Himes, J. 232–3
historical particularism and diffusion
  38–41
Honigmann, J. 75, 203
Hsu, F. 162
Hughes, E. 158, 214

ideology 181
Igbo 20–1, 179

Jorgensen, J. 235

Kardiner, A., and Preble, E. 173
Keesing, F. 212
Kuhn, T.S. 3, 8, 53–62
Kulturkreise school 39
Kuper, A. 26n, 63

Leach, E.R. 180, 196, 202–3
Leaf, M. 199, 203
Lenski, G. 158, 209–10
LeVine, R. 21
Lévi-Strauss, C. 3, 100–41, 175, 200, 228,
  239–40
Levy, M. 35
Lewis, O. 32, 209
Lipset, S., and Raab, E. 173
Lloyd, P.C. 233
Lukacs, G. 13; see also Frankfurt school
Lynd, R. 153–5, 196

Malinowski, B. 8, 28–31, 173, 192–3, 200,
  211, 238n; and kula ring 30
Marx, K. 3, 187, 201–2; as paradigm-
  bridger 12; and racism 226–7
Masterson, M. 57

McClelland, D. 4; see also achievement orientation
Meillassoux, C. 89
Merton, R.K. 31, 156
mock change 189–92
models 240; mechanical and statistical 24; equilibrium 31–2; conscious and unconscious 119–20, 132; conflict 32–5, 87; and middle-range theory 111; and micro–macro dilemma 90–1; ideal and actual 74–6; see also theoretical orientation
modernization theory 85–7
Montagu, A. 223
Murdock, G.P. 16
Murphy, R. 63, 203–4, 240
myth: Asdiwal 105; Oedipus 105; and theory 100–14; and contradiction 149

Nader, L. 219, 233
nature–culture bridge 122; see also structuralism
neo-evolutionism 48
neutralizing mechanisms 5, 177–94
normal science 54; see also Kuhn 53–62

operationalism 96n
order in society 125, 177, 195; scholarly attitudes toward 113–14; breakdown of 139
Ottenberg, S. 21

paradigms 53–72; criteria of 59–61; non-paradigms 61, 70; pre-paradigms 57–62; pseudo-paradigms 62–9; and book reviews 71–2
Parsons, T. 12n, 172, 182, 188
Pelto, P. 8
Penniman, T. 17
Peters, E. 141n, 193

Piven, F., and Cloward, R. 191
Polanyi, K. 30, 89
Popper, K. 55–6, 68
positivism 3, 6, 195
power: and authority 183; and force and consent 183–4; deliberate and non-deliberate 184–6; power élite 177; as stability 5, 182–9; and inequality 220–34; and influence 206; and knowledge 6, 107; see also differential power

racism 51–2, 151, 162–5, 176, 222–8; and mock change 190–2; and South Africa 188, 226–7
Radcliffe-Brown, A.R. 8, 24–8, 196n, 200, 240
Redfield, R. 32, 209
reduced models 123–4; and children 130–1; and primitive society 131–2
reductionism 18; psychological 20–2, 25, 28; neurological 123
replication studies 32
ritual 180–1; and symbolism 208–9
Ritzer, G. 60n
role (or structural) diffuseness 197; and convergence 198
rules: basic 243–4; normative and pragmatic 37
Runciman, W.G. 32

Sahlins, M. 75, 207–8
salvage theory 4, 84, 238
Schaff, A. 171–2
self: meaning of 174–5; versus group 36, 242
Silverman, S. 71–2, 199
simplicity, illusion of 178–9, 195–210
Slater, P. 173, 179
social action 35–8
social problems 220–2

social structure 124; territory of 15–16
Spencer, H. 3, 173
Steward, J. 4, 45–7
strain: between individual and group
  36, 242; see also conflict model
stranger-value 218
structural functionalism 19–32; British
  63–7
structuralism 87–9, 115–41; and Durkheim 115–18; and formal analysis
  121–2; promises of 122–5; problems
  with 125–32; and positivism 132–5;
  and Marxism 136–8; and field-
  work 138–41; and Corsica 138–41;
  varieties of 118

Terray, E. 89
theoremes 114
theoretical orientations: overview of
  8–51; clusters of 10–15; basic 19–50;
  future 97–9, 237–44; the emerging

synthesis 199–201; basic elements
  of 201–2; shifts in 76–8; oscillating
  character of 74; single-factor 127–8;
  see also models
Turner, V. 208
Tylor, E.B. 3, 227

Udy, S. 198
urban anthropology 212–13

vendetta 138–41
Voget, F.W. 75

Weber, M. 3, 187; and structuralism
  135–6; and racism 226; and Protes-
  tant-ethic thesis 21
White, L. 4, 49
Willhelm, S.M. 164
Willis, W.S. 212, 227–8
Wolpe, H. 226